"The truth has been spoken aloud before God and in God's name. Now the world may do to us whatever it wishes. We stand in God's hand. God is faithful. But you, O Land, Land, Land, hear the word of the Lord."

Pastor Julius von Jan,
the Sunday following *Kristallnacht*

Preaching in Hitler's Shadow

Sermons of Resistance in the Third Reich

Edited by

Dean G. Stroud

William B. Eerdmans Publishing Company

Grand Rapids, Michigan / Cambridge, U.K.

Published 2013 by

Wm. B. Eerdmans Publishing Co.

2140 Oak Industrial Drive N.E., Grand Rapids, Michigan 49505 /

P.O. Box 163, Cambridge CB3 9PU U.K.

Printed in the United States of America

19 18 17 16 15 14 13   7 6 5 4 3 2 1

Library of Congress Cataloging-in-Publication Data

Preaching in Hitler's shadow: sermons of resistance in the Third Reich /
edited by Dean G. Stroud.
pages   cm
Includes bibliographical references.
ISBN 978-0-8028-6902-9 (pbk.: alk. paper)
1. Church and state — Germany — History — 1933-1945. 2. National socialism and
religion. 3. Sermons, German. 4. Clergy — Germany — History — 20th century.
5. Anti-Nazi movement — Germany. 6. Christianity and politics — History —
20th century. 7. National socialism — Moral and ethical aspects. 8. Antisemitism —
Germany — History — 20th century.   I. Stroud, Dean Garrett, editor of compilation.

BR856.P74   2013

252.00943'09043 — dc23

2013020718

www.eerdmans.com

Contents

CONTENTS

SELECTED SERMONS OF RESISTANCE
IN THE THIRD REICH

Contents

vii

Preface

In the early 1970s I was studying at Austin Presbyterian Theological Seminary in Austin, Texas, preparing for pastoral ministry. As colleagues from my generation will recall, we devoted much time to reading and discussing the three Bs: Barth, Bonhoeffer, and Bultmann. Although we carried around a copy of Bonhoeffer's *Letters and Papers from Prison*, we did not really dwell much on the background of those prison writings. Instead, we tried to figure out what "religion-less Christianity" might mean, one of the terms he mentioned without providing details. We considered Bonhoeffer the theologian, not only in that book but also in his *Cost of Discipleship*, where he offered his thoughts on the Sermon on the Mount. We read as if Bonhoeffer were addressing us directly, and not the Confessing Church in Nazi Germany. I cannot recall one lecture on the German Church Struggle that would have put his thought in its historical setting.

Even more so than with Bonhoeffer, the historical context of Barth's neoorthodoxy and Bultmann's demythologization of the New Testament never surfaced, at least not in a memorable way. I recall reading long selections from the massive and overwhelming *Church Dogmatics*. And so I left seminary with little historical background, and went into the parish, where occasionally sermon preparation or a discussion group would bring me back to those names. But I knew no more about the situation in which they lived than I had known at seminary.

My first parish was a small Presbyterian church in Mansfield, Louisiana, during the closing years of the civil rights movement. Although I never experienced hostility to my preaching on current events, I do recall sitting in the study working on the sermon for Sunday with a vague sense of unease when I saw the biblical text moving me into areas of controversy. What to say?

Pastors had three ways to deal with demands for civil rights: (1) we could become Jeremiah and proclaim the radical demand for justice and live with the consequences; (2) we could ignore the streets and the headlines and preach "nothing but the gospel" and close our eyes to the marches and our ears to the rhetoric; or (3) we could seek middle ground and balance justice with love, preaching the truth in a way that encouraged rather than outraged the congregation. And behind it all was the question, What business had the church mixing with politics?

Years later, I found myself at the University of Iowa doing graduate work in German. I had majored in German as an undergraduate, so when I left the ministry it was like returning to a first love. At Iowa I read widely in German literature, leaving those names from seminary far behind. Goethe, Kafka, and Brecht replaced Barth, Bonhoeffer, and Bultmann.

In 1984 I came to the University of Wisconsin in La Crosse, where I began teaching German and doing research in literature. But one day, I do not recall just when, I decided to use my German to read theology, thus uniting a current interest with one from the past. I began by reading a historical survey of German evangelical thought in the twentieth century, and saw for the first time the historical context of the theologians whose ideas had challenged me in seminary. Barth, Bonhoeffer, and Bultmann became actors in a terrible drama.

It was then that a question came to mind. If Barth, Bonhoeffer, and Bultmann had been young men living in Nazi Germany, what did they say when they preached? I remembered my days as a pastor living in the South in the early 1970s working on sermons, and I considered how much more dangerous it would have been for them to preach "in Hitler's shadow." I became interested in sermons from the Third Reich. The thought of preaching inside Hitler's Reich, where words were so dangerous, suddenly fascinated me. Anyone could say anything in London or New York, but what about in Bonn or Berlin?

When I began reading sermons from the Third Reich, I wanted to find sermons by outspoken pastors who denounced Hitler by name and condemned Nazi ideas without nuance or irony. I recalled the great sermons of Dr. Martin Luther King and others who used the pulpit to denounce evil. What had German pastors proclaimed on Sundays? This collection of selected sermons offers a response to that question.

Yet the question that always looms in the background is, What should the church have done? The obvious response is that the church should have spoken out directly and boldly against Hitlerism and anti-

Semitism. Leaving aside for the moment the truth that some did, and they suffered for it, the larger issue remains. Sadly, there is the example of Catholic bishops in Holland speaking out against Nazi persecution in that country in 1940, only to see the Nazis respond by immediately arresting and transporting Jews to the camps and the ovens.[1] The case of the Jewish convert Edith Stein and her sister Rose illustrates the hard truth that such public statements enraged the Nazis rather than changed them. The result in Holland was tragic.

Still, there remains the demand of the gospel to speak out against injustice, not only in the hope of converting the oppressor but also under the Christian obligation to speak truth to power. Each sermon in the collection offers an example of Christian speech in the great storm of Nazism.

Sermons in this collection reflect various oppositional responses to Nazism. Because I am honoring resisting pastors for their courage and faith, I have intentionally omitted outright pro-Nazi sermons. However, I have included enough commentary on Nazi Christian attitudes to ensure that readers gain a sense of how they twisted Christianity to fit Nazi views. Knowing what the pro-Nazi Christians believed provides powerful contrast to the sermons and offers critical background.

Each preacher in this collection, and many not represented here, deserves our respect and gratitude for his Christian witness and courage in the face of terrible evil. Some of these preachers died because of these sermons; all risked their lives.

Finally, I offer these translations as primary sources for readers interested in Christianity inside Hitler's Germany. I first began a book *about* sermons in the Third Reich but changed to offer translations *of* sermons in the Third Reich so that readers could draw their own conclusions about Christian opposition to Hitler. I, for one, find these sermons as "preachable" today as they were then. Times and circumstances have changed, but the truth remains as challenging in our time as it was then.

The documentation system used in the book comprises two types of notes: endnotes that contain bibliographic information and bracketed footnotes that contain commentary by the editor/translator on the texts of the sermons.

Acknowledgments

Many people have helped me along the way from concept to final product. To each listed below I give sincere thanks for his or her particular contribution. But in general I want to say how fortunate I was to be a professor at the University of Wisconsin–La Crosse where my research was always supported and encouraged.

Alice Socha edited an early draft of the manuscript during my sabbatical leave (January-May 2008).

Lara Olson, a native of Germany and former Amity Intern Scholar in the Department of Modern Languages, was kind enough to compare my translation of two sermons with the original texts and to discuss my work with me.

Dean Ruthann Benson, College of Liberal Studies, and the CLS Sabbatical Committee provided me a sabbatical leave in the spring semester of 2008 to concentrate on the project.

The Committee on Research and Grants awarded me three research grants that provided vital support for the project.

Anita Evans, Library Director at UW–La Crosse's Murphy Library, her wonderful staff, and especially the fine colleagues in the Interlibrary Loan department were able to find books from the United States and Germany long out of print.

Dr. Leslee Poulton, Chair of the Modern Language Department, provided office space and many kind words over the years.

Dr. Barbara Rusterholz, former department chair, always supported the project while serving as our chair.

Dr. Gregory Wegner, professor emeritus in the Department of History, is both a friend and an expert on Nazi Germany. For years Greg has encouraged my work through conversations and through invitations to be a guest lecturer in his classes.

Dewey J. Bjorkman, M.Div., Th.M., good friend and theological scholar, read the entire manuscript and discussed it at length with me over breakfast meetings at our favorite eatery. Dewey believed in the project from its inception and never grew tired of reviewing the material.

My wife Valentina Virginia offered unfailing support and encouragement, without which the project would not have been finished.

I am very grateful to Jon Pott and William B. Eerdmans Publishing Company for accepting the manuscript and offering wonderful help along the way. Tom Raabe was a great and patient editor whose work makes the final product better than the one he received.

Editor's Introduction

For the time will come when they will not endure sound doc-trine; but after their own lusts shall they heap to themselves teachers, having itching ears; and they shall turn away their ears from the truth, and shall be turned unto fables.

2 TIMOTHY 4:3-4 KJV

Historical Context: Preaching in the Third Reich

Why Read Sermons from Nazi Germany?

Why should we read these sermons from inside the Third Reich? After all, the church in Germany failed to stop Hitler and failed to defend Jewish Germans from ridicule, persecution, and deportation to death camps. In addition, the common thinking is that Christians offered little or no opposition to Nazism. Historians have judged Christians guilty of indifference at best and willing complicity at worst. We wonder if listening to preachers from Nazi Germany can offer anything but confirmation of the dominant view.

Books examining the church in Nazi Germany have seldom had much good to say about Christians and Christianity. We read, for example, in *The Holocaust and the Christian World* the following explanation of the church's failure: "Perhaps at the heart of those failures was the fact that the churches . . . sought to act, as institutions tend to do, in their own narrowly defined 'best' interests. There was little desire on the part of the churches for self-sacrifice or heroism, and much emphasis on 'pragmatic' and 'strategic' measures that would supposedly protect their institutional authority."[1]

On this view, the church was just one more institution whose main interest was survival. Institutional integrity rather than preaching the gospel set the tone. Basically, the Christian community failed to be any more of an opposition to Nazism than any other institution in German society, be it the university, the courts, or the military. While there is certainly enough material against the institutional church to warrant this judgment, institutions are composed of human beings, and each man, woman, and child in Hitler's Germany offered a unique response to events. So an eye for what individuals did or failed to do is a legitimate way to examine the evidence at hand. Without a doubt, the church as a social and political institution failed the test of confronting Nazism (just as, in my judgment, "the church" failed in much the same manner during the American civil rights movement). However, the "institution" — intent on survival rather than sacrifice, as Victoria Barnett emphasizes — was also the mystical body of Christ, and some of her members did challenge Nazism, even at the cost of their lives. Although the majority of pastors in Nazi Germany may well have offered little or no overt resistance that we know of today, we know of some who did. Having conceded that too few did too little, I caution that only God knows for sure. In a terror state secrecy is vital for the protection of oneself and others. And what we will come to call the "Church Struggle" was fought out in the trenches of each parish for control of each pulpit and congregation in the German Reich. As obvious as it sounds, we know only what we know and we do not know what we do not know.

Preaching was one significant way that some pastors did resist. Some radically proclaimed the gospel against Nazi ideology with little or no thought of personal safety. Their sermons provide historical documentation of Christian opposition to Hitler, and they deserve our attention.

Reading these sermons with their cultural context in mind will deepen our appreciation for these texts. We will first suggest the reasons so many Christians in Germany found Nazism appealing, and then we will consider just how hateful Nazi language and thought were. Against powerful appeals from the Nazi leaders to worship the state rather than the Judeo-Christian God and to hate the state's "enemies," Christianity offered a radical alternative. An overview of Nazi religious and racial thinking can sharpen our ears to hear that message.

Evil Calling upon God

When the eighty-five-year-old president of the German Reich, Paul von Hindenburg, handed the German government over to Adolf Hitler on January 30, 1933, he presented Germans with more than a new political leader; he gave Germans a new religious leader as well. Although we do not think of Hitler primarily in religious terms, he seems to have thought about how Christians would view him and his National Socialism. He would never have called himself a "preacher," but he certainly did not hesitate to reference God and to suggest divine support of his Reich. In fact, he made more references to God and to Christianity during the first eight weeks following his appointment as chancellor than at any time thereafter.[2] Getting off on the right foot with Christians in Germany was certainly an early priority.

Just two days after becoming chancellor, Hitler delivered a radio speech in which he asserted that God had removed his blessings from Germany because Germans had disobeyed him by surrendering to Germany's enemies in 1918. Hitler enlisted the Christian God as a divine endorsement for his own nationalism. The new führer then linked his nationalistic view of Christianity to the Nazi program for the future. He assured his listeners that the new government "regards Christianity as the foundation of our national morality and the family as the basis of national life." Hitler identified his nationalistic understanding of Christianity with the foundational institutions of German society. The new führer ended his address with a prayer, "May God Almighty give our work His blessing, strengthen our purpose, and endow us with wisdom and the trust of our people, for we are fighting not for ourselves but for Germany."[3] We should notice his wedding of a militant and nationalistic faith to a militant and nationalistic political program: "we are fighting."

Two weeks later, speaking in Stuttgart, he expressly identified himself and his government with Christianity in words that were surely comforting to Christians. Referring to critical comments by Dr. Eugen Bolz, a member of the Catholic Center Party in the Weimar period,[4] Hitler said, "And now *Staatspräsident* Bolz says that Christianity and the Catholic faith are threatened by us. And to that charge I can answer: In the first place it is Christians and not international atheists who now stand at the head of Germany. I do not merely talk of Christianity. No, I also profess that I will never ally myself with the parties which destroy Christianity."[5] A Stuttgart newspaper gave its coverage of the speech the headline: "Hitler's Affirmation of a Christian State."[6] I believe that quotes like this have misled many to think that Adolf Hitler considered himself a Christian, but surely if we have learned anything at all about Hitler, it is that nothing he ever said could be taken at face value. We must test his every word against what actually took place. These pious words about Christians rather than atheists running the new Germany have no basis in reality. This speech is just another example of propaganda.

In yet another speech, one the Nazi newspaper the *People's Observer* referred to as "the pronouncement of the Gospel of a reawakened Germany," a prayerful Adolf Hitler ended with the pious words "Lord God, never let us become shaky and cowardly, let us never forget the duty we have taken on." Here again we hear reference to a god of combat and weaklings who might become "shaky" and "cowardly." These are not the words of the Sermon on the Mount but of a bellicose divinity of Germanic myth. This speech on March 4, 1933, in Königsberg was broadcast on the radio. As Hitler concluded his remarks, Germans all over the new Reich heard the singing of a well-known prayer from the days of the kaiser and the ringing of the cathedral's bells. But what the listeners did not know was that the church authorities had forbidden the Nazis from ringing the cathedral bells. The Nazis had to play a sound recording of bells ringing to give the audience the mistaken view that the church was endorsing Adolf Hitler.[7]

To illustrate that Christians in Germany had nothing to fear from Hitler and the Nazis, members of the Nazi SA (*Sturmabteilung*) streamed into churches all over the Reich in the weeks following the swearing in of the new chancellor.[8] Photographs abound of uniformed SA troops worshiping in churches. In many churches these hordes of Nazis in their brown uniforms received a warm welcome. These were the first heady days of euphoria for a defeated and beleaguered populace who wanted a restored nation and a sense of pride. In Magdeburg the cathedral became "a forest of Swastika flags," and the pastor told his congregation that the twisted cross of Nazism "has become the symbol of German hope. Whoever scorns this symbol, scorns our Germany."[9] Early on in 1933 Hitler still had to concern himself with Christian response to his new government, and therefore it is not surprising that he did all he could to assure both Protestants and Catholics of his good will toward them.

Hitler's Positive Christianity

In spite of Christianity's total incompatibility with Nazi doctrine, the Nazis did not forget that most Germans in the 1930s still belonged to a Christian church. Although Nazi beliefs and practices offered a pagan religion to Germans who wanted a non-Christian touch of the transcendent to their Nazism, there was also an attempt early on to make Nazism appear Christian. The Nazis did this by advocating what they called "positive Christianity." The idea was not entirely new, because the official Nazi platform from 1920 had included a statement about this in its Point 24:

6

We demand freedom for all religious confessions in the state, insofar as they do not endanger its existence or conflict with the customs and moral sentiments of the German race. The party as such represents the standpoint of a positive Christianity, without tying itself to a particular confession. It fights the spirit of Jewish materialism within us and without us, and it is convinced that a lasting recovery of our *Volk* can only take place from within, on the basis of the principle: public need comes before private greed *(Gemeinnutz geht vor Eigennutz)*.[10]

Profoundly vague and threatening at the same time, the idea of positive Christianity allowed the Nazis to attack whatever aspect of Christianity they deemed "negative." Negativity in Nazi Germany was anything that emphasized the individual's unique worth and dignity over the Nazi herd. Negativity in Nazi Germany was anything that suggested that Jews were human beings created by God and loved by him. Negativity in Nazi Germany was anything that did not fight "Jewish materialism" (whatever that might be) or put the state's well-being before the individual's. Thinking for oneself and nonconformity were strictly forbidden. Christians had to conform to Nazi ideology if they wanted to be seen in a positive light.

Yet the most sinister aspect of Point 24 was that it made Christianity a racial religion. Everything in Nazi Germany was racist, for Nazi Germany was a state based solely on racism. We cannot overemphasize the importance of race in all things Nazi. It is, therefore, essential to notice how the preachers treat race — either directly by mentioning it or indirectly by intentionally ignoring it. It is vital to note how the sermons refer to Jews, Judaism, and the Old Testament.

Along with tying racism to Christian faith, Point 24 made it clear that Nazis would be the sole interpreters of what form of Christianity Germans could practice. Any criticism of the state or of Nazi persecution of the Jews was considered "negative Christianity."

Every sermon in the second part of this book is an illustration of negative Christianity at its best.

If Christians engaged in negative Christianity, they could be put on trial in a "special court" *(Sondergericht)*. One such trial occurred in Schwerin, Germany, and involved pastors who had written or signed a series of circular letters from the summer of 1933 to the spring of 1934 that Nazi authorities found objectionable. In one particular communication, entitled "Our *Non Possumus* for the Sake of Christ's Church," written February 17, 1934, the pastors announced that while obedience to the state was required of Christians, obedience could be limited in the case of the "present church situation."[11] Since Nazis could not allow such freedom of expression, a special court was formed to deal with the offending clergy. Evidently, the pastors' reflections on Romans 13:1 had not been "positive" enough for Nazis. The trial took place in June 1934. The charge was that the pastors had insulted the Nazi state by implying that the state was interfering in church relations! One pastor was sentenced to six months in prison, another to four months, still another to three, and two others were given stiff fines. Interestingly, the charges against one man were dropped, "although he was guilty," because he had "spent a large part of his life abroad and did not understand very well the situation in Germany."[12] The trial made the totalitarian claim on Christian life in the new Germany clear to all.[13]

Early on in the Third Reich any number of articles appeared in religious journals trying to understand just what this official view of the faith could mean in practice. In a collection of essays entitled *The Church in the Struggle for the Gospel*, Pastor Wilhelm Rott wrote an article titled "What Is Positive Christianity?"[14] He found the entire program of positive Christianity a danger to the authentic expression of the faith. To begin with, Point 24 was "too vague" and left interpretation in the hands of the party's organizations (p. 3). Quoting various definitions from Nazi sources, he noted that positive Christianity reduced Christianity to nothing more than "political Christianity" and social work, and that it omitted any faith content (p. 8). Dr. Goebbels then could support his claim at a party rally in Hamburg that the churches had failed the people and had forced the state to take up the work of Christian charity. Hence, "positive Christianity is National Socialism" (pp. 8-9). Furthermore, positive Christianity was "Germanic Christianity," as Alfred Rosenberg made clear in his book *The Myth of the Twentieth Century*. Rott summed up his objections to the current interpretations of positive Christianity by observing that it could, in reality, be expressed with no reference to Christianity at all (p. 10). It was, one might deduce, Christianity with no God, no Christ, and no content. It was the "politically correct" version of an empty gospel.

Yet, as Rott made clear in his essay, Christianity was first and foremost faith in Jesus Christ. Rott asserted that the only way to define Christianity "positively" was to look only at Christ himself, because for Christians there could be no other measurement of the faith (p. 13). Hence, authentic, positive Christianity was simply saying yes to Jesus Christ as the only way to God the Father, and yes to his gospel (pp. 14-15). And because

Jesus became known through the Scriptures, positive Christianity was also a yes to the Bible as the word of God (p. 17). Rott thus returned the traditional and positive content of the faith to Christianity. In his conclusion, he offered Germans the choice between "Jesus Christ" and the "ethics and morality of the Germanic race" (p. 17). In effect, Rott turned the idea of positive Christianity into a confession of faith in traditional Christianity. Perhaps we see here the outlines of the confessing church that would soon emerge.

Belief in Hitler

Although the Nazi program included a counterfeit "positive Christianity" and although Hitler peppered speeches with references to God, neither he nor Nazism had a single thing in common with traditional Christianity. Nazi religion was pagan, containing a pagan savior and creed. The creed knew nothing of sin, and its faith glorified violence. Nazism had no meekness or humility, no love of neighbor, and no thought of forgiveness. Hitler was the German savior and Jews were the devil incarnate. Both Christianity and Nazism spoke of a Reich (empire, kingdom), but they had vastly different understandings about its meaning. Hitler always said the Third Reich would last a thousand years, but Christians knew that it was God's "Reich" that would last forever. In which Reich did Germans want to live? In the Lord's Prayer Christians in Germany were asking for God's "Reich" to come while Nazis were marching to the music of the Reich that had come.

Many books on Nazi Germany discuss the religious nature of Nazism, but one particular scholar offers an insider's perspective. As many know, Victor Klemperer was a Jewish professor who escaped transport to a death camp because his wife was not Jewish. After being forced out of his teaching position at the university, he was ordered to move into Dresden's "Jew House" with his Gentile wife. He survived the thirteen years of Hitler's dictatorship without being transported to a concentration camp. The former professor responded to his situation in a most remarkable manner; he kept a secret journal. His journal, along with his study of Nazi language, provides a rare look inside daily life in Hitler's Germany from the perspective of a Jewish intellectual. In his commentary on Nazi language, Klemperer devotes a chapter to the religious nature of Nazism.

Recalling occasions when he heard Germans profess their "faith" in

Adolf Hitler, Klemperer begins with the story of Paula von B., a working-class young woman at the university. In 1933 she came into the professor's office excited and happy. When he asked why she was so joyful, she responded that she had not felt so great since 1914 and the start of the Great War. She told him the führer "has brought us home again!" and added, "You must recognize . . . that I belong entirely to the Führer."[15] When Klemperer wondered where the source of her confidence in Hitler's leadership lay, she told the professor, "Where all certainties come from: faith."[16]

Although it appears absurd today, many of Klemperer's acquaintances held on to this faith in Hitler even as the war's final bombs were falling in the spring of 1945. As the Russians were pushing deep into the collapsing Third Reich, Klemperer had a brief conversation with a German soldier who had lost an arm on the western front. Amazed at the young man's optimism about a final German victory, Klemperer wondered how he could continue to be confident after losing an arm and seeing the Red Army marching deeper into Germany. His response showed that there was the same "religious" faith at the end of the Third Reich as at the beginning: "I don't understand enough about warfare to be able to judge. But the Führer announced only recently that we are definitely going to win. And he has never lied to us yet. I believe in Hitler. No, God won't leave him in the lurch. I believe in Hitler."[17] Not only was there unswerving faith in Hitler as savior and the new Christ, but the faith had a bible as well. Hitler's *Mein Kampf* was the "Holy Book of National Socialism and of the New Germany." Noting that there were so many references to Hitler in religious terms that he ceased to list them in his journal, Klemperer concluded that in the "holy war" for German salvation, many died still believing until the end.[18]

In an essay on "faith" in the fascinating *Vokabular des Nationalsozialismus (Vocabulary of National Socialism)*, there are a number of references to Nazism as a new faith. Quotations from speeches by Nazi leaders and by Hitler himself demonstrate that faith in Hitler and in Nazism was an absolute commandment. A text by G. Feder, published in the journal *NS Monatsheft* in 1930, offered the Nazi version of the trinity: "The trinity of blood, of faith and of the state." Another quote from an essay by E. Eckert, "Faith in the SA," summed up faith as Nazi certainty that the führer had "come to us by God's will."[19]

Because Adolf Hitler was the expression of God's will for Germany, it followed that his Reich was not comparable to other governments. The

Nazi Reich resembled more the kingdom or Reich of God than a temporal Reich. In fact, there was a trick question on many exams during the Third Reich that Klemperer uses to illustrate the timelessness of Hitler's earthly empire. The question was: "What comes after the Third Reich?" If a candidate answered the Fourth Reich, the candidate failed the exam. The correct answer was that nothing would come after the Third Reich because the Third Reich would last forever.[20]

If Hitler replaced Christ, and if the Third Reich replaced the kingdom of God, then it followed that Germanic blood and not Christ's blood was salvific. As Alfred Rosenberg noted, writing in the foundational text of National Socialism, *The Myth of the Twentieth Century,* the new Germanic faith in Aryan blood had replaced and surpassed the old sacraments.[21] Thus the new faith had all the required elements of a religion: a gospel, a leader, and an eternal nature.

Therefore, Germans who had left the church or had never belonged to one had a religion in which faith was mandatory. In this belief system Nazism had replaced hallmarks of Christianity with the qualities of a good Nazi: strength rather than weakness; domination rather than humility; hatred rather than love; dependence on Hitler rather than dependence on Christ, not to mention the importance of blood, race, and soil rather than the sacraments, and a sense of eternity. Christianity belonged in the dustbin of ancient history. Daily throughout the Reich the radio, the newspaper, the cinema, the school, the university, and men, women, and children were proclaiming the good news that Hitler had come. The new gospel was modern and scientific,[22] and this gave it a persuasive ring. After the devastation and humiliation of the First World War, Germany was coming back from defeat and shame.

In the introduction to his history of Nazi Germany, Michael Burleigh references the insight of an anonymous reporter who called attention to the conflict between Nazism and Christianity in 1937. Nazi religion had "its own intolerant dogma, preachers, sacred rites and lofty idioms that offered total explanations of the past, present and future, while demanding unwavering dedication from its adherents. Acquiescence was not enough; such regimes demanded constant affirmation and enthusiasm from their own populations."[23] Little wonder then that Nazi rallies were filled with music and song, uniforms and banners, cheering throngs as well as impassioned speeches that resembled fundamentalists' sermons. In the 1934 movie of the Nazi Party gathering, *The Triumph of the Will (Triumph des Willens),* Hitler is portrayed as a god coming out of the heavens to his adoring followers, and the first thirty minutes or so have not words but romantic and military music to stir the emotions.

Nazis scripted the important events in family life as well. Marriages and baptisms were given Nazi texts. And when Christmas came, Nazis even had a new text for the most German of Christmas carols. In "Silent Night" Hitler simply replaced Jesus:

> Silent night! Holy Night! All is calm, all is bright,
> Only the Chancellor steadfast in fight,
> Watches o'er Germany by day and by night,
> Always caring for us.[24]

In *The Nazi Persecution of the Churches: 1933-1945,* J. S. Conway reproduces a Nazi Christmas sermon preached in 1936 in Solingen. It is taken from the files of the Old Prussian Union Church in Berlin, and although little information about it is available, the short text speaks for itself. According to the text, Christmas is not the birth of Jesus Christ but an ancient Germanic festival of light in which the Germanic forefathers anticipated the coming of light. Meeting around a Christmas tree, they placed "their burning torches" on the tree's branches as a symbol of light. Then the "preacher" turned his thoughts to Hitler, indicating that after the "Great War" when Germany was falling into ruin and darkness, "he" came who not only talked about light but led the way. Then Germany "awoke and followed the sign of light, the Swastika." All Germans could testify to the benevolence of the new leader in the "Welfare program and the Winter Help" that carried the German "Xmas" into Germans' hearts.[25]

According to this sermon, Hitler came to the Germans in the fullness of time, just as Christ once came in the fullness of time. Ancient Germanic folklore replaced Old Testament prophecy. Before Hitler, darkness covered the land, but now Hitler brings light. The implication is that Hitler, far more than Jesus, is the true light of the world. Whereas Christ and Christians formerly cared for the poor and the hungry, the Nazi benevolent winter help program takes over this social welfare function. The hungry now have Hitler to thank for their daily bread, especially since the Nazis forbade the churches from charitable activities.[26]

The exile from which the new "chosen people" are returning is not Egyptian or Babylonian but the shame of World War One. The Nazis had manufactured an ersatz religion that would bring hell rather than salvation to Europa.

How Nazis Saw the World

Even pagan religion needs content, so Nazism provided a worldview that was straightforward. A core idea of Nazism was the word *Volk*. In German, especially in the German of the Third Reich, the word was more complicated than "folk" or "people." In Nazi language *das Volk* had its root meaning in race and became the key element in identifying nations, societies, and groups.[27] Often we can think of *Volk* in Nazi materials as "race" or the Aryan race with the idea of a Germanic element to it. Hence Nazis saw the world exclusively in racial terms. The purity of the race and the physical features of the racial group were chief concerns. Each race had qualities that were inherited, and confusing or mixing the races weakened them. For this reason, the Germanic race or the Aryan race (often overlapping terms in Nazi thought) was by far superior to all other races on the planet while, of course, the Jewish "race" was the most inferior of the races.

Because of a worldview grounded in racial bigotry, Nazis saw the world as an arena of conflict; the races were engaged in a life-or-death struggle for domination. This certainty of conflict automatically made Jews the enemy, and no matter how they behaved on the surface (or on the street), Germans could be sure that every Jew was plotting the ruin of the superior race. When the world is viewed in such terms, there can no longer be any sympathy for the "other," even if the other is children or the elderly. Once the world becomes a battlefield between the races, compassion and empathy fall away. Even a Jewish child is the enemy, and nothing any child does can change that. Then all Jews, young or old, become simply "the other" who must be eliminated. Removal and ultimately the elimination of the hostile race are the only sure defense of the German *Volk*.

Understandably, such a racial view of the world made Christianity weak, useless, and even hostile to Nazi principles and goals, more of a hindrance than an aid, more suspect than familiar, and far more foreign than Germanic.

In 1937 the central publisher of the Nazi Party in Munich released *The Nazi Primer: Official Handbook for Schooling the Hitler Youth*, which presented the Nazi worldview for the indoctrination of boys in the Hitler Youth. The very first article of the creed was "The Unlikeness of Men." The opening sentence read: "The foundation of the National Socialist outlook on life is the perception of the unlikeness of men."[28] Granting the obvious, that individuals vary in their outward appearance, the primer then connected physical with "mental and spiritual traits" (p. 5). Nazism had to combat the impression that Jews were just as human as Germans, for indeed it was often hard to recognize someone as a Jew (hence the yellow star and the forced changing of names from German to Jewish ones). Nazi education had to teach the differences that lay beneath the skin: "Men must, therefore, be considered with respect to their inner makeup. For the great difference which separates those of German blood from Jews is clearly evident, although physical characteristics seem to designate both as members of the family of white men. We suit our actions accordingly and evaluate what happens according to this knowledge" (p. 7).

Following this insight into the primacy of race and blood, the primer warned of dangers facing Germany from the "Free Masons, Marxists, and the Christian Church" (p. 9). Having lumped these vastly different and irreconcilable groups together (a favorite Nazi ploy) as enemies of National Socialism, the primer took aim at Roman Catholics in particular and Christians in general. Specifically, the authors ridiculed the Christian doctrine of *imago Dei* by emphasizing that a non-Christian German was viewed as inferior to "Jews and blacks and inferior whites in the eyes of the Church" (p. 10). A distortion, to be sure, but the primer cared nothing about distorting actual Christian doctrine. In the end, as the primer noted, "A Jew both in Germany and in all other countries remains only a Jew" (p. 52).

To fortify the indoctrination of racial propaganda, Nazis peppered the media and the schools with lies and caricatures about Jews. Schoolchildren learned that Jews were like poisonous mushrooms; they may look like other people, but they were deadly to Germans. Running through every speech by Hitler, Goebbels, and other Nazis was the two-pronged idea that Jews were the lowest animals in existence and yet due to their remarkable cunning they were the number one threat to German life and culture. Nazis passed law after law to isolate Jews from fellow Germans and to make their lives difficult and miserable. Victor Klemperer noted in his journal each new restriction that came along and commented on how increasingly difficult life was becoming. Among other things, Jews were forbidden to have pets or to own typewriters or to be in public shelters or on the streets at certain times. Even eyeglasses and winter clothing were eventually outlawed. Whatever would make life hard or dangerous for Jews eventually became law, until the "final solution" was put into effect. But for Klemperer and others, the yellow star was especially difficult:

Today I ask myself again the same question I have asked myself and all kinds of people hundreds of times; which was the worst day for the Jews during those twelve years of hell?

I always, without exception, received the same answer from myself and others: 19 September 1941. From that day on it was compulsory to wear the Jewish star, the six-pointed Star of David, the yellow piece of cloth which today stands for plague and quarantine, and which in the Middle Ages was the colour used to identify the Jews, the colour of envy and gall which has entered the bloodstream; the yellow piece with "Jew" printed on it in black, the word framed by the lines of the two telescoped triangles, a word consisting of thick block capitals, which are separated and given broad, exaggerated horizontal lines to effect the appearance of Hebrew script.[29]

Every word in Klemperer's description denotes the shame and humiliation, the otherness and hostility that the star conveyed. Marked off like lepers, these men, women, and children had no hope of ever being accepted into German society again.

But it was not only anti-Jewish laws with which Jews had to contend. Language was a vital part of Nazi hatred. In *The Language of the Third Reich,* Klemperer devoted long sections to Nazi speech against Jews. In the chapter entitled "The Jewish War," Klemperer remarked in detail on this isolation of the Jews. He noted that every aspect of Nazi language referring to Jews was aimed at "segregating them as completely and irreconcilably as possible from everything German. One moment they are characterized as the Jewish people, as the Jewish race, the next as global Jews or international Jewry; in both cases what counts is their non-Germanness."[30] As Klemperer noted, Hitler and Goebbels rarely used the noun "Jew" without a descriptive adjective that belittled them. Adjectives such as "cunning," "wily," "deceitful," and "cowardly" added an air of suspicion and danger, while adjectives like "flat-footed," "hook-nosed," and "water-shy" underscored negative physical features. For the more abstract thinker, adjectives like "parasitic" and "nomadic" were at the ready.[31] These last two implied that Jews, unlike Germans, had no homeland *(Heimat)* and thus were parasites that fed from Germanic blood and sucked the blood from the noble German race. Thus if Germans thrived from healthy "blood and soil," Jews endangered the health of the German *Volk.* This identification of the Jews with parasitic animals would make the final solution of extermination appear logical.

Early in his linguistic study of Nazi language, Klemperer zeroed in on the most insidious and effective element of Nazi vocabulary. He wrote that it was not in the speeches, articles, or pamphlets that Nazis had their greatest effect, but rather in the "individual words, the idioms, the sentence structures, repeated millions of times over that soared up and were absorbed mechanically and unconsciously." Thus the "civilized language" of which Friedrich Schiller wrote, became deadly poison when it was composed of toxic elements. Words in the Nazis' manipulation of German became like "tiny dosages of arsenic" that were "swallowed unnoticed" and that initially appeared to have no effect, but after a while the "poisonous action" was fully present.[32]

Bringing his unique perspective to the question of German anti-Semitism, Klemperer highlighted one aspect of anti-Semitism in Nazi Germany that set it apart from earlier "outbreaks" of the disease. "In earlier times the animosity towards the Jews was directed at a group which stood outside the Christian faith and Christian society; the adoption of the country's religion and customs served as a compensation and (for the succeeding generation at least) as a blurring of differences. Displacing the difference between Jews and Non-Jews into the blood makes any compensation impossible, perpetuates the division and legitimizes it as willed by God."[33]

Michael Burleigh sounds the same theme and mentions a fact about the Jewish-German population that may partially explain Hitler's success in convincing Germans that the Jews really were a threat.

> But the "Jewish Question" was not the most animated issue of the day, least of all in liberal circles, Gentile or Jewish, which had other preoccupations. Beyond bigots, who exist in all times and places, most Germans did not spend their waking hours thinking about Jews, although the impression is inadvertently conveyed by a vast scholarly literature focused exclusively on relations between Germans and Jews. People had to be encouraged to think about Jews at all. Most Germans were probably much more exercised by issues of class and religion than by less than 1 per cent of their population.[34]

Astonishingly, there were so few Jews in Germany that it is likely that most Germans had little personal contact with Jewish neighbors, merchants, doctors, lawyers, teachers, and professors; thus few Germans must have had really close Jewish friends who would have demonstrated how ridiculous Hitler's ideas were. Knowing members of a group easily destroys stereotypes, but with the German population comprising less than 1 percent Jews, few Germans had personal knowledge to go by. Racial hatred feeds on distortions and stereotypes.

Most Jews in Germany had assimilated into German culture. They were musicians, writers, philosophers, professors, physicians, etc. Many had converted to Christianity, and many others did not observe Jewish laws and customs. In the First World War many Jews fought bravely for Germany. This is not to suggest that Jews in Germany faced no problems or prejudice; they did indeed. Talented men and women were turned away from distinguished careers and prestigious positions simply because they were Jews. But Jews in Germany considered themselves to be as much German as any other man or woman in the Reich. This made Nazi hatred and persecution of the German Jewish population all the more tragic and inexplicable.

Was Jesus Really a Jew?

Given the rising tide of anti-Semitic hatred in Germany, Christians who favored the Nazi worldview faced the awkward situation of worshiping a Jew, a man like those the Nazis were railing against. Jesus was a Jew. This basic truth of history made Jesus unacceptable to Nazis. Something had to be done to ease the tension between the Christian faith and the new politics. The solution was to transform Jesus from Jew to Aryan. Those wanting to change Jesus' identity simply asserted that he never was a Jew in the first place. Thus it was that a pro-Nazi teacher of religion in a German school simply told students that Galilee had never been a Jewish region and that the Jews had captured the territory in 104 B.C. Galilee's majority population had been Aryans living under Jewish domination. Jesus was an Aryan, the man told his pupils, whose way of thinking and acting was in sharp contrast to Jewish ways. The teacher then quoted John 8:44, where Jesus tells his opponents that their father is the devil, to prove that Jews were the sons and daughters of evil.[35] Once they had turned Jesus into an Aryan hero, they could make him serve Nazi intentions.

A book published in 1922 and republished in 1933 offers an even earlier example of the Aryan Jesus. Written by a German educator, and friend of Goebbels, *The Original Gospel of Jesus: German Faith,* by Dietrich Klagges, provided the basic outline of Germanic Christianity. According to the book, behind the Gospels stood an original narrative *(Urevangelium)* that had been uncovered through research. Obviously, the anti-Semitic researchers found the Jesus they wished to find. When Jesus debated with the Pharisees, for example, it was not a debate between faithful Jews over a common tradition, but rather Jesus' violent rejection of everything Jewish.[36]

In a chapter entitled "The Enemies," Klagges presented the conflict between Jesus and his opponents in racial terms. Speaking of the "spiritual revolution" that Jesus initiated in Galilee, he wrote, "There they [Jesus' enemies] must have seen their cause threatened. This way of seeing the world and life with its philosophical, religious and ethical principles was the decisive opponent of their way of doing things. They knew that here two completely opposite worldviews stood in opposition and behind them beat the wills of two kinds of beings; two races."[37] On this reading, Jesus did not enter Jerusalem on Palm Sunday to die for our sins but rather he was the Aryan warrior entering the enemy's capital.[38]

Such attempts to make Jesus an Aryan hero, whom the Nazis could accept, were widespread in Germany in the 1920s and 1930s. Members of the Institute for Research and Elimination of Jewish Influence on German Ecclesiastical Life presented by far the most intense "research" into the non-Jewish Jesus. In the course of its existence, membership in the institute included "more than fifty professors of theology at universities throughout the Reich . . . as well as dozens of instructors and graduate students."[39] Thanks to the work of these Nazi "theologians," Germans could buy a "version of the New Testament that was free of Jewish influence." This edited New Testament and a shorter version sold some 200,000 copies.[40]

The absence of hate-filled language against Jews and the frequent reference, either directly or indirectly, to Jesus' Jewishness in the sermons that follow are remarkable, given the pressure in Nazi society to conform to the Nazi narrative. In my view, this was one way in which preachers could subvert the dominant paradigm. The same holds for sermons based on Old Testament texts, especially the prophets and their insistence on justice. How radical and politically incorrect Isaiah, Jeremiah, and the psalmists sounded in Nazi Germany!

A Faith for Weaklings

It was not only Jesus' Jewishness that provoked Nazi hatred of orthodox Christianity. Along with worshiping a Jewish God, traditional Christianity praises virtues that Nazis found repugnant: love of neighbor, forgiveness, peacemaking, and humility, to name but a few. Especially incomprehensible for Nazis was the Christian law to love your enemies and pray for those who persecute you. Michael Burleigh makes the point well: "The Nazis despised Christianity for its Jewish roots, effeminacy, otherworldliness and universality. It appeared life-denying to the life-affirming, mobilizing entirely unwanted sentiments and values. Forgiveness was not for resentful haters, nor compassion of much use to people who wanted to stamp the weak into the ground. In a word, Christianity was a 'soul malady.'"[41]

T4

Nazis despised Christian love for the weak because Hitler and his followers despised the weak. Hitler expressed his contempt for the helpless in 1929 in a Nazi gathering where he suggested that Germany could increase its overall "strength" if Germans had "a million children a year" and eliminated "700-800,000 of the weakest people."[42] The result was the infamous T4 program of mass murder of German citizens whom the Nazis considered "unworthy of life" *(lebensunwertes Leben)*.[43] As if waiting for the cover of war, the T4 program (so-called because its headquarters were located at the Berlin address of Tiergartenstraße 4) began in September 1939 and lasted until the end of the Third Reich in 1945, although it "officially" came to an end in August 1941.[44] One reason the Nazis felt compelled to end the slaughter "officially" in 1941 was that it was becoming common knowledge among the German population as more and more families were receiving the cremated ashes and death certificates of loved ones who had been in mental institutions. Also, the famous sermon by Bishop von Galen (below) confronted the Nazi authorities directly with the horrors of the program and called upon Germans to insist on its cessation. Many pastors and priests were becoming aware of the program as members of their parishes were requesting funerals for their loved ones (see Gerhard Ebeling's sermon below). The euthanasia program became so widely known that in December 1940 Pope Pius XII "unequivocally condemned" it.[45] Yet T4 continued, using starvation and lethal injection rather than gassing to kill its victims.[46]

Nazi murder of Jews, the weak, and the mentally ill certainly illustrates its total incompatibility with Christianity. Therefore, it is not surprising that Nazism completely rejected Christian virtues. There was no longer any attempt to give lip service to Christianity. Christianity came under attack from every side. If Christ died to forgive our sins, then without a sense of sin there is no need for Christ. For Nazis, sin and forgiveness demonstrated weakness and passivity in a culture that honored forceful actions and glorified the hero who bends the world to his will. This was the Germanic hero, not a crucified Jew. The rejection of basic Christian teaching is evident from an SS (*Schutzstaffel*) journal that informed its readers, "The abstruse doctrine of Original Sin, whence the need of salvation is said to arise; the Fall — and indeed the whole notion of sin as set forth by the Church, involving reward or punishment in a world beyond — is something intolerable to Nordic man, since it is incompatible with the 'heroic' ideology of our blood."[47] Not even the problematic and often tragic history of relations between Christians and Jews could improve Christianity's standing in Nazism. Again, Michael Burleigh makes the point forcefully:

> Whatever Christianity's ambivalences and antagonisms towards the Jews, its core concerns with compassion and humility were anathema to a politics of racial egotism, and worship of brutality and strength. These "aspects" of Christianity would have to be expunged. In Nazi eyes, Christianity was "foreign" and "unnatural," or what has been described as the Jews' "posthumous poison," a notion the Nazis picked up from Nietzsche. Viewed pseudo-historically, it was an eastern Mediterranean "servant ethic" imposed upon the credulous ancient Germans by force and subterfuge. Christianity had obliterated their values and traditions, sapping their "racial" vitality.[48]

With so little sympathy for Christian virtues, every sermon that advocated basic Christian virtues challenged the Nazi way of being. This simple fact, overlooked by critics of the church in this period, is simply remarkable. As Christians know from the New Testament, especially the Acts of the Apostles, simply preaching the gospel in the face of evil is sufficient to provoke violent response. The most basic of Christian truths — that God is love, that we are to be imitators of Christ whose love for us reaches its pinnacle at Golgotha, that we are to forgive "seventy times seven," and that God will judge each of us against his standards rather than the world's — presented a fundamental challenge to everything Hitler and his followers represented. It is amazing that Nazi Christians could find enough support in the New Testament to publish even a thin version!

The German Christian Movement

Although Christians today are horrified that the Nazis tried to sever Jesus from his Jewish heritage, there was a particular group of Christians in Germany who welcomed and encouraged the idea that they could believe in Jesus without having to accept his Jewishness, humility, or virtues. While it should have been obvious that there was no real compromise between Christianity and Nazism, that did not stop some from trying to mix the two into a new Germanic gospel. Those who attempted to write this new gospel called themselves German Christians *(Deutsche Christen)*. For the sake of clarity, I will refer to members of this movement as "German Christians" and those Christians who did not identify with them as "Christians in Germany" or "Confessing Christians," where appropriate.

In some ways the German Christian movement was progressive. Christianity in Germany was in crisis between the wars because many thought Christian teachings had little to say to Germans in the modern world of science and progress. Following the First World War, many Christians in Germany found the church lifeless and meaningless. What could a text that was over 1,900 years old say to Germans after Versailles? What did Jerusalem have to do with Berlin? Unless a new Reformation occurred, pastors might as well close the Bible and walk away.

It was in this context that the German Christian movement began. The movement predated the Third Reich by three years, and in general it was working for a "non-denominational German Reich Church" founded on radical German nationalism and racism *(völkisch)*.[49] The hotbed of the movement was in Thuringia, where the "Thuringian movement" of the German Christians remained independent from the larger group and managed to grow in number even as the larger one began to fade.[50] This group was started through the efforts of two young pastors, Siegfried Leffler and Julius Leutheuser.[51] It is very telling that Leffler "did not shy away from calling Germany the 'Counter Chosen People to the Jews' *(das Gegenvolk der Juden)* chosen to 'take the veil from the cross and to provide the world the redemptive service that until today no people *(Volk)* had been capable of providing.'"[52] This statement strongly suggested that Hitler and the Germans would save the world from the Jews and thereby redeem humanity, something that Christ on the cross had been unable to do. For Nazis, the cross was truly a symbol of shame, weakness, and humility. It was the sign of signs that the Jews had won. Now with Hitler, the time had come for Germans to do what Christ himself had failed to do.

Klaus Scholder sums up the appeal of the German Christians as follows: "What fascinated contemporaries in this approach was the apparent recovery of the unity of thinking and doing, of faith and action, of church and politics. German Christianity no longer existed apart from the *Volk* and its history." And he notes that the Thuringian German Christian movement "was the first of those spontaneous church movements which provided a direct connection between church and Party, and which owed their emergence to the religious enthusiasm of pastors and communities, not to any political calculation of the Party."[53]

On May 26, 1932, the German Christians issued their "Guiding Principles." The movement advocated the "unification of the 29 churches . . . into one Protestant Reich Church." The new united church would be "a dynamic national church *(Volkskirche)*" that stood "on the basis of positive Christianity." This, they maintained, was a "truly national faith in Christ, in the Germanic spirit of Luther and heroic piety." Race, too, was an essential element in their reading of Christianity; therefore, "racial mixture" was forbidden. For them, the Christian faith did not destroy race but rather made race sacred.[54]

The German Christians, then, were Christians who read the gospel through extremely nationalistic and anti-Semitic lenses. These Germans eagerly sowed thorns of hatred and bigotry among the wheat. Strangely enough, Hitler was never much in favor of the movement. Even a revision of Christianity with Nazi ideas was still too much Christianity for the führer, but German Christians delighted in finding in Adolf Hitler a Christlike figure. If Hitler did not need them, they certainly wanted Hitler. The German Christians were mostly laity, and they numbered some 600,000 soon after Hitler came to power.[55]

These Germans found in Hitler just the redeemer they had been waiting for. In an allusion to Saint Paul's conversion on the road to Damascus and to Hitler's temporary blindness during the First World War on the battlefront, they proclaimed, "We put our trust in our God-sent Führer who was almost blinded when he heard God's call: 'You must save Germany.' And who, once his sight was restored, began that great work which led us to the wonderful day of 30 January 1933."[56]

Meeting in Berlin on June 6, 1932, the group issued a set of public guidelines. The first stated that their guidelines were not designed to replace doctrine but were a "confession of a way of life."[57] Point 4 echoed Point 24 of the Nazi program: "Our standpoint is one of positive Christianity. We declare ourselves for an affirmative faith in Christ, such as accords with the

German spirit of Luther and heroic piety."[58] Point 7 explicitly embraced racist and nationalist thought: "We see in race, national heritage (*Volkstum*) and the nation an order of life that has been given and entrusted to us by God. . . . Therefore the mingling of races is to be opposed."[59] Other guidelines made clear German Christian hatred of Communists and Jews, even going so far in Point 9 as to forbid marriage between Germans and Jews.[60] So the German Christians redrew the doctrines of the faith to fit the worldview of the Nazis: an Aryan Jesus; no Old Testament in the Bible, at least not as an authentic part of the canon; the elimination of the Jew Paul and all his letters; and a watered-down New Testament that would present Germans with a Germanic Christ who fought the Jews in the same way as the Nazis. German Christians stood shoulder to shoulder with the Nazis and saw no contradiction between faith in Christ and faith in Hitler, so long as they were free to interpret faith in Christ according to the new realities in Germany.

But ultimately the attempts by German Christians to wed Christianity to Nazism failed, and not even Hitler was impressed. Try as they might, the two just did not fit together. While many of their ideas remained in circulation, the movement itself fell apart because Hitler and others simply could not be bothered with propping up even a weakened form of Christianity. After the notorious rally in the Berlin Sports Palace on November 13, 1933, where a large crowd enthusiastically cheered their anti-Semitic ideas, the influence of German Christians waned. The radical revisions of the gospel proclaimed on that day horrified many Christians in Germany. In 1935 German Christian gatherings in Regensburg were "prohibited by the Gestapo,"[61] and by 1938 the movement was as good as dead. Since the majority of Nazis, as well as the Nazi leadership, had never supported the idea, few Nazis mourned the passing of the German Christian movement. Once the German Christians exited the scene, Nazism was "a purely Nazi ideology."[62]

Martin Luther Day 1933

For many Protestant Christians the advent of the Third Reich seemed to be the completion of the Reformation that Martin Luther had begun. It is little wonder then that Nazis and nationalistic Protestants were eager to make the occasion of Luther's 450th birthday in 1933 a day of national renewal and rededication. It seemed providential to many that this special anniversary of the birth of the leader of the German Reformation should fall during the initial year of Hitler's Reich. A photograph from that day shows the Luther statue in Berlin guarded by ten SA men and carries the caption, "The SA stands guard at the Luther memorial in Berlin."[63] As celebrations throughout Germany that November made clear, the new Reich was bringing Luther's reformation to completion. In his classic work on the Third Reich, William Shirer reminds us that it "is difficult to understand the behavior of most German Protestants in the first Nazi years unless one is aware of two things: their history and the influence of Martin Luther."[64]

Luther was far more than a religious figure; he was a German hero whose heroism and Germanic traits both Hitler and the Nazis were eager to promote. Hitler had already singled out Luther, along with Frederick the Great and Richard Wagner, as one of the three great figures in history that had combined grand vision with political realities. Here for Hitler was the idea of the great leader, and he was happy to view himself as a member of that select group.[65]

Along with various anti-Jewish statements by Luther, there was one quote pro-Nazi Christians used time and time again: the Latin sentence *Germanis meis natus sum, quibus et serviam*, which, somewhat loosely translated, is "I was born for my beloved Germans: it is them I want to serve."[66] Thus Nazis saw Luther as a servant not so much of Christ or of the church but of the German race and nation *(Volk)*. Such references linking Luther and Hitler were quite acceptable in Nazi Germany, and this allowed Protestants to feel right at home in the new Reich, and the Nazis could appeal to an honored German tradition.

In 1933 a conference of pro-Nazi Christians drew up the Rengsdorfer Theses, stating seven principles illustrating the compatibility of National Socialism with "German" Christianity. The fourth thesis reads: "For us Germans *(deutsche Menschen)* the Reformation made the gospel accessible in accordance with our national character *(Volkscharakter)*. History confirms that this proclamation of the gospel of the Germanic race is appropriate."[67]

Of course, not every Protestant Christian went along with this view of Luther. In the same publication in which the Rengsdorfer Theses appeared, Karl Barth wrote seven oppositional theses. His counterthesis to the one quoted above reads: "The Reformation as renewal of the church based on God's word is 'made accessible' for Germans *(deutsche Menschen)* not in accordance with their character but rather in accordance with the wisdom and will of divine providence. It was and is as appropriate and inappropriate for the Germanic race as for any other race. Whoever treats the Reformation as a specifically German affair today interprets it as propaganda and places himself outside the evangelical church."[68] Similarly, Dietrich Bonhoeffer and Hermann Sasse, among others, wrote the Bethel Confession in that same year.[69] In a section on the Reformation, they, like Barth, suggested that a Nazi reading of Luther was far off the mark:

> Martin Luther is for the church of the Reformation the loyal witness of the grace of Jesus Christ. As such he is the "prophet" and "evangelist" to the Germans. But to understand his actions as a breakthrough of the Germanic spirit, or as the origin of the modern feeling for freedom, or as the establishment of a new religion is to completely misunderstand his mission. He fought against the modern religiosity in that he demonstrated the fanaticism of people who wished to come to recognition of God based on their own preparation and without the preached word. And he fought against the modern longing for self-sufficiency in that he taught that blind trust on human reason and on human freedom was blindness.[70]

As with Luther, so with virtually every aspect of traditional Christian faith and teaching, there was a fierce battle in the opening years of the Third Reich over just what application Christianity had for the present moment in German history. Should and could a Christian in Germany confess Hitler as a manifestation of God's will, or would Christians have to hold firm to the ancient confessions and see Hitler as a demonic expression of evil?

Confessing Christ

As Barth's counter to the Rengsdorfer Theses and the Bethel Confession illustrates, opposition voices began to warn about Nazism's false understanding of Christianity. The orthodox response to false Christianity was to be confessional *(bekennen)* in nature, rather than political. But in Nazi Germany, as we have seen with "positive Christianity," theology and politics were never far apart, and politics quickly began to intrude on faith matters.

On March 24, 1933, the Nazi Reichstag (Parliament) passed "the Enabling Law." This law ended constitutional government. New regulations began to tighten Nazi control of daily life, and for the remaining days of his Reich, Hitler had no constitutional opposition and Germans had no constitutional protections. Germany passed from a state of laws to one of terror.[71] From that day on, each new law added pressure on the population to conform to the new order or suffer the consequences. Of course, German Jews received "special treatment" as legal measures increasingly harassed and segregated them from the majority population until the ultimate dehumanization of being transported in overcrowded cattle cars to concentration camps where they were gassed or worked to death.

Few, if any, foresaw the steady descent into hell that began in January 1933. Michael Burleigh summarizes a remarkable essay written by a critic of National Socialism in 1937 in which the writer compares living in Nazi Germany to being a passenger on a train who is unaware that a bridge is being rebuilt — little by little and piece by piece — until it is no longer the old bridge but a completely new one. Only the most observant passenger traveling across the bridge every day would notice that a total transformation had occurred.[72] In the weeks and months of those first two years of the Third Reich, the National Socialists were slowly transforming Germany from a democratic society *(Rechtsstaat)* into a terror state *(Terrorstaat)*.

Yet, while the vast majority of Germans either failed to notice the radical changes or failed to object to them, some Christians did notice and did object. These discontents would soon be known as the Confessing Church. Confessing the traditional Christian faith, pastors began to speak out against Nazi influences on church life and governmental attempts to take over control of churches.

To understand the Confessing Church and those pastors who preached from that perspective, it is necessary to say something about church politics in the first two years of Hitler's government. When Hitler became chancellor in January 1933, the Protestant churches were organized in regional groups called *Landeskirchen.* In 1934 there were twenty-two *Landeskirchen:* thirteen Lutheran, two Reformed, and seven United churches, with the largest among them being the Evangelical Church of the Old Prussian Union with eight provinces.[73] There was no single German church structure for Protestants as there was for Roman Catholics. The independence among these regional churches was an irritant to Nazis. A hallmark of Nazism was the idea that every institution in Germany had to conform to Nazi ideology in a manner that made it structurally clear that all paths led ultimately to Hitler. This conformity was called *Gleichschaltung,*

26

which means something like "synchronization." We can understand the word's root meaning if we recall that the German word *gleich* means "equal" or "same." Therefore, *Gleichschaltung* meant that everyone and every institution had to express a Nazi orientation and perspective. In this way, everyone and everything in the Third Reich had to conform to Nazi principles or be destroyed. The first years of Nazi rule were devoted to conforming German society to Nazism. Ideally, each German should bring his or her thinking into line with Nazi ideology; this was called an "internal" *Gleichschaltung*. Nazis worked for enthusiastic and voluntary adjustment of ideas, views, beliefs, and actions to the wishes of the leader. Yet if Germans, for any reason, failed to fall into line on their own, then an "external" *Gleichschaltung* would be required. This latter term was pejorative and required political action and the passing of harsh laws to ensure that everyone and everything in the Reich reflected Hitler's principles.[74] Propaganda sought to achieve internal *Gleichschaltung* whereas terror sought to ensure external *Gleichschaltung*. Whether internal and voluntary or external and coerced, the idea was that every man, woman, and child along with all institutions in Nazi Germany would live according to Nazi expectations.

Gleichschaltung received a veil of legality when the Nazi parliament passed two laws requiring all political power in the various regions of Germany to be brought into line with the "desire and direction" of the new government. The first law was passed on March 31, 1933, and the second on April 7, 1933.[75] Perhaps the best short explanation of the term is a remark by Goebbels in the summer of 1933: "What one means today by that often-misused word *Gleichschaltung* is nothing less than the radical reorganization of the state and all parties, all interest groups, all associations into one huge whole. It is the necessary step to a totalitarian state, that in the future can be only one party, one conviction, one *Volk*. And all the other powers and forces have to subject themselves to this state or be pushed aside without mercy."[76]

Accordingly, the Protestant churches in Germany required this political adjustment. Certainly a single Reich church headed by a Nazi Christian could accomplish this conformity easier than working with the scattered regional churches. While voluntary readjustment was preferred, as noted above, Hitler went along with the "German Christian" idea of a unified Reich church, so long as the leaders were politically correct in their Nazi worldview.[77] Hitler agreed that Ludwig Müller, a leading force in the German Christian movement, would be an ideal Reich bishop and that plans to reorganize the German Evangelical Churches could begin with the understanding that the "methods of its creation must be non-controversial, inoffensive to the Church leaders, and such as to give rise to no unwelcome comments in the foreign press. Above all, the leaders of the Church must be prepared to accept the political leadership of the Nazi Party and to regulate their affairs accordingly."[78] Hitler wanted no unfavorable press that could embarrass the new regime early on, but he was clear that control would be in Nazi hands. Not attracting international attention could lend credence to Hitler's propaganda that Germans were welcoming the new government with open arms.

What has come to be known as the "Church Struggle" (Kirchenkampf) was in large part the "struggle" or "battle" over church leadership and Nazi influence on Christian life. This attempt to force Protestant Christians to surrender control to the German Christians led to conflict over structure and doctrine. It became quickly apparent that Hitler's demands that church matters not attract negative attention were unrealistic.[79] German Christians were more than willing to unite in a new Nazi Reich church under a mini-führer (Reich bishop) whose loyalty to the real führer was unquestioned. Confessing Christians were unwilling to fall into line with the new thinking. Preferring Jesus Christ to Adolf Hitler, they rallied around the historical theological confessions and doctrines that had shaped Christian thought in Germany long before the new age of Nazism. Initially they did not oppose the new church organization, and their candidate for Reich bishop, Friedrich von Bodelschwingh, actually won the May 1933 election.

Willing to have an election, but unwilling to abide by nondesirable results, Hitler became furious, even refusing to meet with the winner.[80] Demanding that the election outcome be overturned and that Müller be declared Reich bishop, the German Christians, working hand in hand with the police, began to subvert church leaders. Eventually, Bodelschwingh resigned, Müller declared himself the new bishop, a pro-Nazi church constitution was approved, and new church elections were scheduled for July 1933.[81] Given the full support of the government, including the Gestapo, the press, and the police, as well as the impetus from a last-minute nationwide radio address by Hitler, the German Christians won this election and Müller became the new Reich bishop.[82]

The Pastors' Emergency League

Somewhat earlier, on April 7, 1933, the Nazi parliament passed what has become known as the "Aryan Paragraph," which made it illegal for non-Aryans to work in any bureaucratic capacity. All public servants who were not "racially pure" could no longer work in the public sector.[83] For many, including the German Christians, the spirit of this law was as important as the letter; therefore at the "Brown Synod" (brown being the color of Nazism) in September 1933, the German Christians demanded that churches of the Old Prussian Union incorporate the Aryan Paragraph.[84] Thus Nazi racial laws, not the Christian gospel, would dictate who could or could not preach the gospel in Germany. A Jewish Christian pastor would now have to lose his pulpit because of a government regulation. No longer was it true that Christian baptism incorporated a believer into the body of Christ, where there was no longer Jew or Gentile.

In September, Pastor Martin Niemöller founded the Pastors' Emergency League, whose first official protest was issued at the National Synod of the Church in Wittenberg on September 27, 1933. In the statement, the members of the league, numbering some two thousand pastors, protested the Aryan clause. One of the members was Dietrich Bonhoeffer. Amazingly, the number of pastors who signed on as members of the league reached some seven thousand, and, despite harassment and persecution, the Pastors' Emergency League existed for the entirety of the Third Reich.[85] As with any group of this nature, the members' resistance to the totalitarian claims of the state varied, with most members falling somewhere between radical opposition on the one hand and compromise on the other.

One example of the kind of thinking present in Germany at the time that would lead Christians to believe that Jewish Christians should be excluded from the office of clergy is the report by the theological faculty at the University of Marburg dated September 25, 1933. As one would expect from a group of German university professors, the report was detailed in every respect, but the conclusions were amazingly Nazi. For example, citing the New Testament's proclamation that in Christ there was no longer Jew or Greek, the report maintained that this was a spiritual statement that had nothing to do with biological and social differences.[86] Noting the difference between German Protestant churches and Roman Catholics, the committee stated that the Reformation had emphasized not only the universality of the gospel but also its "historical and national/racist" *(historisch-völkisch)* aspects. This meant that Christians in Germany need not consider the universal nature of the gospel, but could emphasize the Germanic, nationalistic, and racial themes of Nazi Germany in deciding how Christians should treat Jewish Christians. The church was more German, nationalistic, and racist than universal and welcoming. Hence, the Germanic character of the Reformation rather than the Christian message was the decisive feature in the expulsion of Jewish Christians from church office. Further, it found that "the German people *(Volk)* today perceive the Jews in their midst more than ever before as a foreign nationality." The church in Germany needed to be a national and racially pure church *(Volkskirche),* and for this reason, Jewish Christians had to be removed from church office.[87]

Yet, in the same collection of theological reflections in which the Marburg theologians published their essay, a group of pastors and theologians from across Germany, including Rudolf Bultmann of Marburg, signed a statement entitled "The New Testament and the Race Question." Noting that the New Testament itself provided no answer to the "race question" because the construct of "race" was foreign to it, they stated that the opposites of "Jew and Greek" or "Jew and Gentile" were based on God's election of "the Jewish people" *(Volk)*. But in God's eyes both "Jew and Gentile" were sinners. Therefore "the contrast of Jew-Gentile as opposite racial groups was shown to be irrelevant in light of the saving act of God in Christ."[88] Consequently, full equality among all believers in the faith community was assumed in Christian baptism. Therefore, the idea that a church office could be controlled by nationalistic-racist considerations was completely foreign to the church.[89] Because the church consists of both Jews and Gentiles who have come to the same faith and been baptized together, the theologians concluded that the Christian church could not part from its New Testament identity. The church was founded on the New Testament alone.

The difference between the two sides was great. For Christians with Nazi sympathies, the church was primarily German and nationalistic, while for others Christ was the Alpha and Omega of Christianity. The New Testament and not history, race, or nationality defined the believing community.

Enter Karl Barth

Along with the founding of the Pastors' Emergency League, a young Swiss professor and theologian was beginning to influence the conversation. In

1930 Karl Barth began teaching at the University of Bonn, and not long after that he was calling Christians to radical opposition to the "German Christians." But even before his arrival in Bonn, Barth's commentary on Paul's letter to the Romans had caused a stir. The first edition had appeared in 1919, and then expanded editions followed from 1921 through 1932. In his reading of Romans, Barth challenged readers to hear the epistle as God's word directly addressing the present moment. No longer was the letter a relic of the past whose message was more historically interesting than contemporarily relevant.

Heinz Zahrnt, whose history of Protestant theology in the twentieth century contains a lengthy and appreciative discussion of Barth's commentary, called it "a great explosion," in that Barth "proceeds with the single assumption about the text 'that God is God.'"[90] For Barth, secular history was not an "idealized pantheistic" course of grand events so much as a record of "naturalistic" and "materialistic" forces.[91] In short, human history was nothing to brag about, and certainly it was no hymn of praise to human achievement and progress, given the recent events of Europe's first world war. So, as Zahrnt expressed it, Barth "turned nineteenth century theology on its head" and then went "not from the bottom up but from the top down."[92] We do not reach God by starting with man, his accomplishments and victories, but rather, God reaches out to us in revelation. Already we can anticipate Barth's objection to the pro-Nazi theology that wanted to start with Hitler and work from there up to God. For Barth "God is the subject and predicate of his theology all in one."[93] Neoorthodoxy sounded radical to those trained to view Scripture as a curious example of ancient history, not the sacred word of God.

According to Barth's interpretation, no longer is the reader in charge of the biblical text but the text judges the reader. And so when the "German Christians" insisted on inserting Hitler and racial hatred into the Scriptures or removing Paul and robbing Jesus of his Jewish identity, Barth was ready to object with a vigorous regard for biblical authority. Nineteenth-century liberal theology had weakened biblical foundations,[94] and German Christians had simply taken advantage of this human-centered interpretation. Barth's commentary condemns this approach and seeks to rebuild a solid biblical foundation. His neoorthodox interpretation of the epistle repeatedly hammers away against the idolatry of self-worship in the human form of nation or a leader. Easily linking God with human desire is an insult to God and blasphemy against the first commandment. As Barth wrote, "The kingdom of men is, without exception, never the kingdom of God" (*Menschenreich ist nie Gottesreich).*[95] The gulf between humans and God is too wide for the human eye; only God in his revelation and in his word may cross that divide. Hence every human effort to identify a leader, a nation, a fatherland, or a race with the divine always results in the worship of the "No-God."[96] Barth simply reminds his readers that God is not the god of (German) history.

This call to a neoorthodox manner of interpretation characterized Barth's lectures on homiletics that he gave during the 1932-33 academic year. Some 110 students signed up to hear him, and according to one student, these presentations, along with his sermons in the university church, had a "strong influence on a large number of our generation of preachers."[97] For this reason I think it helpful to devote some space to these lectures.[98]

Barth urged future preachers in Germany to take the biblical text seriously, to submit themselves to it, and not the other way around. By focusing on the text through exegesis, pastors would hold up an alternative rhetoric to the culture.

From his lectures it is clear that for preachers in the Barthian tradition, the biblical text reigns supreme. Not even great political upheavals or headlines from the daily newspapers can nudge the text from its central place in the sermon. At one point in the lectures, the professor related that when the *Titanic* sank he strayed from the text and preached a "Titanic sermon," and when the First World War broke out he brought that into sermon after sermon. Finally, a woman in his congregation asked him to talk about something other than things everyone could read in the newspaper. For Barth these examples were mistakes that the preacher makes in attempting to be "à jour." The preacher does not have to bring daily events into his sermon to be relevant.[99] Yet, as long as the text controls the sermon, it may be appropriate to mention events that have a bearing on the interpretation.[100] This being said, when the preacher exegetes the biblical text faithfully and in obedience to the biblical text, he may find himself challenged to say dangerous words that will demand from him "civic courage" *(Zivilcourage).*[101] This is the risk of all faithful preaching. Without the preacher intending to be controversial or political, the Holy Spirit may make him so in the faithful hearing and proclaiming of Scripture. Barth's sermon and others in the second part of the present volume are fine illustrations of this interpretative method.

But Barth did not limit his views on preaching to the classroom. In the confusion brought about by the church elections in the summer of 1933, Barth founded a theological journal whose monthly publication would add a neoorthodox voice to the Church Struggle. The first issue of

Theological Existence Today appeared on June 25, 1933, and quickly sold over thirty thousand copies.[102] The journal's title reflected how seriously Barth took the preacher's and the teacher's role. The question of the moment was how "preachers and teachers of the church" were to live their theology today, not yesterday or tomorrow.[103] Barth insisted that the clash of theologies (confessional and Nazi) presented an urgent crisis in the church's life in which orthodox theology must combat demonic heresy. God was demanding radical faith rather than resignation or conformity to Nazi Christianity.

In the first essay, which carried the same title as the journal itself, Barth issued a call to arms against the German Christian movement and against any marriage of Christianity with Nazism. He warned that "what under no circumstances is allowed to happen is this, that we in zeal for a new thing we consider good, lose our theological existence." Then repeating the phrase "in the church we are unified [in believing] that . . . ," he offered a number of unconditional stances for the church. The last was "that God is nowhere present for us, nowhere present in the world, nowhere present in our realm and in our time as in his word; that this word of his has no other name and content than Jesus Christ and that Jesus Christ for us is nowhere in the world to be found as new every day except in the holy scriptures of the Old and New Testaments. About this we in the church are unified or we are not in the church." "Theological existence today" was being bound *(Bindung)* to God's Word and to Jesus Christ alone and to no other name or race or land. The German Christians were attempting to cut away this binding.[104]

Each issue contained sermons and Bible studies by leading pastors throughout Germany. Leaders in the Confessing Church, as well as pastors not so well known, offered Bible-centered and exegetical interpretations of Old and New Testament passages. Even after Barth's forced exile from Germany, the journal continued until 1941, when Nazi authorities shut it down. It resumed publishing in 1946, and its last volume appeared in 1984.

"Lord, Where Shall We Go?"

On one occasion Barth invited a student to contribute an essay to the journal. The student was Max Lackmann, who was only twenty-four years old at the time. The essay, "Lord, Where Shall We Go?" appeared in the summer of 1934 and clearly drew a line between faithfulness to God's word and faithfulness to the Nazi state. While many at the time found themselves in conflict over their loyalty as Germans and their identity as Christians, Lackmann insisted that for Christians there was no conflict; they must side with Christ and against the Nazi state. The essay, some forty-two pages long, caused an uproar in Germany, and Lackmann lost his right to study! Ordained in 1940, his sermons drew fire from the authorities, and the young pastor ended up in Dachau, in the cell block reserved for Catholic priests.[105] It was there that he came to wish for the two Christian confessions to be united, and after the war he devoted himself to this work.[106]

Throughout the essay, Lackmann addressed his readers directly as "Dear Brothers and Fellow Students." He reminded them that soon they would be Germany's preachers and theologians, taking the place of the current pastors and professors. Therefore it was time to declare on whose side they stood. He told his fellow students that in Nazi Germany Christians had to decide either to follow "the Jew Jesus of Nazareth" or stand with the German *Volk* that wanted to follow its own "longings and ideas."[107] The decision facing Christians in Germany in 1934 was simply the decision to proclaim the gospel — nothing more. Yet even this basic function of Christian proclamation, he wrote, could land Christians in prison (p. 6). Then he wrote, "And now I ask my brothers and fellow students, the young theologians at German universities: *How do things stand with you?*" (italics in original). In a reference to Jeremiah 7:4, he warned his readers that Germans dare not "plug their ears and call out in self-satisfaction 'This is the temple of the Lord, this is the temple of the Lord,'" for such self-deception would "mean the damnation and destruction of all our brothers and sisters and children" (p. 7).

As early as 1934 Lackmann saw the threat National Socialism posed for young people. More and more, Nazism was spreading its influence through a host of "educational" activities in an effort to ensure that the next generation of Germans would be completely inundated with the Nazi worldview, which Lackmann termed "the incarnation of Nazism." In the direct manner that characterizes this frank assessment of Nazism's threat to Christianity, he wrote, "Dear brothers and fellow students: We in particular as young theologians stand in the front line against this claim of the [totalitarian] state and the ever expanding world view of the Third Reich" (p. 8). As the "total claim" on all of life was becoming more and more evident, Lackmann reminded his generation of Christians of "Christ's total claim." There was no compromise possible with Nazi views (pp. 8-9). The need of the hour was not for the church to become political, but theological: "Dear brothers and fellow students! This hour of German history compels us now more than ever to be theologians who in this hour now as before are bound *solely* by God's Word in the Holy Scriptures" (p. 9, italics in original).

Being bound to the Scriptures was no refuge from the world; it threw the Christian directly into the conflict. Lackmann made it clear that the call was to live with both feet firmly planted on the soil of the Third Reich. He told his readers, "You are not permitted to find your own way but you must journey to where the God of Abraham, who is also your God, calls you to walk, to stand, and to live. The theologian does not walk in heaven but on the earth, where his fellow brothers and sisters — the non-theologians and non-Christians and the pagans — also walk. For the German theologian in the present time this means the Third Reich. But he walks this path as *theologian,* which means as 'servant of the word'" (p. 13, italics in original).

Just one year into Hitler's dictatorship, Lackmann could see dark clouds gathering. He warned his readers that their experiences as Christians in the Third Reich would resemble those of Jeremiah among his people and Christ in the garden, forsaken by his disciples (p. 20). Christians in Germany have become such "bizarre people," he writes, that "none of the *men and women of this world* will walk with them" (p. 20, italics in original).

We see Barth's influence on Lackmann's thinking, but the courage to live out his Christian faith in the most dangerous of circumstances was his own. What is remarkable about the essay is that Lackmann saw very early, along with Barth, Bonhoeffer, and others, how dangerous life was becoming for Christians who did not go along with the new thinking. Also, Lackmann was firm in his conviction that Christian theologians were not to join in political battles but were instead called to proclaim the gospel and to entrust the rest to God. And the most important way for Christians to do that remained the preaching of the word. It was in the Sunday sermon that young theologians were to make the claims of God clear in a Germany where the claims of Hitler were enforced by law and terror.

The influence of Barth, and others who agreed with him on his approach to homiletics, would be hard to overemphasize. Writing a preface to a collection of postwar sermons, Helmut Gollwitzer underscored the liberating effect of "text sermons":

As a way to secure the freedom required if preaching is to be taken seriously, my friends and teachers — here I have especially to name Karl Barth, Eduard Thurneysen and Hermann Diem — recommended in the Reformed tradition text-sermons, that is, the attachment of the sermon to a biblical text. They taught that the Bible text should not be merely a motto placed at the head of the sermon, not merely the occasion for all sorts of associations, not merely a peg on which to hang a theme chosen by a preacher, but should be in concrete control of the preacher. The sermon should make this text more perspicuous to the hearer than it was before. At the same time it should give pleasure, so that one is thankful for it, and be a source of guidance for life today. The preacher's subordination to this text frees him from all other authorities, from ecclesiastical authorities — that was the liberating experience of the Reformation — and from political authorities — that was the liberating experience at the time of Hitler's dictatorship.[108]

Dietrich Bonhoeffer and the "Jewish Question"

Along with Karl Barth, the young theologian and preacher Dietrich Bonhoeffer began to speak out on church and political issues during that first year of the Third Reich. In a paper remarkable for its boldness and insight into the dangers of Nazism and the coming Holocaust, Bonhoeffer addressed the church's responsibility to care and advocate for the Jews in Germany. The essay appeared in the June 1933 edition of *Vormarsch*, a journal of Reformed theology, and Bonhoeffer gave an oral presentation on its principal points to a group of pastors in Berlin. Sadly, a few of the pastors stormed out of the room while Bonhoeffer was speaking.[109] As Ferdinand Schlingensiepen writes in a recent biography of Bonhoeffer, the piece showed how difficult it was for Bonhoeffer and other pastors and theologians to formulate a forceful response to the state's threats.

German tradition had no room for political resistance from a theological perspective, because for more than four hundred years the evangelical churches in Germany had been closely tied to the state for protection. Using Luther's teaching of the "two kingdoms" *(zwei Reiche),* the church and state had long agreed that the church would not reach into the political sphere and the state would not violate the spiritual realm.[110] Today, as we read the sermons below, and as we look back on the timid Christian response to the Holocaust and other Nazi crimes, we need to remember how unforeseen the evils of Nazi Germany were and how unprepared Christian tradition was to respond to them. At the time, Bonhoeffer was himself beginning to flesh out his ideas on how the church should engage a state that was destroying the innocent. Many Christians simply did not know what to do. They did not know what they could do, or even what they should do. Bonhoeffer offered three radical responses to injustice that would place Christians in real danger from the state if they were to take the side of the Jewish victims.

The first response to injustice would be for the church to ask the state if "its actions are legitimate" in view of the state's responsibility to ensure the welfare of all its citizens.[111] If the state were willing to correct its errors, the matter would be settled. But if the persecution continued, then the church would take a second step. Christians would have to help the victims. "The church has an unconditional obligation to the victims of any ordering of society, even if they do not belong to the Christian community."[112] Here Bonhoeffer was crossing into dangerous territory. Although many Germans agreed that Christians ought to aid fellow Christians, including Jews who had converted to the faith, many others stopped at the notion of helping Jews who had not converted. The gap between the Jewish and Christian communities was too wide for many Christians to recognize Jews as their neighbors in Christ. Bonhoeffer told the Christians that they had to aid victims of Nazi persecution, regardless of religious affiliation or status in the Nazi state. If persecution continued, then Bonhoeffer suggested yet a third step. This measure was one that he ultimately would take himself, and it would cost him his life. "The third possibility is not just to bandage the victims under the wheel, but to jam a spoke into the wheel itself."[113] Here Bonhoeffer's Christian faith required political and self-sacrificing opposition. His way of "jamming a spoke" into the Nazi wheels that were crushing Jews would be to join those plotting to kill Hitler. The thought "that the legitimate state *(der Staat)* could become an illegitimate state *(Unrechtsstaat)* never appeared in [Lutheran] theology, not even as a hypothetical question."[114]

That Bonhoeffer was "the first Lutheran theologian to think his way through this question means that already in 1933 he had seen the church's situation clearer and had drawn more radical conclusions than most of his teachers and friends, and even more than Karl Barth, whom he admired greatly."[115] In this essay Bonhoeffer challenged Christians in Nazi Germany to become radical in their love of neighbor in a dangerous way. The Jews in Germany had a nonnegotiable claim on Christians in the way that the wounded man in the parable had a nonnegotiable claim on the Good Samaritan.

The Nazi Persecution of the Jewish People

As we recognize from Bonhoeffer's insistence on Christian aid for Jewish victims of persecution, life for German Jews was growing more unbearable by the day. There were daily attacks in the press, in the schools and universities, on the radio and in the cinema. Soon the anti-Jewish laws would bring the full force of the state down on Jews living under Nazi authority. In 1935, just two years after Hitler's rise to power, the Nazis enacted the Nuremberg Laws that set German Jews apart from other Germans for "special treatment" through increasing discrimination. Thus began what would end in the Holocaust. Berlin tightened the restrictions almost daily, denying Jews the right to work for the government, teach in schools, or move freely.

In November 1938, the Nazis let loose a wave of massive persecution against Jews throughout the country. Storm Troopers (SA: *Sturmabteilung*) and other thugs attacked Jews, broke store windows, and burned shops, homes, and synagogues in every corner of the empire. Jews were beaten, and many killed. Historians remember the night as *Kristallnacht* (Crystal Night); like many words from Nazi German, the word is lovely; the reality terrifying. While the police watched and did nothing, the Nazis inaugurated the beginning of the Shoah — the great storm of devastation. In one night, Germany ceased to be a land of laws and turned into a state of terror, a nightmare country where Kafkaesque madmen ruled with impunity.

On that horrible day Dietrich Bonhoeffer opened his Bible to Psalm 74 and underscored verse 8b, "They are burning all the houses of God in the land." Along the margin of verse 9 he drew a long black line: "We do not see our signs, and no prophet preaches any more, and there is no one with us, who knows for how long" (my translation of the German verses).[116] Certainly after that night no one in Germany, not Christian or Jew, could pretend that life in the country was civilized. Bonhoeffer's challenge to Christians in Germany to bind up the wounds, help the persecuted, and sacrifice their own lives if need be looms large over the entire Church Struggle. For as Christ reminds us, "What good does it do to save your own life if you lose your soul?"

Bonhoeffer, however, was not entirely correct in underscoring the words of the psalm that lamented the lack of preachers and prophets. Many Christians and others of good will were horrified at the lawlessness and violence against their Jewish neighbors. The historian Ian Kershaw notes that "Jewish eye-witness accounts abound with references to the kindness of 'aryan' [*sic*] and 'Christian' neighbors" and they "point out the overwhelming rejection of the pogrom by the vast majority of the population."[117] Kershaw quotes at length an account by a Jew in Munich: "The mood among the Christian population in Munich is wholly against the action. . . . Despite the ban on sales to Jews, grocers asked Jews whether they needed anything, bakers delivered bread irrespective of the ban etc. All Christians behaved impeccably." Kershaw comments, "There were few occasions, if any, in the Third Reich which produced such a widespread wave of revulsion — much of it on moral grounds — as the 'Crystal Night' pogrom."[118] Such actions as those on *Kristallnacht* to protect and aid Jews during the Hitler years, of course, were extremely rare, and Kershaw reflects that it may in part have been due to the "conditions of extreme terror and intimidation in which people lived. . . . Reports of arrests and recrimination for pro-Jewish comments, assistance to Jews, or criticism of Nazi actions abound in the sources."[119]

Bonhoeffer's Preaching

On the following Sunday a few courageous preachers did preach on the previous week's events across the nation (two sermons on the *Kristallnacht* are included below).

Although the Confessing Church never went as far as Bonhoeffer had hoped in resisting Nazi oppression or in defending German Jews, the young theologian continued to work within the church, even teaching courses on preaching at the underground seminary in Finkenwalde. While Barth came to the classroom via the pulpit, Bonhoeffer came to the pulpit via the classroom, as has been noted by Bonhoeffer's friend and biographer Eberhard Bethge.[120] Just as Barth emphasized the supremacy of the biblical text in the pulpit, Bonhoeffer too conveyed a high regard for the "lordship of the text" and the christocentric understanding of the sermon to the seminarians. This view of proclamation was the Confessing pastor's shield against the darts and arrows of the enemy — it was the rock on which Christian orthodoxy could make a stand against pagans inside and outside the church.

In the years following the war, scholars and general readers alike admired Bonhoeffer's writings from prison and his theological work, but we should note too his love of preaching. He preached his first sermon when he was only nineteen years old, and when he learned a few years before his own death that an acquaintance was terminally ill, he wrote, "What would I do, if I knew that in four to six months the end would come? I believe, I would try to teach theology as I used to do and to preach often."[121] At Finkenwalde he had the opportunity to talk at length about preaching and about the sermon's importance. In his biography of Bonhoeffer his friend Eberhard Bethge made a wonderful observation from these days. Since Bethge himself was one of Bonhoeffer's students in the seminary, the observation may well be based on personal experience. Bethge wrote, "It had a highly unusual effect on his students to see how seriously he took the timid and shabby sermon of each candidate as the authentic and spoken *viva vox Christi* — even for himself. Nothing, he made quite clear, is more concrete than the actual and present voice of Christ in the sermon."[122] In his lectures Bonhoeffer went so far as to talk of the sermon in sacramental terms: "The sacrament of the word *(sacramentum verbi)*. Because the word is Christ accepting men, it is full of grace but also full of judgment. . . . If we ignore the spoken word of the sermon, then we ignore the living Christ. There is a sacrament of the word."[123]

This high estimation of what the sermon could do is evident also in the preaching of those whose sermons we read below.

The Barmen Declaration

The high value placed on preaching and on the Scriptures as the word of God shines through the Barmen Declaration as well. Tensions between Ludwig Müller, Reich bishop, and the "Confessing Front" of pastors and laity, led chiefly by Barth, had grown worse as the first anniversary of Hitler's coming to power approached. Meeting in Barmen, this first Confessing Synod had over three hundred pastors and laity in attendance.[124] Barth authored a first draft of a confessional document in which he targeted the "German Christian" teachings that "there are areas of . . . life in which we belong not to Jesus Christ, but to other lords."[125] The final document was the Barmen Declaration, which questioned the totalitarian claims on the church by the Nazis and the heretical teachings of the German Christian movement. In the first article the Confessing Christians, following Barth's lead, established that the gospel of Jesus Christ as found in the sacred Scriptures was the inviolable basis of the German Evangelical Church.[126] The Protestant writer and theologian Heinz Zahrnt considers the first article of the Barmen Declaration to be a perfect summary of Karl Barth's theology, and he quotes it verbatim in his account of this episode in his history of Protestant theology in the twentieth century: "Jesus Christ, as he is witnessed to in the Holy Scriptures, is the one word of God that we are to hear and in whom we are to trust and obey in living and dying. We reject the false teaching [of the German Christians] as if the church could and must recognize as the source of her proclamation other events and powers, figures and truths as God's revelation outside and along side this one word of God."[127] Nothing on the human horizon could contradict, subtract from, or add to Christ as the word of God as set forth in the Scriptures.

The second article stated that the German Evangelical Church was organized in regional churches *(Landeskirchen)* and therefore was not a part of a new church under Müller and the German Christians. Indeed, the German Christians had endangered the very existence of the church by going outside the historical confessional bounds.[128] Then the Barmen Confession went on to list five positive confessions (articles of faith) and five heretical teachings held by the German Christians. To each affirmation there was an opposing rejection. The Barmen Declaration became "the basic statement of the whole Confessing Church, a theological lifeline in the stormy seas which lay ahead, forged to hold the Church true to its mission and to allow it neither to become a propaganda weapon of a political movement nor a society for the propagation of views about the next world."[129]

Barmen also declared that Jesus Christ alone had claim to a Christian's entire existence and thus rejected the notion that there were other "areas" of life in which Christians had "other lords."[130] Dietrich Bonhoeffer, who was in England at the time of the synod, considered Barmen "one of the most important events of his life, and it became the reason he could return to Germany" from the safety of England.[131]

Barmen as Rhetorical Guide

The Barmen Declaration was a statement of Christian faith and not a political agenda.[132] If the German Christians were eager to worship the golden calf of Hitlerism, the Confessing Christians were adamant that such activity was idolatry. While many critics of the church, looking back on the Hitler years, criticize both Catholics and Protestants for not being more political, we have to remind ourselves that neither church understood itself as a political organization with a political agenda. If the churches objected to the German Christians for being too political, they were not going to err by becoming political themselves.

Hearing the Sermons

Given the concerns of the Confessing Church pastors, there could be no mistaking Hitler for a contemporary messiah or Germans as the chosen people; nor could membership in the church be racial. Making this clear became the chief task of the Confessing pastors and elders meeting at Barmen. While such a task may appear to many of us today, who are so far removed in time and context from Nazi Germany, as too little too late, in the 1930s such a proclamation placed the preacher in great danger. Hitler allowed no dissent, no criticism, and no deviation from the forced conformity to Nazi thought and speech *(Gleichschaltung).* Every "confessional" sermon left the pastor open to arrest or worse.

It is important, therefore, to read each sermon in the light of the christocentric emphasis of Barmen. To speak of Christ as the authentic Führer and, by implication, not Hitler, was subversive speech. To speak of sinners and not of victors was also subversive, for Nazis insisted on the victorious outcome of the cultural struggle during its first years and then later the victorious outcome of the war. To say something good about the people of the Old Testament or to identify Christ with the Jews or as a Jew was inflammatory rhetoric. To suggest that the weak and helpless were deserving of God's love and Christian charity was to go against the Nazi teachings about the mentally ill and the handicapped, whose lives did not have the same value as did the healthy and strong. To mention the suffering brought on by the war was to be a traitor who doubted the genius of the führer. To place God's kingdom above all earthly kingdoms (i.e., the Reich) was to side with the international conspiracy against the German *Volk.* And to alert the congregation to the suffering of the Jews or to the suffering caused by the war was to place oneself in immediate danger.

Along with what was said in sermons, we must be alert for what was not said. As the preceding paragraph suggests, to say the one thing was not to say the other. These rhetorical silences served the purpose of sharing subtle and sometimes not so subtle criticism of the regime. For this reason,

Christian vocabulary, so different from the poisonous words of Nazi rhetoric, offered pastor and congregation a subversive language through which to share the faith and extend comfort.

Nazi Speech

As indicated above in discussing Nazi faith and the mandatory conformity to the new way of life in Germany, the Nazis developed a unique vocabulary through which they presented their constant propaganda.

Again, Victor Klemperer's book on Nazi language is worth reading for its detailed look at certain words and expressions as experienced firsthand by a Jew living in the midst of Nazis. And as a professor of languages, his insight is particularly valuable. To mention one example, as we read the sermons it is helpful to recall Klemperer's insight that Nazi speech dealt in superlatives. Hence, Hitler was the "smartest" leader of the "bravest" people of the "purest" blood, and Germany was the "greatest country" and "most glorious" of nations in the most "heroic" of wars and struggles against the "worst" of enemies in the "most dangerous" of times. As Klemperer often does, he combines linguistic insight with personal experience. In discussing "a well-stocked subgroup of the general use of the superlative," Klemperer writes:

> This [the superlative] could be referred to as the most prevalent linguistic form of [the language of the Third Reich], which is not surprising given that the superlative is the most obvious means by which a speaker or agitator can achieve a desired effect, it is the quintessential advertising mode. That is why the NSDAP [the Nazi Party] reserved it for its own special use by eliminating all competition and maintaining sole right of disposal: in October 1942 Eger, our neighbor in the next room, the former owner of one of the most respected clothes shops in Dresden, at the time a factory worker and soon to be "shot attempting to escape," told me that a circular had forbidden him from using superlatives when advertising his business.[133]

Another invaluable resource for studying Nazi speech is the *Vocabulary of National Socialism (Vokabular des Nationalsozialismus)*, which to date is available only in German. This study of Nazi words, expressions, and concepts underscores what Klemperer points out in his study of Nazi language and in his lengthy diary; the Nazis took language seriously and sought to refine its use for political ends. As is well known, Goebbels, as head of Nazi propaganda, worked tirelessly at getting the words right to convey the ideas of Nazism as well as to cover up its crimes with euphemisms. While there is not space here to discuss the many examples and essays on Nazi language in either Klemperer or the *Vocabulary of National Socialism,* a few examples might serve to illustrate the pervasive tone of Nazi language.

Christians hearing the term "original sin" think naturally of the Genesis story of the Fall. Nazis, hearing the same reference, might well think of Hitler's definition of the term in *Mein Kampf,* where it becomes the "sin against blood and race."[134] Göring justified the Nuremberg race laws by referring to original sin as "disgracing one's blood" *(Blutshande)* and by acknowledging, "we Germans have been forced to suffer terribly from this original sin" (p. 205). Preachers who took their text from Genesis and not *Mein Kampf* would automatically challenge a basic Nazi concept just by reading the Genesis story and allowing the inspired Hebrew author to remind congregations that original sin had to do with hubris and disobedience rather than with blood and racial purity.

As noted by Klemperer, Germans "believed" in Hitler much as Christians and Jews believe in God. It does not surprise us therefore to note that the noun "faith" *(der Glaube)* became a central idea in Nazi vocabulary. In general, Nazi faith was the "new political faith" of "unquestioned, devotional trust in all matters pertaining to National Socialism and the abilities of the Führer always to do what is right" (p. 274). As Hitler noted in a speech on April 4, 1922, "the most powerful thing *(das Gewaltigste)* that our movement *(Bewegung)* ought to create is a new faith for these diversified, searching and erring masses" (p. 274). Nazi leaders were not alone in confessing faith in Adolf Hitler. The German Christian bishop Müller went so far as to declare faith in Hitler's policy to be like Christian faith in Jesus' Sermon on the Mount (p. 275). In an article entitled "The Faith among Storm Troopers" ("Der Glaube in der SA"), the author mixes religious faith and Nazi faith into one cup when he declares that faith in the SA is "faith in the Führer sent to us by God's will" (p. 276). Certainly every recitation of the Apostles' Creed and every mention of faith in God, in Christ, or in the power of prayer in a sermon in the Third Reich would challenge the Nazi understanding of this central Christian virtue.

The word "brutal" appears to have been a favorite adjective. We tend to see brutality as a negative idea, and when used against the enemies of Nazism the Nazis were ready to allow it this connotation, but when applied to the Nazi trait of being unwilling to compromise or to accept anything short of victory, brutality was a positive virtue (pp. 129-30).

As is well known, the swastika was the symbol of Nazism. Yet, in my opinion, part of the reason this symbol was omnipresent in the Third Reich is that its literal meaning in German is "hook cross" *(Hakenkreuz)*. Nazis twisted and distorted the cross into a pagan symbol to challenge and replace the Christian cross. As suggested in *Vocabulary of National Socialism,* the swastika was in direct competition with the Christian cross (p. 289). I am persuaded that the mention of the cross of Christ *(das Kreuz)* in sermons of opposition often had this competing cross *(das Hakenkreuz)* of the Nazis in mind.

"Hard and hardness" were great virtues in Nazism. Softness and weakness were for inferior races. Noting that the word in German had long had a negative connotation, as in Luther's translation of Luke 19:21 where the servant fears his master because he knows him to be "a hard" man, Hitler saw it as one of the most desired qualities in German youth (pp. 294, 295). Himmler, speaking in 1943 to a group of SS leaders in Posen, told them that ridding the world of Jews, these men would know what it was like to walk over the corpses of a hundred or five hundred or a thousand, and this would make them "hard" (p. 296).

As with so many words and ideas, the Nazis turned human values upside down and ridiculed Christian virtues and commandments. So when a sermon lauded a Christian trait, background noise was blaring the accepted perversion of words, meanings, and attitudes. Love, forgiveness, sin, redemption, salvation, prayer, humility, and weakness all have their place in the Christian vocabulary, but in Nazi speech these are replaced by hatred, rejection, brutality, final victory, obedience to Hitler, and rejection of the weak, the ill, and the marginal.

In the Third Reich these two languages were set against each other every day. Indeed, the central question for Christians was "cross or swastika" *(Kreuz oder Hakenkreuz).*

Christian Rhetoric of Silence

In the cacophony of hatred, sometimes the best response was to be quiet. In a remarkable insight, the Confessing pastor Wilhelm Niemöller wrote of how the best response to Nazi talk may have been the "silence" of preaching and teaching in the parish. Commenting on the outrageous idea of the German

Christians that the work of the nation was to "become German! Not become Christian," Niemöller responded, "Now it seemed there was nothing left to do but to be silent and yet [in so doing] to open our mouths all the more faithfully. The place for that was the congregation."[135] I take this "silence" to be orthodox preaching and orthodox behavior in every parish as incarnational opposition to National Socialism and its oppressive conformity to evil. Christians countered Nazi political speech with gospel rhetoric.

The Confessing Church placed great trust in the local parish, as Niemöller makes clear from his own parish's experiences during the Church Struggle. Along with the Confessing pastors, the members of each congregation carried on the Church Struggle (p. 48). A pastor does not preach to an empty church, and during the years of the Church Struggle, Niemöller writes that attendance at Sunday services grew so much that often extra chairs had to be brought in and many were forced to stand (p. 53). He adds that the number of members taking communion grew from 1,476 in 1932 to 2,070 in 1936 (p. 53). Also, lay Christians could be counted on to contribute money, both to the work of the Confessing Church and to missions of charity (pp. 50-51). In his own parish church, some 3,319 laymen and laywomen signed their names to a document in which they "joyfully" placed themselves under the authority of the Confessing Church, and this at a time when the Nazis were stepping up harassment against the two pastors of the church (p. 50).

Another "hotbed" of Christian opposition was the church in Berlin-Dahlem. Although Hitler Youth activities were intentionally scheduled to conflict with worship services for the young people on Sunday mornings, the "boys came running covered in sweat and dust from Grunewald to the village church in Dahlem and took their places."[136] As persecution of the Jews grew in intensity, members of the parish engaged in dangerous activities to help both Jews and non-Jews, even though this work was never "sufficient."[137]

Admittedly, the "hardest blow for the congregation" came with the arrest of their pastor Martin Niemöller in the summer of 1937. Pastor Helmut Gollwitzer was at the St. Anne parsonage on that evening, and under his leadership parish members joined in petitionary prayers for their pastor. This gathering for prayer continued on a regular basis thereafter.[138] Gollwitzer became the pastor of the Berlin-Dahlem church and continued to preach oppositional sermons until the Nazis removed him from the pulpit and exiled him from Berlin. As the names Niemöller and Gollwitzer suggest, Berlin-Dahlem was blessed with extraordinary preachers. Not these alone, but others also contributed to the congregation's oppositional stance to Hitler and its confessional loyalty to Christ. As a member of the congregation recalled, "In addition to all these preachers who preached in their distinctive styles on a regular basis to the congregation, there were always certain worship services that became unforgettable for the congregation because of their powerful text or the special day the service was held, or because of their great poignancy or their crucial sharpness and power."[139] Elsie Steck then lists the names of preachers who continued to preach powerful sermons throughout the war: "Father Niemöller [the pastor's father], Hans Asmussen and Heinrich Vogel, Klappenroth and Martin Fischer, Günther Dehn, Hans Böhm, Jannasch, Bibelious and Lilje, but also of so many other pastors from the Dahlem neighborhood and from all over Germany."[140]

Preaching as Provocation

In March 1935 the Second Confessional Synod of the Old Prussian Union church met in Berlin-Dahlem. At this meeting pastors and laity issued a declaration that stressed preaching the gospel as "the central mission" of the church.[141] In part, the declaration stated, "we see our nation *(Volk)* threatened by a great danger. This danger is the new religion of National Socialism."[142] Pastors were told to read the text of the declaration the following Sunday from the pulpit. When word got out about the resolution, the government forbade the reading because of the statement about a "new religion." Moreover, all pastors were to notify the state in writing that they would refuse to read the text. When many pastors refused to comply, a "wave of arrests" took place, with 715 pastors being arrested. Among them was Paul Schneider, the first pastor to die in a concentration camp.[143] Although the pastors spent but one day in jail, the episode showed how important the Confessing Church viewed preaching and the importance of using the pulpit to meet the challenge of the "new religion." It also demonstrated the coming dangers.

The preachers whose sermons appear in this book, and many others, both Protestant and Catholic, could not look the other way as the "new religion" began to take its toll. Not even personal safety excused timidity in the pulpit. In a letter to his wife from his jail cell on November 14, 1937, Pastor Paul Schneider wrote about preaching in Nazi Germany: "It is not that I and all the rest of us have said too much in our sermons, but rather that we have said far too little."[144]

Reading these sermons in the twenty-first century, one cannot help but marvel at the confidence these preachers placed in the proclaimed word of God. Not only are many of the sermons radical and prophetic, they are also lengthy by contemporary standards. By today's standards it is simply amazing that congregations listened to such lengthy sermons that required close attention while just outside the church walls Nazi terror ruled. Once the nightmare of persecution began, followed by war and then bombs falling on German cities, and unimaginable casualties both at the front and at home, we might think that the preacher would turn to brief, comforting utterances of a pious nature. But this was not so. The preacher expected concentration and attention. Even more, the preacher expected the courage of faith. Urgent as things might be outside the church, preaching the word of God was even more urgent inside the church.

Each preacher in the second section of this book, in his own unique circumstance and style, reminds us of Jeremiah, whose lament must have sounded like the voice of a distant brother:

> If I say, "I will not mention him,
>   or speak any more in his name,"
> then within me there is something like a burning fire
>   shut up in my bones;
> I am weary with holding it in,
>   and I cannot.   (Jer. 20:9 NRSV)

Throughout the Reich, the Church Struggle took place in both pulpit and pew. Preaching in Hitler's shadow was risky business. But always Jesus Christ was real and uncompromising in his claim on preacher and congregation alike. Compared to Christ, how small Hitler appeared. Against the horrible distortion of words by Goebbels and his propaganda machine, the Christian in the pulpit offered the truth of the gospel and the integrity of the "word made flesh." In so doing, certain themes stand out in these sermons of opposition: the authority of Jesus Christ; the sovereignty of God; both the Old and New Testaments as Holy Scripture; the purity of the church; the certainty of God's judgment on Germany for immorality and for the failure to love the neighbor, especially the Jewish brother and sister; the relevance of the gospel after the European Enlightenment and in spite of Nazi pseudoscience and paganism; and the gospel's insistence that Christians must risk even their lives for the truth of Christianity.

SELECTED SERMONS OF RESISTANCE
IN THE THIRD REICH

Proclaim the message; be persistent whether the time is favourable or unfavourable; convince, rebuke, and encourage, with the utmost patience in teaching.

2 TIMOTHY 4:2 NRSV, CATHOLIC EDITION

Except for the Bonhoeffer sermon, the sermon translations are by the editor.

Gideon

Born in Breslau in 1906, the twins Dietrich and Sabine were among the eight children of Karl and Paula Bonhoeffer. The father was a professor of psychiatry in Berlin where the family lived in a large home in an upper-class section of the capital. For Dietrich, his family was the center of his life.[1] But the First World War shattered the idyllic environment of the Bonhoeffers when Walter, one of the children, was killed in battle.[2]

As a student, Dietrich was simply brilliant. He finished his doctoral studies at the age of twenty-one and his dissertation, *Sanctorum Communio*, continues to be read and discussed. During the academic year 1930-31 he studied at Union Theological Seminary in New York, where he came into contact with the African American community of Harlem. He attended worship services and was moved by the vitality of the spirituals. But contact with a community of citizens suffering discrimination sensitized him even more to the sufferings of German Jews under Hitler. At Union the German theologian became friends with the French pacifist Jean Lasserre, who helped him to see the "absurdity of Christians killing people for the sake of national pride or territorial ambitions."[3] Furthermore, it was his new French acquaintance who helped Bonhoeffer understand that Jesus' radical insistence that his followers practice peace (love of the enemy, nonresistance, going the second mile, etc.) was meant not for the first century alone but for all Christians in all times until the end of time.[4] At the time, these ideas pointed Bonhoeffer toward Gandhi, and soon he had plans to travel to India to study, but the trip never took place because he was called back to Germany to aid the Confessing Church in the training of seminary students.

Confessing Church seminarians were forbidden to attend German universities, and members of the Confessing Church were not allowed to teach at universities either. Therefore the Confessing Church established an underground seminary in the secluded village of Finkenwalde near the Baltic Sea. In his lectures at Finkenwalde, Bonhoeffer offered future pastors in the Confessing Church a startling interpretation of Jesus' call to radical discipleship. Here too the seeds planted in America by his French friend bore fruit in German soil. Bonhoeffer would later revise and publish his lectures under the title *Nachfolge* (discipleship).

The police closed the seminary at Finkenwalde in September 1937. Soon thereafter some twenty-seven of his Finkenwalde students were in Nazi jail cells. In January 1938 the Nazis forbade Bonhoeffer's presence in Berlin, and it was only with special permission that he was permitted to visit his parents.[5] As life became more and more difficult in Germany, Bonhoeffer accepted an invitation to teach in the United States, but soon after his arrival he decided to return to Germany. Bonhoeffer left New York for Germany on July 27, 1939.

A little more than a year later, in September 1940, Bonhoeffer, like so many other pastors, was officially banned from preaching and speaking in the Third Reich.[6] Soon thereafter he joined a small group of conspirators whose chief goal was to murder Adolf Hitler and negotiate an end to the war, primarily with England. As part of this activity, the group was able to rescue a few Jews from the Nazi terror.[7]

Bonhoeffer's work with the *Abwehr* allowed him and others in his circle to have firsthand knowledge of the severity of Hitler's policy against Jews.[8] Certainly this information only increased his sense of obligation for personal sacrifice for this oppressed minority. His willingness to join what became the July 20 plot was foreshadowed by his essay "The Church and the Jewish Question," which he wrote in the early days of the Church Struggle (see the editor's introduction). He had been greatly disappointed by the timidity of the Confessing Church in the face of Nazi persecution of the Jews.[9] At the time of the Barmen Confession, Bonhoeffer was serving as pastor to a German-speaking church in London. Although absent, he followed the developments of the Confessing Church closely, and the Barmen Confession pleased him in its radical affirmation of the unique Lordship of Christ in the church, but its silence in the face of Nazi persecution of the Jews greatly disappointed him.[10]

This increasing violence against Jews certainly influenced his shift in thinking from pacifism to violent resistance.

After his arrest in April 1943, Bonhoeffer continued to be a model of Christian courage. The prison offered new opportunities to practice obedience to Christ in the midst of great suffering, danger, and even torture. His writings from prison, published as *Letters and Papers from Prison,* have equaled his book on discipleship in popularity. Like Paul Schneider in Buchenwald (see below), Dietrich Bonhoeffer refused to allow prison confinement to silence Christian witness.

By special orders of Hitler, Bonhoeffer was hanged on April 9, 1945, just days before Germany surrendered.

The sermon in this collection comes from the early days of the Third Reich. As early as 1933 it had become obvious to Bonhoeffer that the new Reich was evil. Hatred of Jews and preparation for war were daily fare for Germans. When Bonhoeffer preached his first sermon following Hitler's coming to power, he surely must have known that Jewish Gideon would present a sharp contrast to German rhetoric against Jews and for war. His repeated emphasis on Gideon's lack of military forces in the face of greater military strength must have made an impression on the congregation. Also, the talk of altars reflected the altars in German churches that had been profaned with Nazi flags and pictures of Hitler. The sermon on Gideon offered Germans in the new Reich a radical choice between the Judeo-Christian God of tradition and Germanic paganism.

Gideon[1]

February 26, 1933[2]

Berlin, Germany

And he said unto him, Oh my Lord, wherewith shall I save Israel? behold, my family is poor in Manasseh, and I am the least in my father's house. And the Lord said unto him, Surely I will be with thee, and thou shalt smite the Midianites as one man. . . . And the Lord said unto Gideon, The people that are with thee are too many for me to give the Midianites into their hands, lest Israel vaunt themselves against me, saying, Mine own hand hath saved me. . . . And Gideon said unto them, I will not rule over you, neither shall my son rule over you: the Lord shall rule over you.

Judges 6:15-16; 7:2; 8:23 KJV[3]

[1] This translation of Bonhoeffer's sermon is the copyrighted translation of Fortress Press, © 2009, and is used with their permission. Notes on the German text are mine, as is the inclusion of the biblical text from the King James Version of the Bible.

[2] The German text indicates that this was Estomihi Sunday. "Estomihi" is from the Latin *esto mihi* (be to me) and is from Ps. 31:2:

> Incline your ear to me;
>   rescue me speedily.
> Be a rock of refuge for me,
>   a strong fortress to save me. (NRSV)

This was the psalm of the day, and Bonhoeffer's reading of the Gideon story offers a beautiful commentary on the psalm's emphasis on God as our only refuge in times of trouble.

[3] The use of Old Testament texts by Bonhoeffer and others in the Confessing Church is noteworthy, given the Nazi hatred of anything Jewish. See Doris L. Bergen, *Twisted Cross: The German Christian Movement in the Third Reich* (Chapel Hill: University of North Carolina Press, 1996).

This is a passionate story about God's derision[4] for all those who are fearful and have little faith, all those who are much too careful, the worriers, all those who want to be somebody in the eyes of God but are not. It is a story of God's mocking human might, a story of doubt and of faith in this God who makes fun of human beings, who wins them over with this mockery and with love. So it is no rousing heroic legend — there is nothing of Siegfried[5] in Gideon. Instead it is a rough, tough, not very uplifting story, in which we are all being roundly ridiculed along with him. And who wants to be ridiculed, who can think of anything more humiliating than being made a laughingstock by the Lord of the world? The Bible often speaks of God in heaven making fun of our human hustle and bustle, of God's laughter at the vain creatures he has made. Here it is the powerful Sovereign One whose strength is unequaled, the living Lord, who carries on this way about his creatures. For him, who has all power in his hands, who speaks a word and it is done, who breathes forth his spirit and the world lives, or takes it away and the world perishes, who dashes entire nations[6] to pieces, like potters' vessels for this God, human beings are not heroes, not heroic, but rather creatures who are meant to do his will and obey him, whom he forces with mockery and with love to be his servants.

So that's why we have Gideon and not Siegfried, because this doubter, mocked by God, has learned his faith in the school of hard knocks.

In the church we have only *one* altar — the altar of the Most High, the One and only, the Almighty, the Lord, to whom alone be honor and praise, the Creator before whom all creation bows down, before whom even the most powerful are but dust. We don't have any side altars at which to worship human beings. The worship of God and not of humankind is what takes place at the altar of our church. Anyone who wants to do otherwise should stay away and cannot come with us into

[4] The German word is *Spott,* whose range of meanings includes ridicule, derision, sneer, sarcasm, and mocking, among others. Certainly so soon after Hitler's assuming of power, God's mocking and ridicule are not what Germans expected to hear.

[5] Siegfried is the hero of the *Nibelungenlied,* a medieval epic poem and the basis of the opera by Wagner. Here Bonhoeffer draws a stark contrast between a Jewish and a Germanic hero.

[6] The German word is *Völker,* which is here in the plural form and is *Volk* in the singular. *Volk* was/is a common word that the Nazis overused and distorted with racial meaning and hatred.

God's house.[7] Anyone who wants to build an altar to himself or to any other human is mocking God, and God will not allow such mockery. To be in the church means to have the courage to be alone with God as Lord, to worship God and not any human person. And it does take courage.[8] The thing that most hinders us from letting God be Lord, that is, from believing in God, is our cowardice. That is why we have Gideon, because he comes with us to the one altar of the Most High, the Almighty, and falls on his knees to this God alone.

In the church we also have only *one* pulpit, from which faith in God is preached and not any other faith, not even with the best intentions. This again is why we have Gideon — because he himself, his life story is a living sermon about this faith. We have Gideon because we don't want always to be speaking of our faith in abstract, otherworldly, irreal, or general terms, to which people may be glad to listen but don't really take note of; because it is good once in a while actually to see faith in action, not just hear what it should be like, but see how it just happens in the midst of someone's life, in the story of a human being. Only here does faith become, for everyone, not just a children's game, but rather something highly dangerous, even terrifying.[9] Here a person is being treated without considerations or conditions or allowances; he has to bow to what is being asked, or he will be broken. This is why the image of a person of faith is so often that of someone who is not beautiful in human terms, not a harmonious picture, but rather that of someone who has been torn to shreds. The picture of someone who has learned to have faith has the peculiar quality of always pointing away from the person's own self, toward the One in whose power, in whose captivity and bondage he or she is. So we have Gideon, because his story is a story of God glorified, of the human being humbled.

[7] Following Hitler's becoming chancellor there were many church services throughout Germany honoring Adolf Hitler. Churches filled with Nazi flags and clergy with swastikas on clerical robes were common sights. Bonhoeffer's biographer writes that in the Marburg cathedral there was a "forest of Swastika flags around the altar." The cathedral's preacher pointed to the flags and noted that the swastika "has become the symbol of German hope. Whoever defames this symbol defames Germany." Eberhard Bethge, *Dietrich Bonhoeffer: Eine Biographie*, 8th ed. (Gütersloh: Chr. Kaiser/Gütersloher Verlagshaus, 1994), p. 305.

[8] Certainly Bonhoeffer's life bears vivid testimony to the truth of this simple and profound thought.

[9] Again, Bonhoeffer's life would underscore this truth.

Here is Gideon, one person no different from a thousand others, but out of that thousand, he is the one whom God comes to meet, who is called into God's service, is called to act. Why is he the one, or why is it you, or I? Is it because God wants to make fun of me, in coming to talk with me? Is it God's grace, which makes a mockery of all our understanding? But what are we asking here? Isn't God entitled to call whomever God chooses, you or me, the highly placed or the lowly, strong or powerless, poor or rich, without our being entitled to start arguing about it straightaway? Is there anything we can do here other than hear and obey?

Gideon is supposed to liberate Israel from its bondage at the hands of the Midianites, an enemy nation with superior power. He, who is just like any of a thousand others, is called upon to do a phenomenal deed. He looks at himself and his own strength and then at the unconquerable might of the opposing side. He has nothing on his side — the enemy has it all. "He responded, 'But Lord, how can I deliver Israel?' How am I supposed to accomplish this thing that you are calling me to do? Lord, it's too big a job; don't be cruel. Take it back, or let me see some help, give me armies, weapons, riches! God, you don't realize how wretched we are; look at this starving, weakened people;[10] see how homelessness and lack of bread makes them doubt you; look how they bow down to other gods and not to you. How can I deliver Israel?" This Gideon is someone we know, isn't he? He has suddenly become very much alive for us. Gideon, we recognize your voice only too well; you sound just the same today as you did then. The call comes to our Protestant church, just one like many others in the world: You are to redeem Israel; you are to set the people free from the chains of fear and cowardice and evil that bind them. This call startles the church and troubles it profoundly, this church without influence, powerless, undistinguished in every way — why is it the one to be burdened with this call? It looks at the hopelessness of its proclamation; it looks at the apathy and the misery of those who are supposed to be listening and recognizes that it is not equal to the task. It looks upon its own inner emptiness and barrenness, and it says fearfully and reproachfully, *with what* am I supposed to redeem this people? How am I supposed to do this phenomenal thing?

And then suddenly the call comes to us: Put an end to the bondage in which you are living; put an end to the mortal fear that gnaws at you, to the power of human desire that is burning you up, to your tormented and self-

[10] The German here is *Volk.*

satisfied keeping to yourself. Put an end to your fear of other people and your vanity; set yourself free. Who would be willing to say that he or she has never heard this call and has never answered, as Gideon did: "Lord, *with what* am *I* supposed to do such great things?"

But then Gideon is silenced; today just as in those days, he's told to shut up. You're asking, "With what?" Haven't you realized what it means that this is God calling to you? Isn't the call of God enough for you; if you listen properly, doesn't it drown out all your "with what" questions? "I will be with you" — that means you are not asked to do this with any other help. "It is I who have called you; I will be with you; I shall be doing it too." Do you hear that, Gideon of yesterday and today? God has called you, and that is enough. Do you hear that, individual doubting Christian, asking and doubting Christian? God has plans for you, and that does mean you. Be ready and see to it. Never forget, even when your own powerlessness is grinding you down to the ground, that God has phenomenal, immeasurable, great plans for you. "I will be with you."

What does Gideon do? He goes out and has the trumpets blown, calls up an army from all the tribes, gathers around him whatever fighting forces he can find. Compared to the superior forces of the enemy, it is still only a small army, and Gideon hesitates to go into battle. Then, just as he is pitching his tents opposite those of the enemy, there comes God again, blocking his path. "Gideon, what have you done? Gideon, where is your faith? Look at this army of yours; it's too big; Gideon, it was fear and doubt that made you call up this army. The troops with you are too many for me. I'm not going to give you the victory this way. Then you would only take the credit for yourselves and say, 'We have delivered ourselves; we have gained the victory.' But I will have none of it." Fall down before your God and let God be your Lord; know that only God can save you.[11] This is God's promise, and the word of God is more powerful than all the armies in the world.

Here the crucial question has been put: "Gideon, do you seriously believe in God your Lord, even here face-to-face with this terrifyingly dangerous enemy? Then, Gideon, send your massive army home; you don't need it. God is with you; the victory belongs to God and not to your army." What a phenomenal thing to ask, what a confusing encounter with the liv-

[11] Given the enthusiasm for Adolf Hitler and the new, powerful Third Reich at the time, this was a radical, anti-Nazi idea. Nazi worship of the führer and of the power of the human will was sweeping the nation, and this deification would only intensify.

ing God! There stands Gideon with his little army, hesitating to go out against the enemy's superior forces, and then God comes and laughs rudely in his face, makes fun of him: "Gideon, the troops with you are too many for me." Instead of bringing on huge amounts of weapons and armies, he calls for disarmament, meaning faith, faith; let your armies go home! How cruelly God makes fun of all human might; it's the bitterest of all tests of faith and makes God an incomprehensible lord and despot over the world. Isn't it crazy? Wouldn't Gideon have been torn apart inwardly, to have to give up the only forces that, from a human viewpoint, he could count on, here in the face of the enemy? What kind of wild God is this, zealous for his own honor, always standing in human beings' way and frustrating their plans, before they know it? Why does God frustrate us? Because God is opposed to the proud, because human beings keep getting it wrong, however they do it? Why do we always get it wrong? Because we are always trying for our own credit, and don't want to believe in God.

But Gideon believed and obeyed; he let his troops go home, and with every man who left him, his faith grew in this God who had made fun of him. And when they had all gone except for a tiny remnant, the victory was given into his hands. He believed, he obeyed, he gave God the glory, he renounced the honor for himself, and God kept the promise made.

Is this a tall tale like all the others? Anyone who says so has failed to understand that Gideon is still with us, that the old story of Gideon is being played out in Christendom every day. "I will be with you in the face of the enemy. . . ." What does Gideon do? What do we do? We rustle up all our own forces; we reach out for every means of help; we calculate, we weigh, we count; we arm ourselves with offensive and defensive weapons. Until then, suddenly and unexpectedly — nobody knows the hour — the living God is there and assails us again: "If you have faith, lay down your weapons; I am your weapon. Take off your armor; I am your armor. Put away your pride; I am your pride." Do you hear that, church of Gideon? Let God alone; let the word and the sacraments and the commandment of God be your weapons; don't look around for other help; don't be frightened. God is with you. "Let my grace be sufficient for you." Don't try to be strong, mighty, famous, respected, but let God alone be your strength, your fame and honor. Or don't you believe in God?

It does seem crazy, doesn't it, that the church should not defend itself by every means possible in the face of the terrible threats coming at it from every side. What madness brought this Gideon into the world? But all this is only the foolishness of the Christian faith itself; that is what this story is [about]. It's not about the particular command that was given; it's not that which is valid for all the ages, but rather the foolishness, the stumbling block of living faith, which confesses, "With might of ours can naught be done, soon were our loss effected. . . ." And you as an individual, you who have heard the call to free yourself from bondage, to loosen its chains and the grip of fear, you are already right back into acting from lack of faith. You think that by straining to exert all your energies, you can do it yourself, by putting all you have into it, because you want to control your own destiny. Then suddenly God himself is standing in your path, and there go all your fine plans again. "Lay down your weapons, for I am your weapon, and a thousand of your weapons are not equal to one of mine. Let me do what you cannot do. You want the honor of saying, 'I have delivered myself,' but this is not for you; give me the honor and the glory, believe in me. Let my grace be sufficient for you, for my power is made perfect in weakness."

Gideon's warriors must have been flabbergasted; they must have shuddered when he gave them the order to go home. The church is always astounded, and shudders, when it hears the voice of the One who commands it to renounce power and honor, to let go of all its calculations and let God alone do God's work. We shake our heads and are scandalized as we watch many a Gideon among us going his way. But how can that confound *us* who see in the midst of our church the cross, which is the sign of powerlessness, dishonor, defenselessness, hopelessness, meaninglessness, and yet is also where we find divine power, honor, defense, hope, meaning, glory, life, victory? Do we now see the direct line from Gideon to the cross? Do we see that the name of this line, in a word, is "faith"?

Gideon conquers, the church conquers, we conquer, because faith alone conquers.[12] But the victory belongs not to Gideon, the church, or ourselves, but to God. And God's victory means our defeat, our humiliation; it means God's derision and wrath at all human pretensions of might, at humans puffing themselves up and thinking they are somebodies themselves. It means the world and its shouting is silenced, that all our ideas and plans are frustrated; it means the cross. The cross over the world — that means that human beings, even the most noble, go down to dust whether it suits them or not, and with them all the gods and idols and lords of this world. The cross of Jesus Christ — that means God's bitter mockery of all

[12] The German word here that Bonhoeffer repeats for emphasis is *siegen,* the verb from which comes the Nazi slogan *"Sieg heil,"* or sacred victory. How radically different the idea of victory or conquest is for the Christian.

human grandeur and God's bitter suffering in all human misery, God's lordship over all the world.

The people approach the victorious Gideon with the final trial, the final temptation: "Be our lord, rule over us." But Gideon has not forgotten his own history, nor the history of his people. . . . "The Lord will rule over you, and you shall have no other lord." At this word, all the altars of gods and idols fall down, all worship of human beings and human self-idolization. They are all judged, condemned, cancelled out, crucified, and toppled into the dust before the One who alone is Lord. Beside us kneels Gideon, who was brought through fear and doubt to faith, before the altar of the one and only God, and with us Gideon prays, Lord on the cross, be our only Lord. Amen.

KARL BARTH
....

A Sermon about Jesus as a Jew

Many consider Karl Barth (1886-1968) the greatest Protestant theologian of the twentieth century. Countless seminarians and pastors, both in Germany and elsewhere, identify themselves as Barthians. While his massive *Church Dogmatics* influenced theological thinking for most of the twentieth century, not everyone is aware of his early life, especially his leadership in the Confessing Church and his influence during the early days of the Church Struggle. Yet Barth's voice and peaching are as important to Christian resistance to Nazism as Bonhoeffer's.

Born in Basel, Switzerland, Karl Barth rose quickly to international acclaim with the publication of the revised edition of his *Epistle to the Romans* in 1922. In this significant commentary on Paul's letter, Barth underscored the immeasurable gap between the biblical God and human culture, leaving no room for men and women to boast of their best achievements as anything worthy of God's approval. Certainly this theme took on even more radical tones in Hitler's Third Reich (as sketched in the editor's introduction).

Barth's father taught church history and New Testament in the capital city of Bern. It was there that Karl entered school, and it was there too that he announced his desire to become a theologian.[1] He studied first in Berlin under the most famous German theologian of the day, Adolf von Harnack, with whom he later disagreed. Leaving Berlin, he completed his studies in Marburg under Wilhelm Hermann, whose view of Jesus echoed the "liberal quest" for the historical Jesus that was so important to the theology of the day.[2]

In his native Switzerland, Barth served a small congregation as pastor. From 1911 to 1921 he preached regularly in Safenwil, where his love for his congregation and the problems they faced daily made him an advocate of social justice, but he never went so far as to confuse Christian concern for social justice with Marxist concerns for revolution.³

Christian concern for others is rooted in knowledge of God, and this must come from his revelation in Jesus and not from human desires and historical progress. In all his work Barth forcefully reminded Christians that God's unique revelation in Christ nullifies our human-centered attempts to discern the meaning of Christ from history and culture. God addresses us in his word and our responsibility is to respond and obey, not to change and adjust the gospel. Barth insisted that the gap between God and his creation was far too wide to be closed by mere men. Only a divine revelation could close the divide.⁴

When Hitler came to power in January 1933, Barth was a professor at the University of Bonn, where his lectures on preaching (1932-33) were both popular and influential. As the "German Christians" and the Nazis took more and more control of society and made their hatred of Jews evident, they began to demand untenable compromises from the churches and sought to poison the gospel with Nazi ideology. Barth became a chief advocate for a noncompromising response to these heresies.[1] He was forced to leave Germany in 1934 after refusing to swear the loyalty oath to Hitler that was required of university professors as civil servants.⁵[2] After leaving Nazi Germany for Switzerland, Barth continued to exert tremendous influence on Christian thinking in Germany. It is fair to say that his neoorthodox theology along with sermons and publications provided a foundation on which to oppose the Nazi paganism and its influence in the German church.[3]

Beginning in 1932 and continuing for the remainder of his life, Barth worked on his massive interpretation of Christian teaching in volume after volume of his *Church Dogmatics.* He did not live to complete the work, but these important writings shaped theological discussion for many years. In these contributions Barth presented an understanding of the Christian revelation in terms of what God has done in Christ and not in terms of any "natural theology."⁶

[1] See the editor's introduction. Also, James B. Torrance, "Karl Barth," in *The Encyclopedia of Religion,* vol. 2, editor in chief James Lindsey (New York: Thomas/Gale, 2005), provides a good overview.

[2] See the appendix below for context of the controversy and the text of a sermon on swearing the oath.

[3] Along with his sermons, books, and lectures, his journal *Theologische Existenz heute* was an ongoing forum for the church's voice to be heard.

The sermon included here was preached just at the end of Hitler's first year as chancellor. Its theme is Jesus as a Jew.[4] Copies were made the following day, and Barth even sent the sermon to Hitler.[7] The Jewishness of Jesus offended some in the church, and they walked out. Writing later to a woman from the church, Barth insisted that one simply cannot sever Jesus from his Jewishness: "anyone who believes in Christ, who was himself a Jew, and died for Gentiles and Jews, *simply cannot* be involved in the contempt for Jews and ill-treatment of them which is now the order of the day."[8]

[4] Eberhard Busch offers a detailed discussion of the importance of this sermon for Barth's views on Judaism and the Jewish citizens in Nazi Germany. See Eberhard Busch, *Unter dem Bogen des einen Bundes: Karl Barth und die Juden 1933-1945* (Neukirchen-Vluyn: Neukirchener Verlag, 1996), pp. 165-74.

A Sermon about Jesus as a Jew

December 10, 1933
Second Sunday in Advent

Schlosskirche in Bonn, Germany

Now the God of patience and consolation grant you to be like-minded one toward another according to Christ Jesus: That ye may with one mind and one mouth glorify God, even the Father of our Lord Jesus Christ. Wherefore receive ye one another, as Christ also received us to the glory of God. Now I say that Jesus Christ was a minister of the circumcision for the truth of God, to confirm the promises made unto the fathers: And that the Gentiles might glorify God for his mercy; as it is written, For this cause I will confess to thee among the Gentiles, and sing unto thy name. And again he saith, Rejoice, ye Gentiles, with his people. And again, Praise the Lord, all ye Gentiles; and laud him, all ye people. And again, Esaias saith, There shall be a root of Jesse, and he that shall rise to reign over the Gentiles; in him shall the Gentiles trust. Now the God of hope fill you with all joy and peace in believing, that ye may abound in hope, through the power of the Holy Ghost.

Romans 15:5-13 KJV

Dear Friends![5]

The church of Jesus Christ is a crowd, a throng, a gathering — a "community" as that beautiful, old word expresses it; it is a word that we have to learn to understand all over again in a completely new way — a commu-

[5] German *Liebe Freunde.*

nity that is not held together by common interests and that is not held together by common blood and not even by common opinions and convictions but certainly a community held together rather by that voice that we
hear at the beginning and at the end of our text, a voice that sounds repeatedly and that is never to be falsified nor ever confused with any other tones
in the world, *"The God of patience and of comfort give you all . . . ! The God
of hope fill you all . . . !"*[6] The voice that speaks to us in this way, so
pleadingly and at the same time so giving, so serious and also so friendly,
is, in the words of the apostle Paul, the voice of the divine Word himself,
from whom the church of Jesus Christ is born and from whom she[7] must
always feed and from whom alone she may be fed. God knows who God is;
and in his Word he *tells* us: he is the God who gives patience, comfort, and
hope. *God* knows that we need him as we need nothing else and yet we
have no power over him;[8] and in his Word he *tells* us this, he pulls our
thinking and longing together and brings these to himself, that we must
implore: May *he* grant us! May *he* fill us! And *God* knows how close to us
and how ready he is for us; and in his Word he *tells* us this by placing on
our very lips as a deep sigh from closest proximity and in deepest and most
sure trust in him this petition: May *he* grant us! May *he* fill us! May this
voice, with which God tells us what he knows of himself and of us, ring out
from the past. The apostle Paul is really very far away from us, and the
whole Bible is very far away from all the books and newspapers that we
read.[9] If the Bible still rings out with *its* sounds, *its* news, *its* claim and encouragement, then the church of Jesus Christ is present, in which even I, by
hearing this voice, "am a living member and will remain so forever" (Heidelberg Catechism, question 54).[10]

But in this Advent season we have reason to reflect: the fact that there
exists a word of God for us as well as a church of Jesus Christ as place of

[6] I follow Barth's italics throughout the sermon. Unless the King James Version is
noted, all biblical quotations are my translation of the German text.

[7] In German the word for church is feminine. I have used the feminine pronoun
because in English the church may be referred to as "she" or "it," depending on one's view of
the *ecclesia*.

[8] Here Barth challenges the Nazi notion of the powerful Aryan whose victory is due
to his power and will.

[9] A Nazi criticism of Christianity was that it was ancient, out of date, and
prescientific. Barth recognizes the historical fact yet draws on the contemporary presence of
the Holy Spirit in the living community of the church.

[10] The reference to the catechism is in the text.

comfort, of patience, and of hope, a church that comes from God; this we cannot take for granted. That is not like air that is everywhere and every place. That is not a truth that is placed in our hand either through nature or history so that we can simply live with it as with something that belongs to us. The fact that God's word exists in the church is founded neither on the spiritual life of man nor is it a cultural accomplishment, nor does it belong to the ways and nature of a *Volk*[11] or of a race, and neither is it founded in the necessary course of world history.[12] It is rather a mystery with which our very existence is coated from the outside in and not from the inside out; a mystery that in no sense is within us but rather is completely founded in a foreign power and force that is above us.

That there is a church and a word of God is something that is only true because, as our text says, *"Christ has received us,"* received us as a beggar is received off the street, received as people who did not even think it possible nor who could have thought it possible to receive him but rather as people who really could only have been *received*. We can even go so far as to say: *accept,*[13] like an orphan is accepted into an orphanage, accepted to be something that we innately are not, namely, accepted as his brothers and children of his father. We could even say *taken along* or *taken into* the district where he, the Son of God, leads, governs, carries the responsibility, and creates so that except for him no one should have worries or cares.[14] Based on our own will, we would never have been taken along and taken into this district.[15] Yet he has taken us there. That is the message of Christmas that we will soon celebrate once again: Christ has accepted us! And to be sure, accepted *for the praise of God:* not as if this simply had to be

---

[11] Throughout the sermons I have left the German word *Volk* in the text or have placed it in parentheses. I have done so because this word is a key word in Nazi vocabulary, pointing as it does to a "community of people formed and shaped by race from a common lineage or origin" (Cornelia Schmitz-Berning, *Vokabular des Nationalsozialismus* [Berlin: Walter de Gruyter, 2007], p. 642). I see each use of the word in the sermon as a confrontation between Nazi and Christian rhetoric.

[12] Barth here rejects the anti-Nazi rhetoric of both *Volk* and race.

[13] Barth's emphasis on the German *nehmen* in: *aufnehmen, annehmen, mitnehmen, hineinnehmen.* God "takes" us in in each sense of the various verbs that Barth uses. Again, a challenge to Nazi hubris that would never see Germans as needing anyone to take them in in love or pity. He continues hammering away at this idea of Christians not being worthy of God's mercy.

[14] If Christ rules, then we ought never to fear and fret over anything.

[15] Here again Barth attacks the Nazi idea of Aryan worth as opposed to unworthy and inferior individuals and groups.

this way, not according to any natural law or because God has need of us, and not for the sake of our needs and desires, rather because it was right for him in his freedom to be great and wonderful in this respect, that we would be accepted, received, taken along, and taken in by his Son.[16] For this reason the angels sang in the holy night: Glory be to God in the highest and peace on earth among men of good will (Luke 2:14) — because of his, the divine good will! But all of this is true according to our text in a double sense that we do well to note.

It surely means something all-encompassing; namely, that he has taken on humanity in order — as God — to be our neighbor and at the same time — as man — to be God's neighbor. So that in him God's kingdom[17] has come near to us, who are but human (Matt. 4:17). And it means that we, who are only human, might stand before God's throne as people pleasing to God. Because God himself in Jesus Christ has clothed himself with humanity, we are therefore clothed by the mystery of God's Word and the church.

But beyond this we are given here something truly remarkable to consider. It is not self-evident that we belong to Jesus Christ and he to us. *"Christ was a servant of circumcision for the sake of God's truth to confirm the promises given the fathers."* This means that Christ belongs to the people *(Volk)* of Israel.[18] *This* people's *(Volk)* blood was in his veins, the very blood of God's Son. *This* people's *(Volk)* way of life he took on by taking on humanity, not for the sake of this people *(Volk)* or from a preference for this people's *(Volk)* blood or race, but rather for the sake of truth, that is, for the sake of demonstrating the truthfulness and faithfulness of God. And because with *this* people *(Volk)* and with this people *(Volk)* only — an obstinate and bad[19] peo-

[16] Again Barth dismisses any notion of human merit or worthiness to account for the miracle of incarnation.

[17] Here I have chosen to translate the German word *Reich* as "kingdom." Yet it is important to note that in German *Reich* means both "kingdom" and "Reich," as in Hitler's Third Reich. Certainly the two were in conflict and Christians in Hitler's Reich had to decide to which Reich they owed their loyalty. It is hard to know if the Christians in German congregations heard the word as oppositional terms or if it was only the common translation of the Greek *basilea* without political overtones.

[18] Barth forcefully reminds his listeners that Jesus was a Jew, a real Jew in flesh and blood. Jewish blood was of course ridiculed by the Nazi view of racial purity. At this point many in the congregation left the church in protest. Busch, *Bogen*, p. 168.

[19] The German here is *ein böses Volk*, which in its strongest sense could be "an evil people." Barth here is on thin rhetorical ice to characterize Israel with language that comes very close to echoing Nazi ideology. Yet, again, Barth's purpose seems to be to emphasize the

ple *(Volk)*, to be sure (Exod. 32:9)[20] — but precisely with *this* people *(Volk)* God had formed a covenant, had given them his presence and the promise of an unparalleled redemption. Jesus was a *Jew* in order to confirm and to fulfill this free and merciful promise of God "given to the fathers" and not to reward the Jews or to honor them. He himself once said of himself that he was sent to the lost sheep of the house of Israel, and to them only was he sent (Matt. 15:24; compare 10:5f.). This means for us, who are not Israel, a closed door. But if the door is now open, if Christ now belongs to us as well as we to him, then this verse must certainly assume a special meaning: "Christ has received us to the praise of God." The existence of the Jewish people down to the present day has constantly reminded us of this.[21]

Frederick the Great is supposed to have asked his physician Zimmermann once whether he could give him a single completely certain proof for the existence of God, and he is said to have received the laconic answer, "Your majesty, the Jews!" The man was right. The Jew reminds us through his very existence that we are not Jews and therefore really "without Christ, alien and outside the commonwealth of Israel and alien to the covenants of promise, without hope and without God in the world" (Eph. 2:12). The Jew reminds us that it really is something special, new, and wonderful if we "are no longer guests and strangers, but fellow citizens with the saints and members of the household of God" (Eph. 2:19). We are not this innately.[22] The Jew — in his so puzzlingly foreign and just so puzzlingly indestructible existence — is living proof in the midst of all the peoples *(Völkern)* of

---

grace and mercy of God over any idea at all of human merit on the part of either Jew or Christian. Also, as the reference to Exodus indicates, unflattering references to God's people are not uncommon in prophetic literature. In Deut. 32:5 the author refers to the Israelites as a "perverse and crooked generation" in the King James translation.

[20] At this point in the sermon Barth refuses to sentimentalize or romanticize Jews. Referencing Old Testament criticism of Israelites, he emphasizes that God's acceptance of Israel then, and Jews in Germany, is no different than his acceptance of Christians. It is pure, unmerited grace. God has no need of Israel then and no need of Christians today. But that links Christian and Jew rather than separates them. Both Israel and the church share in the same grace.

[21] The survival of the Jewish people throughout history and throughout the world, especially in Nazi Germany and eastern Europe in 1933, is reason for joy and celebration of God's faithfulness to his covenant from which Jew and Christian should take comfort. Rather than persecute Jews, Christians in Germany should honor, respect, and welcome them. This is not a thought that Nazis would welcome but one that Christians needed to hear and ponder.

[22] The German is again *vom Hause aus*.

the world that God is free to choose whom he will and that he is under no obligation to choose us either. It is sheer grace if he also chooses us. For it could well be that if we resist this strict proof of God's existence, that if we resist too passionately the Jews, we resist this God of free grace![23]

But exactly here is the special, new, and miraculous thing about Christ receiving us — although he is a "servant of circumcision for the sake of God's truth" (note: cf. Rom. 15:8) — it is that Israel, the chosen and pardoned people *(Volk)*, did not treat the redeemer any differently than all peoples *(Völker)* of every time and place would have treated him had they been in Israel's position.[24] That is to say, they rejected him and nailed him to the cross, not in foolish haste, not from misunderstanding, but rather in the exact same way that they had always treated God.[25] "My people" *(Volk)*, as God so often named this people *(Volk)*, proved itself once more and finally as "Not my people *(Volk)*" (Hos. 1:10). But the prophet Hosea had just said the very opposite thing, and now it became true in the crucifixion of Christ! "It will happen in that place where they were told, 'You are not my people,' they will be told, 'O you children of the living God'" (Hos. 1:10). "Father, forgive them for they do not know what they are doing!" (Luke 23:34) — this is exactly what is said to this people *(Volk)* on Golgotha. It is just that this can no longer be said only to this people *(Volk)*. While Israel was making itself like all the other nations *(Völker)*, all the other nations *(Völker)* were making themselves like Israel. The closed door opened. Israel herself had to open it. God's covenant and truth were not broken but rather were fulfilled by those in Israel — but also by those among the Gentiles, who now recognized and accepted God's mercy as the work of his covenant and of his truth. For here was the fulfillment of the covenant, the faithfulness of God precisely in the crucifixion of Christ: "For God sealed them *all* under disbelief that he might have mercy on *all*" (Rom. 11:32).

That is why it can be said further, *"The Gentiles glorify God for his mercy"* (Rom. 15:9). Hear this well: not because they were better, purer, more righteous than the Jews! If the Jews had had an advantage then, they

[23] God's grace unites Christian and Jew, while Nazi hatred separates German from Jew.

[24] One argument the Nazis used against the Jews was that they were "Christ killers." Yet Barth asserts that any culture would have done the same. The rejection of Jesus by some first-century inhabitants of Judah reflects the human rejection of God.

[25] Clearly a reference to Israel's rejection of God. Barth wants his listeners to identify with Jewish rejection of first God and then Jesus rather than judge that troubled history as different from Christian behavior.

would still have it today, not because of any good characteristics but because it has pleased God to select *them,* to make the covenant with *them* that he has fulfilled in Christ that he might have it with us too. This then is the reason that the Gentiles glorify God, because God has shown and confirmed his *mercy also to them* in Christ crucified in the midst of Israel. Because the covenant with Israel — both for Israel and for the Gentiles — was revealed as the covenant of *grace* for *sinners,* who cannot boast of having maintained faithfulness, who can live only by mercy but who also are now allowed to live by mercy. Here is where Israel's advantage and our disadvantage end. That is what an orthodox Jew even to this day cannot understand: that the covenant God made with his people and only with his people has been revealed in the rejection of Christ by his own people as the free, innocent goodness that God wills to do for everyone. Exactly this covenant! says Paul, and then he lets the book of this one ancient covenant speak and testify for the glory of God among the Gentiles: *"Therefore I will praise you among the Gentiles and sing your name." "Rejoice, Gentiles, with his people!" "Praise the Lord, all Gentiles, and praise him, all peoples." "There will be the root of Jesse, and he will arise to rule over the Gentiles; on him shall the Gentiles hope." In this way* Christ has accepted us to the praise and glory of God. "Salvation comes from the Jews" (John 4:22). Jesus Christ was a Jew.[26] But by his bearing and carrying away the sins of the whole world, including our own (compare John 1:29), in the sin of the Jews, this salvation that comes from the Jews has come also to us. We rejoice at this door opening so wide if we can also rejoice that there is a word of God and a church of Jesus Christ. And each time that we think about the Jews, why should we not think especially of this, "the Gentiles glorify God for his *mercy*"?

Now we are able to understand the other thing our text has to tell us about the church of Jesus Christ: "As Christ has received us to the glory of God, so *receive each other.*" This is a law without exceptions. This is an order, a strict and inflexible order.[27] But the Gentiles and the Jews, all who have been received by Christ and praise God because of his mercy, fulfill this command. They all receive one another.[28] "To receive each other"

[26] This short, simple sentence is the sermon's key point.

[27] Nazi Germany certainly knew about laws and order. Here Christian obedience is set against Nazi obedience.

[28] The notion in Nazi Germany that Germans were to receive rather than reject Jews was radical. But Barth goes even further. Christians in Germany must allow themselves to be received by their Jewish neighbor. Jew and Christian are linked together, and Nazi teaching about race cannot separate the two whom God has joined in the covenant.

means to see each other as Christ sees us. He sees us all as traitors of the covenant but also as those with whom God intends to maintain his covenant. He sees us in our pious and worldly godlessness, but also as those to whom the kingdom of God has come near. He sees us as those who are absolutely instructed to be merciful but also those who have already experienced mercy. He sees us as Jews in conflict with the true God and as Gentiles living peacefully with the false gods, but he sees us both united as "children of the living God" (Hos. 1:10).

Surely we cannot view each other in this way on our own strength. If we look at each other from our personal point of view, then the first truth, that we are violators of the covenant, and the second truth, that God keeps the covenant in spite of this, totally pass us by. We take far too seriously both the excellences and the mistakes we perceive in each other. We praise ourselves too loudly and we scold ourselves far too severely. Either way, we do not accept each other. Then we are in the marketplace and not in the church.[29] Then certainly God's word falls silent. But when it does *not* fall silent, when we consider that we have been received by Jesus Christ to the glory of God, then we see each other with the eyes of Jesus Christ, and that means, for sure, that our deeply fragile faithfulness to the covenant, our godlessness and wretchedness become visible, but so too does the prevailing faithfulness of God that rests immovable over every one of us and we simply have to be able to welcome each other regardless of any excellence or errors, praise or blame — however important such things may be in the proper place — and with each other praise God's faithfulness to us who are unfaithful. When we see each other so, then we will accept each other, and then we are in the church of Jesus Christ. For that is the church of Jesus Christ: the community of those who accept each other as Jesus Christ has accepted us, hearing the word of the God of patience, consolation, and hope. That is "communion of saints." The praise of God for the sake of his mercy has brought them together and will hold them together through everything that happens. And will hold them together as no friendship, no community of common thought, no national or racial community, no political state

[29] Barth uses the metaphor of the marketplace and the merchant in his commentary on Romans. The marketplace is the world where human values reign, but God as the "divine Merchant" uses far higher standards: "There is no form of human righteousness to which the divine Merchant will assign so high a value that He will certainly purchase it for Himself." Karl Barth, *The Epistle to the Romans,* trans. Edwyn C. Hoskyns (Oxford: Oxford University Press, 1968), p. 63.

can hold them together.[30] It will hold them together in the way the members of the body of Christ in the whole world are held through the Lord himself (see Col. 2:19). And now we can close with a short reference to those things in our text for which we are to *pray*.

It is first of all this: *that you are agreed among yourselves in regard to Jesus Christ so that with one voice you may in unity glorify the God and Father of our Lord Jesus Christ.* This means that from the mutual accepting of one another as Christ has accepted us, we would have to conclude that in the church of Jesus Christ only *one* thought and *one* will would be alive and powerful in everyone — to be sure, not any single human unity of thought and will but a unity likely very different from human ways of thinking and willing — with the intention of letting the praise of God for his mercy's sake become loud, to be passed on, to be awakened also in those who do not yet know that they have received mercy.[31] This intention would then by necessity have to be carried out "with one voice and in unity." This means that the church of Jesus Christ would have to be one community that with each other *discerns* the word it has heard in order to *confess* it with one another.

The church must do so! But does it? If it does, then where is its discernment and confession? And if not, then why not? Our text tells us simply to pray for the church that it *become* a church of discernment and confession. If only we then would once again *pray for this unanimously!* What does it mean then to pray? To scream, to call, to reach out so that what is true once and for all time might be true for us: Christ has accepted us. Ecclesiastical discernment and ecclesiastical confession would indeed follow such a prayer, if earnestly offered, as thunder follows lightning.

The other thing we pray for is this: that *"God fill you with all joy and peace in the faith, that you have complete hope through the power of the Holy Spirit."* This means that from the mutual accepting of each other as Christ has accepted us, it must follow that in the church of Jesus Christ all joylessness is on the way to becoming joy, all discord is at least on its way to becoming peace, all distress of the present moment would somehow finally be engulfed by the hope for the Lord's presence. Do we lack this confession and discernment in our church because there is within us so much dispassionate and rigid joylessness, discord, lack of peace, and misery? Or is there so much rigid joylessness and lack of peace and misery in us in spite of our

---

[30] Christian faith binds far more strongly than Nazi or national ideology.
[31] One of Barth's great sentences — to be read slowly and enjoyed greatly.

alleged faith because our church lacks both discernment and confession?[32] It is certain that there is a definite connection here. And therefore it is understandable that we are here simply told that we must pray for the church, to pray that joy and peace in her faith gain the upper hand, that we — not through the power of our minds but through the power of the Holy Spirit — might partake of a full and overflowing hope. And our praying will simply have to be a sighing that it not remain so hidden from us that Christ has accepted us to the glory of God. If this does remain hidden from us, then we will find it hard to accept each other, and as long as we do not accept each other, then how can we ever obtain peace, joy, and hope? These are certainly waiting at our door. And they will be given to us if we earnestly pray for that one thing for which we must ask.

The thoughts of many people are occupied in this particular time more seriously than before with what it is that the church misses and what we miss in the church. Let us note that our text does not speak about this, but rather where it could speak of such things, simply prays and tells us to pray to this God of patience, of comfort, and of hope, who is the Lord of the church. If we hear this and allow it to be said to us that we simply are supposed to pray, are permitted to pray, and can indeed pray, then it might become clear to us that the one thing and indeed the decisive thing is *not* lacking in the church or in us who are in the church: namely, this *word* from which the church is born. If we hear this, that there is one *prayer* that is capable of much (compare James 5:16), then we surely *have* the word of God. Let us *hold* to this in that we do what is suggested through the word of God! Perhaps this time has come upon us in the church[33] so that we might learn to pray differently and better than ever before and thereby to keep what we have (compare Acts 3:11).

[32] Confession *(Bekenntnis)* in the sense of confessing one's faith in word and deed. Hence the Confessing Church.

[33] The Church Struggle in the Third Reich.

....

Christ Crossing the Stormy Lake and Jesus' Glory

Paul Schneider (1897-1939) was the first Protestant pastor to die in a concentration camp. Unfortunately, he is not widely known in the United States, perhaps because he was not a brilliant theologian like Dietrich Bonhoeffer or Karl Barth. He was a small-town pastor who loved his people and his Lord more than life. For him, there never was a question of compromise with Nazis nor of looking the other way as paganism engulfed Germany. He was simply fierce in his opposition to Nazism, and he expected no less from his parishioners. In his view, one could not be Christian and Nazi. His radical devotion to Christ and to the gospel was evident from the first days of the Third Reich and continued to his final day in Buchenwald.

Paul Schneider was born on August 29, 1897. He was the second of three children born to Pastor Gustav and Elisabeth Schneider in Pferdsfeld. He described himself once as a "simple country preacher's kid," and he did indeed spend his life mostly in the rural area of his birth.[1] But an otherwise idyllic childhood was marred by his mother's illness. She died in 1914, and the way she endured her suffering deeply affected Paul (p. 1). His relationship with his father was distant.

When he was eleven years old, his father sent him away from the village home to study at the humanistic high school in Bad Kreuznach. When his father became pastor in Hochelheim, Paul was able to live at home and attend the high school in Giessen (p. 2). At the age of seventeen, Paul took "an emergency diploma" (Notabitur) that allowed him to join the German army, where he saw three years of service on both the eastern and the western fronts. He was discharged in 1918 with the Iron Cross, 2nd Class (p. 3).

Between 1919 and 1922 Schneider studied theology at the university in Giessen. He wrote that his war experiences deeply influenced his decision to study theology. Here alone, he found, was the power that could help rebuild a "heartbroken nation (Volk) and a heartbroken humanity" (p. 3). Rather than the war making him hard and cold, it made him sympathetic and tender toward the suffering of others. This certainly was the case when he had a practicum to work for a year with coal miners. In his diary he explained his decision to engage in this hard, dirty work as an opportunity to get to know workers in their joys and in their needs, and to see "into what little corner of their hearts religion had hidden itself" (p. 9).

As a consequence of a preaching seminar following his practicum with miners, Schneider had to wrestle with his own faith, not because of what he had experienced in the war or in the mines, but because of the liberal theology that he had earlier embraced. In his faith crisis, he had to determine once and for all what was true about Christianity. In a 1926 letter to his future in-laws — he was to marry Margarete Dietrich, a pastor's daughter — he explained that his answer to the scholarly question in an assignment about the meaning of miracles was simply that "our faith stands [or] falls with the miraculous events of the cross and the resurrection." He noted too that the paper helped him get beyond the popular liberal theology of the day (p. 13). Just as Bonhoeffer was changed by his contact with the African American Christian community in Harlem, Schneider was changed by his social ministry with the poor in the eastern part of Berlin. He spent ten months in Berlin working with poor and working-class men and women, and he came to know personally men and women for whom Christ was a living presence; and this led him to the personal decision to give his life totally to Jesus Christ (p. 17).

After his father's death, Schneider took over his father's congregation in Hochelheim and was pastor there from 1926 to 1934. His sermons against the German Christians as well as essays against Goebbels and other Nazi leaders proved too much for the local community and Nazi authorities (pp. 45-47). The first Schneider sermon in our volume, preached on January 28, 1934, caused uproar both in the congregation and among the local Nazi authorities. The sermon pits the Christian worldview against the Nazi worldview, especially the Nazi faith in "blood and soil" as the source of "salvation" in the new Germany. The following day Schneider wrote in a letter that he no longer believed that "our evangelical church" could avoid direct conflict with the Nazi state (p. 69). Following the sermon, the pastor read a communication from the Confessing Church warning that the attempts by the German Christian Reich bishop Müller to force the evangelical *Landeskirchen* to be under his control *(Gleichschaltung)* would be met with a reminder that "we must obey God more than men."[2] Paul Schneider was alerting his congregation to the increasing governmental threats to Christians.

Less than a month after he preached this sermon, Schneider was forced out of the pulpit and reassigned to the churches of Dickenshied and Womrath, where the congregations were more supportive of the Confessing Church.[3]

Christ Crossing the Stormy Lake
and Jesus' Glory

January 28, 1934

Hochelheim, Germany

Now it came to pass on a certain day, that he went into a ship with his disciples: and he said unto them, Let us go over unto the other side of the lake. And they launched forth. But as they sailed he fell asleep: and there came down a storm of wind on the lake; and they were filled with water, and were in jeopardy. And they came to him, and awoke him, saying, Master, master, we perish. Then he arose, and rebuked the wind and the raging of the water: and they ceased, and there was a calm. And he said unto them, Where is your faith? And they being afraid wondered, saying one to another, What manner of man is this! for he commandeth even the winds and water, and they obey him.

Luke 8:22-25 KJV

And straightway Jesus constrained his disciples to get into a ship, and to go before him unto the other side, while he sent the multitudes away. And when he had sent the multitudes away, he went up into a mountain apart to pray: and when the evening was come, he was there alone. But the ship was now in the midst of the sea, tossed with waves: for the wind was contrary. And in the fourth watch of the night Jesus went unto them, walking on the sea. And when the disciples saw him walking on the sea, they were troubled, saying, It is a spirit; and they cried out for fear. But straightway Jesus spake unto them, saying, Be of good cheer; it is I; be not afraid. And Peter answered him and said, Lord, if it be thou, bid me come unto thee on the water. And he said, Come. And when Peter was come down out of the ship, he walked on the water, to go to Jesus. But when he saw the wind boisterous, he was afraid; and beginning to sink, he cried, saying, Lord, save me. And immediately Jesus stretched forth his hand, and caught him, and said unto him, O thou of little faith, wherefore didst thou doubt? And when they were come into the ship, the wind ceased.

Matthew 14:22-32 KJV

Dear Friends in Christ![1]

I am certain no thinking and alert Christian has failed to notice that we in the Evangelical Church[2] are being challenged to struggle and to witness and to confess our faith. I am certain that we realize that we cannot simply enjoy the fruit that others have harvested for us. Moreover, we now are forced to wrestle with the church of Christ, with the true Evangelical Church herself, for the soul of our people *(Volk)*. To be sure, many people are still asleep and have not recognized that it is the hour to rise up. They still think that since all around us things have changed, certainly in the church, of all places, things must remain exactly as they were before. Or perhaps they just want to subject the church to the political authority of the state and shape the life of the church to fit the current political views as the "German Christians" are currently doing.

To be sure, they can only support this practice by preaching the heresy that the gospel does not rest solely on the good news of our savior Jesus Christ and the kingdom *(Reich)* of God, but that somehow race and the gospel together constitute the church. Insofar as they place "blood and race" alongside the Word of God as authentic sources of revelation, alongside the will of God revealed alone in the words of Scripture, alongside Jesus as the only mediator between God and men, they, in all truth, fall away from the living God and his living Christ.[3] In our church a blazing fire has broken out over these matters, and there can be no peace until those who have betrayed the pure teaching and those wolves who have come into

[1] The German is *Liebe Gemeinde,* literally "Dear congregation."

[2] The Protestant church is most often called simply the Evangelical Church in German to distinguish it from the Catholic Church.

[3] Here one sees Schneider lashing out against the new teaching of the German Christians that God's revelation included Nazism. One thinks too of Barth's rejection of such thinking. The Barmen Declaration in May 1934 will again attack this heresy.

the sheepfold in sheep's clothing have vacated their bishops' chairs and their seats as our representatives — or at least until the Confessing Christians have abandoned this falsified church of Christ.[4] But these people are still in power and would like to silence those who oppose them, and even render them harmless with the help of the political powers by denouncing them as reactionaries and enemies of our fatherland — which they are not. The little boat of the church of Christ is traveling on stormy seas.

All this has not come upon us out of nowhere, nor has it come upon us overnight and without our own guilt. Disorder and lack of church discipline have been widespread now for a long time in the Evangelical Church.[5] There is no longer a fence between saints and pagans who adamantly want nothing whatsoever to do with God's word and who want to hear nothing at all of God.[6] We have tolerated the teachings of Balak,[7] of liberalism that praises the goodness and freedom of men and women while minimizing the honor of God and letting the seriousness of eternity fade away into a misty haze.[8] We do not despise enough the deeds of the Nicolaitans of which the letters to the churches in Revelation warn us,[9] these who mock morality, these who are mean and tightfisted, these who scorn Sundays and who go to Holy Communion as obvious sinners who refuse to repent. We are auctioning away the forgiveness of sins, this most precious good of Christ's church, like mass-produced pieces of junk that anyone can buy for a penny.[10] And now the rising floodwaters have come over the church and the tiny boat is filling with water, and we can barely bail it out.

[4] Here a handwritten note in the margin reads "with the help of political powers and methods," making clear that this Nazi church has political backing.

[5] The pastor was adamant that his responsibility included oversight of Christian life and morals. This generated numerous conflicts with both parishioners and Nazi authorities.

[6] Margin note by Schneider: "I mean especially the custom of the Eucharist in our parish being a village custom." The pastor had recently canceled a community celebration of communion at Christmas for young people, because the Nazis were joining in and unbelievers were partaking. Sharp conflict resulted from the cancellation of the event (Rudolf Wentorf, *Der Fall des Pfarrers Paul Schneider: Eine biographische Dokumentation* [Neukirchen-Vluyn: Neukirchener Verlag, 1989], pp. 78-79).

[7] Num. 22:6 where Balak wants to curse the Jews. Schneider may be referencing Nazi anti-Semitism.

[8] Margin note by Schneider: "Effects of a liberal proclamation of the gospel still evident in Hochelheim." Recall that as a student he admired liberal theology.

[9] Rev. 2:6, 15.

[10] Margin note by Schneider: "the practice of confession at our open celebrations of Holy Communion."

The church of Christ sails upon the ocean of national life *(Völker-leben)*, and our German Evangelical Church sails upon the waters of our particular national identity *(Volksleben)* as Germans.[11] With thanks to God, we Evangelical Christians have accepted whatever has appeared to be healthy in the recent turn of events in our nation *(Volk)*, that is: the will for political unity, for national honor, for a social community[12] in which the poorest and least important individual in our nation *(Sohn des Volkes)* is loved and honored, and we have joined in with the festivals and measures that seek to bring these things about. But we cannot close our eyes to the high storm-waves we see surging toward our people in the Third Reich. What is now coming together in the German Christian Faith Movement under the leadership of influential Nazis — among them Rosenberg,[13] the editor of the *People's Observer* — is nothing less than naked paganism with which, according to Christian understanding, there can be no agreement. We simply cannot believe what the great newspaper of North Rhine–Westphalia has written when it states that the thoughts in Rosenberg's book *The Myth of the Twentieth Century* should become the world-view of national socialist Germany. Let us never say that this does not concern us, for the German Christian Faith Movement is now claiming to be the religion of all Germans. Let us say it bluntly: we Evangelical Christians can never say that we agree with these things that many leading figures of the new Germany are voicing and declaring in speeches.

We are not concerned in the least about their accusation of hypocrisy. We are not asking that people be "moral prigs," but we do have the clear commandment from God against harlotry and adultery that Luther explains in our Smaller Catechism: "We are to live chastely and decently in both words and works." Only authentic and modest conduct is consistent with this, as Scripture, which gives the woman greater honor, shows us,

[11] Protestants were more nationalistic than international. Schneider viewed this as strength rather than weakness. The key, as Schneider develops it in the sermon and in his life, is to distinguish the good from the bad of one's culture.

[12] *Volksgemeinschaft.* Here the pastor is using Nazi language. It is still early in the Third Reich, and he seems to be looking for areas of cooperation between church and state, as one would expect of a good Lutheran pastor nourished by the "two kingdoms" teaching of Protestantism. The reference to national unity may refer to the chaos of the Weimar years, and the mention of national honor may refer to German objection to the Versailles treaty that concluded World War I and shamed the Germans with war guilt.

[13] Alfred Rosenberg was an influential Nazi who edited the Nazi newspaper the *People's Observer* and whose book *The Myth of the Twentieth Century* was extremely popular. The book is hostile to Christianity.

and it is not consistent with the freedoms that Dr. Goebbels is now granting to German women.[14] We know a joy that rests on the deepest foundation and has given hundreds and thousands of believing Christians the
power to sacrifice themselves for the Fatherland.[15] Shrovetide Carnival is
foreign to Evangelical Christians, and they will have nothing to do with
such things, as the Scripture says: "Let foolishness and silliness not be said
of you." Our faith brings a greater joy.[16]

We, as evangelical parents, want to know that our children are unequivocally being raised in our evangelical faith and taught its content, and
we want to be sure that they have not been contaminated with the current
racist religious spirit.[17] We want Sunday to remain the day of the church
and especially that Sunday morning be reserved for our young people's
church attendance.[18] We want the state to stay in its political sphere and
not intrude into the sphere of faith and our worldview. We want the state
to be humble enough to listen to God's word that comes to it through the
service of the church. We rely on Hitler's word that he will use the powers
of Christianity to construct the national life. We are ready to help, but only
in the freedom that obeys only God.[19]

But now you are challenged to confess and bear witness, dear evangelical church. Do not be a silent dog because the Savior says: "Only the
one who confesses me before men will I confess before my heavenly father." Now, you Christian in your church, you are surrounded by waves
that are coming over you from the church and from the nation and the

[14] A margin note by Schneider reads: "check the hypocritical/creepy (Muckererlass)
edict of Chief of Staff Röhm." Perhaps Schneider is referencing a Kraft durch Freude comment based on the following sentence? Kraft durch Freude, or "Strength through Joy," is a
term taken from Hitler that referred to Nazi free time activities intended to unify racially
pure Germans of all classes and to conform all activity to the National Socialists' worldview
(Gleichschaltung). Cornelia Schmitz-Berning, Vokabular des Nationalsozialismus (Berlin:
Walter de Gruyter, 2007), p. 437.

[15] Perhaps a reference to German war dead from 1914 to 1918. Schneider himself was
a decorated and wounded veteran of WWI.

[16] Catholic regions of Germany delight in the carnival celebrations that precede
Lent.

[17] [M]it völkish-religösem Geist. A margin note reads: "Among members of Emergency Pastors League it is being said that the Rosenberg book has been recommended for
availability in school libraries."

[18] Hitler Youth activities were often organized to conflict directly with church activities.

[19] Certainly Schneider is referencing the "two kingdom" tradition, but especially
Hitler's early appeals to Christians as sketched in the editor's introduction.

state. And we are anxious and we are afraid. We are experiencing what the disciples were going through on the stormy lake. We call out, "Lord, help us. We are perishing."

We do not see how the poor, unprotected little boat of the church can be preserved amid the powers and forces of the world. But then we must remember that in this boat of the church the Lord is with us; even if a Rosenberg does write about the myth of the twentieth century, the church has the promise that "The gates of hell and of death shall not prevail against her." And it only looks as if our Lord is asleep and is not concerned about us. But soon he will be up, for the storms are now coming over his church and over the lives of Christians so that HIS [*sic*] glory might be revealed, so that his strong and powerful arm might become visible and so that the world has to confess in amazement: "What kind of man is this whom wind and sea obey," who safely steers the little boat of the church through the stormy waves of the world *(Völkerwelt)?* We should be ashamed of our little faith and disbelief, of our fear of men and the world. Or is it rather that he who overcame the world on the cross is unable to comfort us? Should we think that the Lord who himself founded his church on this earth might leave her or neglect her in such an hour? Oh, let us refuse all weariness and all cowardly and lazy fear![20] The Lord comes to you in the boat, the sea grows calm, and you may be still and secure.

This is how it is with all the storms that come upon you, O Christian, which you must suffer for Jesus' sake and because you follow him. You should know: "He, the Lord, is with you, he awakens. When the power of the waves tries to cover the little boat of your heart in the dark night, then stretch out your hand. Listen to me, watchers in the night!" Where is the storm? It is not so much around you as in you, in your heart.

There, deep in your heart, you see, as Peter did, the heaving winds blowing against you, and you become afraid and begin to sink. But even then the Lord holds out to you his saving hand and holds you firm in order to strengthen your weak faith. But just what is it then that you have to do alone in order to experience Jesus' glory in the storm, in this storm over the church, in this storm over your life as a Christian? You must believe, trust, and abandon yourself to the miraculous power of the Lord in whom you believe. But perhaps you do not believe? Then never say that you are a Christian, for then you are only a Christian in name or in your head or

---

[20] Schneider would soon demonstrate his courage in Buchenwald, where he was brutally tortured for his faith.

maybe a hypocritical Christian. "Faith is the bulwark of the heart," says Luther. Whoever will not live his faith and acknowledge his Lord, will sink and lose his soul; even were he to win the whole world, he will be condemned with the whole faithless world. I would rather die for my faith than live a cowardly and cultured life with the rest of the world. For nowhere is it said that God will allow us in all circumstances here to live the little span of earthly life without going through loss of money, property, honor, life and limb, wife and child. Even more, such sorrows must come upon the Christian at times; but the Lord brings the little boat of the church through the stormy seas of human events, which must grow calm at his word. He calms the storms in your heart as in the song that you ladies love to sing: "Even if I know not the path, you know it well. This lets the soul be quiet and peaceful." "You know the way the stormy wind blows, and you command it, and you never come too late. So I will await thee, your word is without deception; you know the right path for me. That is all I need." In the peace of this song the Baltic mariners went comforted and happy to their death. The Lord guides the little boat of his church, the little boat of your Christian life — not toward a temporal port but an eternal one. That is our great hope and our joy. Shouldn't we squeeze closer together in the boat of Christ's church, even closer than we are right now in these pews in a unity of faith of our hearts? Don't we want to rejoice that we have been given this ship? See, this is not a story from of old, this gospel, but a story of today, about the living Lord and his church as you used to sing in our village in the song: "O church of Christ, O noble ship, how wonderful your course, true, many a shipwreck threatens, true, many a wave roars. Yet God is with you, be of good cheer, the Lord will bring you safely to your goal. No matter how angry the sea, it dies down when he commands." "O Jesus, hear our pleas, turn to dust the hordes of the foe, let all the world behold it — with us is indeed our God. Guide your children always toward the safe harbor, and let your people in unity rejoice in eternal peace!" Amen.[21]

[21] Following the sermon was a reading of the *Kanzelabkündigung* (message from the pulpit) from the Confessing Church, which was read from many pulpits that Sunday: "We raise before God and this Christian congregation the complaint and charge that the Reich bishop in his decree has threatened violence against those who have been unable to keep silent for the sake of their conscience and their congregation concerning the present danger of the church. And in addition has set into force laws that run counter to our confession of faith which he had earlier lifted in order to satisfy the church. — We must hold the Reich bishop accountable to the scripture: 'One must obey God more than men.'" Wentorf, *Der Fall des Pfarrers Paul Schneider*, p. 98.

A Sermon about the Relevance
of Christianity in Nazi Germany

The early life of Martin Niemöller (1892-1984) hardly indicated his later opposition to Nazism, but after a very nationalistic beginning, his opposition
to Hitler cost him seven years in a concentration camp. His father was a Lutheran pastor, but Martin did not follow in his father's footsteps immediately.[1] He joined the German navy and during the First World War served
on a German U-boat, which he later commanded. Later he wrote a book
about his experiences entitled *From U-Boat to Pulpit*.[2] He married Else
Bruner in 1919, and the couple had six children. In 1920 Niemöller began
theological studies in Munster.

Because of his nationalistic views and his bitterness over the defeat of
Germany and the collapse of the Kaiser Reich, he was no supporter of de-
mocracy or of the fledgling Weimar Republic. He even joined a right-wing
student group that supported a failed attempt to overthrow the Weimar
government. When the putsch failed, the group was dissolved. During the
harsh economic times of the Weimar years, the young Niemöller worked for
the Lutheran Home Mission in Westphalia that involved him in helping the
poor with social services. In 1931 he left the Home Mission to become one of
three pastors at the prestigious Berlin-Dahlem church.

His sermons reflected his political leanings, and he voted for Hitler
because of the Nazi pledge to honor Christianity and to provide Germany
with a strong leader who would restore German pride. Niemöller did not
initially oppose Hitler's anti-Semitism, yet he did object to Nazi attempts
to bar Jewish Christians from full membership in the church.[1] His oppo-

---

[1] See the editor's introduction on the Aryan Paragraph, under the heading "The
Pastors' Emergency League."

sition to this move by "German Christians" led him and others to form the Pastors' Emergency League, from which the Confessing Church later grew. Many pastors and parishioners objected to the state's attempt to apply its racial laws to church matters. Although many would concede that the state had authority to impose such requirements in its political domain, they reasoned that the church did not fall under the state's political rule. His views were more anti-Jewish than anti-Semitic in that he did not view matters in racial terms but in theological terms. He had no difficulty in accepting Jews who converted. This was the main problem with the Aryan Paragraph. It excluded converted Jews from the Christian community.

A decisive moment came in January 1934 when Martin Niemöller and two Protestant bishops met with Adolf Hitler. They were upset by the government's efforts to influence Christians with Nazi anti-Christian thinking. But "at the meeting it became clear that Niemöller's phone had been tapped by the Gestapo" and that he and the members of the Pastors' Emergency League were "under close state surveillance."[3] Thereafter he was an opponent of Nazism. In 1934 Niemöller joined others in forming the Confessing Church, whose members confessed the absolute Lordship of Christ over the church.

Although Niemöller knew full well that he was under close scrutiny by the Gestapo, his sermons contained sharp criticism of Nazi paganism and its anti-Christian worldview. After repeated arrests, in 1938 Niemöller was sent to the concentration camp in Sachsenhausen, near Berlin. His crime was "abuse of the pulpit."[4] While there he tried to win permission to join the navy. In 1941 he was transferred to Dachau, where he was housed with Catholic priests.

Niemöller's cell mate at the Sachsenhausen concentration camp was a Jewish prisoner, Leo Stein. After the Nazis released him to go to New York, Stein wrote an article about Niemöller for a Jewish journal. In the article he quotes Niemöller's response to his question about the pastor's anti-Jewishness and support of Hitler:

> I find myself wondering about that too. I wonder about it as much as I regret it. Still, it is true that Hitler betrayed me. I had an audience with him, as a representative of the Protestant Church, shortly before he became Chancellor, in 1932. Hitler promised me on his word of honor, to protect the Church, and not to issue any anti-Church laws. He also agreed not to allow pogroms against the Jews, assuring me as follows:

"There will be restrictions against the Jews, but there will be no ghettos, no pogroms, in Germany."

I really believed, given the widespread anti-Semitism in Germany, at that time — that Jews should avoid aspiring to Government positions or seats in the Reichstag. There were many Jews, especially among the Zionists, who took a similar stand. Hitler's assurance satisfied me at the time. On the other hand, I hated the growing atheistic movement, which was fostered and promoted by the Social Democrats and the Communists. Their hostility toward the Church made me pin my hopes on Hitler for a while.

I am paying for that mistake now; and not me alone, but thousands of other persons like me.[5]

After the war he emerged as a prominent church leader in Germany. He spoke out against Nazi crimes but in many ways remained a controversial figure, due mainly to his continuing nationalism. This led him to become a strong advocate for German reunification. Before his death in 1984, this former U-boat commander became a pacifist.

There is one quote by Martin Niemöller, taken from an address to the Confessing Church in January 1946, that sums up his stance on human rights:[6]

THEY CAME FIRST for the Communists,
and I didn't speak up because I wasn't a Communist.
THEN THEY CAME for the trade unionists,
and I didn't speak up because I wasn't a trade unionist.

THEN THEY CAME for the Jews,
and I didn't speak up because I wasn't a Jew.
THEN THEY CAME for me,

and by that time no one was left to speak up.[2]

[2] The poem is attributed to Niemöller. Regardless of its author, it certainly is in the Niemöller style.

A Sermon about the Relevance
of Christianity in Nazi Germany

December 20, 1936

Berlin-Dahlem, Germany

John bare witness of him, and cried, saying, This was he of whom I spake, He that cometh after me is preferred before me: for he was before me. And of his fulness have all we received, and grace for grace. For the law was given by Moses, but grace and truth came by Jesus Christ. No man hath seen God at any time; the only begotten Son, which is in the bosom of the Father, he hath declared him.

John 1:15-18 KJV

"Let all who are devout rejoice."[3] "Rejoice in the Lord alway: and again I say, Rejoice."[4] It is the joy and jubilation of Christmas that is anticipated, so to speak, in the hymns and Scripture passages of the fourth Sunday in Advent. This means, dear friends, we never really bring off pretending to be waiting on someone to come whom we do not know. On the contrary, the one who is coming and for whom we are waiting is no other than the one who was already here and whom we know. That is the reason for the joy and jubilation that will not be dampened. The Lord who was and who is to come has never for an instant stopped being with us as the living and present Lord. Whether Advent or Christmas, passion week or Easter, Ascension or Pentecost, whether we are hearing the news of his coming or of

---

[3] The German text, *Nun jauchzet all ihr Frommen,* is the opening line of a German advent hymn. Likely written by David Denicke (1603-80) and published in the *Nürnbergisches Gesangbuch* (1676). http://www.musicanet.org/robokopp/Lieder/nunjauch.html; accessed August 9, 2012.

[4] Phil. 4:4 KJV.

his having come, whether we are hearing the news of his dying or of his raising from the dead, of his exaltation or of his living presence in the Holy Spirit, in all this we find good news: this Lord is our Lord, and the Lord is near.

Now today we are being called to account in a peculiar manner in that they are contesting our right to continue to carry on and to testify to the gospel of him who was and who is and who will come again as the *one*[5] message of salvation. And the more unbridled the public attacks against Christianity become, they show us that it is not at all against the Old Testament or against the apostle Paul[6] — as they always want us to believe — but rather it is against the one Lord in whom we believe, even Jesus of Nazareth. And all the more clear becomes the one question they aim at us, about which we ought to be very clear and to which we must always render an answer: Why should he of all people be indispensable? Why can't you make do without him? Isn't it rather like at that self-proclaimed "Christian" assembly that took place a few weeks ago: "We are able to believe only in the God of real life who encounters us in our national life together *(Volk)*, in war and in the confusion and wretchedness of the postwar years and whom we meet in such a vivid manner in our recent German awakening and new beginning that no honorable German can avoid him."[7]

We cannot so simply dismiss the matter with a reference to the Christian past of our nation. No, we don't get past the problem so easily. We see how wretchedly little of the Christian past has survived in Germany, and it appears to us that in the matter of religion and faith nothing is so constant as change. We see — to use the words of the last Nazi Party Day — that the Christian age has been replaced by another.

It all has to do with Jesus of Nazareth. Since the days of the Enlightenment he is no longer the One, but rather one among many, a prophet, to be sure, but no more than *one* among many. A founder of a religion, one of the greatest, to be sure, but still just one among many. For a hundred years, since the days of Karl Marx, Jesus of Nazareth has been nothing more for

[5] Except for the German word *Volk,* all words in italics appear so in the German text.

[6] Pro-Nazi Christians rejected both the Old Testament and Paul as Jewish influences on Christianity.

[7] Typical pro-Nazi pagan theology that saw the postwar years leading to the new German awakening and rebirth of the Nazi era. Niemöller is most likely referring to a "German Christian" rally.

the disenfranchised and oppressed than "the preacher's fairy tale aimed only at comforting stupid people with the great beyond and to keep them in good spirits."[8] Jesus of Nazareth is for the former "Christian" middle class a discounted greatness. Christian citizens have noticed that they now have blood and spirit: "and Jesus of Nazareth is not bone of our bone, and not blood of our blood, and not spirit of our spirit."[9] German citizens are saying — as a rebuff at one of those rallies of self-proclaimed Christians: "We no longer believe in the Jewish Messiah whom they call Christ, and the Lion from Judah, or the Passover Lamb of Jehovah."[10]

So are we supposed to live our Christmas faith in a harmless and happy way as if the happy news "Christ is born" would tie a ribbon around our people (Volk) and would have something for everyone? That's not the way it can be anymore! Our people (Volk) no longer celebrate Christmas. We see it in the newspaper and at the public Christmas celebrations: our people (Volk) celebrate the myth of the eternal birth; our people (Volk) celebrate the myth of the reawakening light, its own unbridled hope of newly awakened life, but not the birth of the Son of Mary. Our people (Volk) celebrate consciously and with care, but they do not celebrate him who said, "I am the light of the world,"[11] not him of whom it is attested, "In him was life."[12]

And with that the question of faith is put to us and we cannot avoid it: Myth or Jesus of Nazareth? Winter solstice or the birth in a stable at Bethlehem? God, as he is supposedly experienced today by our people (Volk), or as he is attested to in the Bible as the Father of Jesus Christ? We certainly know that this cannot be proven and that here faith stands against faith, opinion against opinion, conviction against conviction. It is still true that "no one has seen God."[13]

And now the question is whether we have a right to see God in the manner we conceive him to be or to dispense with him altogether. The world in which we are living no longer knows God. It proclaims God only

[8] I have been unable to locate the source of this quote, but it does illustrate that Marxist and Nazi rejection of Christianity shared some important ideas.

[9] Here Niemöller may be referencing Nazi slogans: "blood," "spirit," "kind"/"sort"/ "species," etc., were key terms in Nazi vocabulary. Jesus does not fit the Nazi ideal type.

[10] Typical German Christian rhetoric against the Jewish roots of Christianity. Nazis often used the name Jehovah because they thought it sounded Hebrew.

[11] John 8:12.

[12] John 1:4.

[13] 1 John 4:12.

where it seems fitting and useful. It proclaims godlessness where that appears more pious and better. But the world remains — whether it proclaims God or godlessness — true to itself and its convictions. "I am the Lord, my own god! And where there are other gods, they live because of my grace and die from my wrath." This human-secular self-glorification, this insistence that "I am the Lord, my own god," stands in opposition to the one fact that we cannot avoid — that no one can avoid — on which all human self-glorification shatters, no matter how powerful it acts, and that is the law under which we all stand and which no violence can control, the law "thou shalt! and thou shalt not!" which brings to naught all self-glorification and self-worship. A law that a *foreign*[14] voice speaks: "I am the Lord! I am your God!"

We would like to deny that such a will that is not our own will stands over us. A prisoner can indeed dream that he is free, but the chain remains and the dream comes ultimately to an end.[15] The wages of sin is death,[16] and that is the final word. Thus must this myth arise that romanticizes death as passing into the nation's life. But the nation has no eternal life — even when they proclaim it a thousand times — and one cannot run away from death.[17]

It is certainly true that "no one has seen God." But where we try to free ourselves from his rule, we have to first disavow this law. And in turn, where we do not disavow it, where we allow it to be valid, the rule of God becomes unbearable for us. For this law shows our self-rule to be rebellion, a slaves' revolt against God. Thus we flee from this law into the lie that it will not become our judgment and condemnation.

Dear friends, in the face of this law there is nothing at all to harmless faith that acts as if things do not matter much to God, as if sin were nothing but a psychological obsession, as if death were nothing more than a

[14] The God of the Hebrew Scriptures. Note earlier in the sermon where Niemöller addresses the Nazi rejection of the Jewish roots of Christianity. Yet it is this God whom Jews and Christians worship that ultimately rules.

[15] The Nazi dream of self-willed domination lasted thirteen years. Here we find Christian faith in God's providence in the early days of the Reich. God, not Hitler, rules history.

[16] Rom. 6:23 KJV.

[17] "The eternal life of our nation (people)" [*das ewige Leben unseres Volkes*] was a common Nazi idea based on a reading of Darwin that justified "every sacrifice and crime"; Cornelia Schmitz-Berning, *Vokabular des Nationalsozialismus* (Berlin: Walter de Gruyter, 2007), p. 221. Here again Niemöller is demonstrating how Christian theology directly challenges Nazi ideology.

harmless disfigurement of creation as in the melody, "It's not all that bad."[18] The question presents itself in the face of this law, whether this holy judging is God's only word to us. In the face of this law we begin to understand that little word "grace" not only as an attack on our pride but as a soft glimmer of hope, as the *only* possibility to be brought out of the lie about life back to the truth of life before, under, and with God.

But it is just here that the gospel applies, just here that the good news applies: "Grace and truth have come through Jesus Christ."[19] If that is the *one* truth vis-à-vis the old reality — namely, that we deny the law and take a chance on death — then the new reality is this: God forgives sin and shows mercy. And it has pleased God to make this new reality dependent on this one man, this Jesus of Nazareth, whom we confess as the Christ, the only begotten Son of God.

And that has been and remains foolish talk. That is a long way from offering proof. We do not see God's truth and mercy. What we see is a poor child, a Jewish itinerant teacher from Nazareth who is abandoned by God and dies as a criminal on the cross. But it was he who brought us the happy news, "Come to me, all of you. Your sins have been forgiven you. Who sees me, sees the Father. My body given for *you*, my blood shed for *you*, and my peace I give to you."

We know no one who speaks like this. We know no one who could speak like this in the face of the law, who would find faith among any of us.[20] Does it harm him at all when the people around us begin to fall away from him, does it affect him when the people begin looking for another savior! Should that impress us when tone-setting leaders in our nation *(Volk)* turn their backs on him in ever increasing numbers and consort with those who despise and slander him? Will we permit these things to diminish our joyfulness of our faith?

"And of his fulness have all we received, and grace for grace."[21] Thus confessed the apostles with John at their fore, and thus ring out the words of the creed and of those men and women who have witnessed to their faith throughout the centuries. So too we hear it today, "From his fulness

[18] "Es ist ja alles halb so schlimm." Perhaps a line from Bertolt Brecht's poem "Ballad of Marie Sanders, the Jew's Whore" that relates the fate of a Gentile whom the Nazis punish for being with a Jew in violation of the Nuremberg Laws. The text was set to music by Hanns Eisler (see http://www.thejewishmuseum.org/; accessed August 23, 2012).

[19] John 1:17, my translation of the German text.

[20] Perhaps an allusion to Luke 18:8.

[21] John 1:16 KJV.

we have all received grace upon grace." This is how a young academic who has been sitting in jail for weeks now writes to his family: "Be of good cheer and in high spirits and do not worry yourselves about me. It is after all advent. And every evening when outside the noise of the day subsides, I hear the chimes of the parochial church proclaiming 'Open up the door, make wide the gates.'" Nothing has changed — in truth nothing! — since Paul wrote from prison to the Philippians, "Rejoice always in your hearts, and again I say 'rejoice'"![22]

He, Jesus of Nazareth, is the one who is coming, the one in whom alone the world is offered God's mercy — even to us — from whom we want to take that we might have the fullness. If we experience persecution, let it be so that joy alone rules. "But I say unto you, Love your enemies, bless them that curse you, do good to them that hate you, and pray for them which despitefully use you, and persecute you."[23]

Take from his fullness grace upon grace! We ourselves *have* received grace upon grace. We will and should and may take! "Let all people know your tenderness. The Lord is near."

O Lord of graciousness and faithfulness,
O come thou now again anew
To us, who are so sorely distressed.
It is urgent that you yourself come down to us
To renew your peace,
Against which the world revolts.[24]

[22] Phil. 4:4, my translation of the German text.
[23] Matt. 5:44 KJV.
[24] The fifth verse of the Christmas hymn "Your King Comes" by Friedrich Rückert, 1788-1866. Full text at http://www.liederportal.de/adventslieder/dein_koenig_kommt.php; accessed August 9, 2012.

···

A Sermon about Giving Thanks in the Third Reich

When Paul Schneider preached this his last sermon, he was serving the two parishes of Dickenshied and Womrath in the Rhineland area of Germany. He had been arrested many times in his first parish, and arrests continued in his new assignment. Twice the Gestapo took him into custody, but his numerous battles with local Nazi authorities continued. It was certainly no secret that this decorated veteran from the First World War was prepared to fight the battle over Christianity in Nazi Germany with no thought of surrender or compromise. The Nazi terror state had several methods of dealing with unruly and outspoken clergy. The most gentle was to forbid them to preach *(Redeverbot)*. After that might come arrest and confinement in the local or regional jail. But if these methods proved unsuccessful, the pastor could be ordered to vacate the area — meaning he was forbidden to live or preach in his parish. This was termed "internal exile," and after his third arrest, Paul Schneider was ordered to leave the area on July 24, 1937.[1]

Schneider had always considered such measures unacceptable because the relationship between a pastor and the congregation was outside state control or influence. Consequently, he tore up the order and threw it into the nearest wastebasket. In defiance of the Gestapo, he preached as usual on July 25, 1937. Only when pressed by his wife and close friends to obey the order did he consent to travel to Baden-Baden.

Life without their pastor soon proved to be unbearable for the church members. In a letter to their pastor, dated September 19, 1937, the ruling elders *(das Presbyterium)* in Womrath urged their pastor to return to the parish, for since his absence no one was seeing to the spiritual and pastoral needs of church members.[2] On October 3, 1937, Paul Schneider returned to his parishes. After preaching the following sermon at the Dickenshied church, he was driving to the Womrath parish to give the sermon a second time when the Gestapo halted the car and arrested the pastor.

According to Rudolf Wentorf's biographical documentation, the pastor had delivered the sermon in Dickenshied, but inside the Gestapo jail in Koblenz he wrote out a complete manuscript for his Womrath congregation. The text was smuggled out of the Gestapo prison in a bag of dirty laundry. His wife then duplicated the text and distributed copies to the parishioners.[3]

On the same day as his arrest, the pastor wrote a letter in which he expressed his regret for not being able to deliver the sermon at Womrath and his hope that the congregation had not allowed his arrest to prevent them from holding a worship service. This, he said, was what God would expect of them. He wrote that he was happy he had been able to lead worship and to preach in the first parish, and assured the Womrath congregation that next time he would go there first. He closed the letter urging the congregations to hold on to their faith and to entrust themselves to "God's miraculous power." Although they were alone and isolated, they were all the more compelled to depend utterly on God.[4]

He remained in jail until November 27, 1937, when he was transferred to the concentration camp Buchenwald, where he was later murdered. His courage in the camp and his refusal to be silent as he witnessed one Nazi atrocity after another are almost beyond belief. Beaten and hung by the arms for days, he continued to "preach" God's love for inmates and judgment on the criminals committing murder and mistreating inmates. When the Nazis finally murdered him, the body was so disfigured that the family was told not to open the coffin.[5] Paul Schneider was the first evangelical pastor to die for his faith in Nazi Germany.[6]

While there is no Thanksgiving Day in Germany, traditionally Germans observe the first Sunday in October as a day of thanksgiving for the harvest *(Erntedankfest)*.[1] In this sermon Schneider once again rails against Nazi ideology and the desperate situation of the church in Nazi Germany. He alerts his congregation to forthcoming, difficult days of persecution for faithful Christians in Germany, but as other pastors in this collection do, he warns Germans that God's justice will destroy Germany if Germans fail to repent. Also, the pastor reminds Germans that God, not the state, is both creator and benefactor. Paul Schneider's use of the poem "Belshazzar" by

---

[1] See cultural note on *Erntedankfest* in W. Scholze-Stubenrecht and J. B. Sykes, eds., *Oxford-Duden German Dictionary* (New York: Oxford University Press, 2005), p. 236.

the nineteenth-century German Jewish poet Heinrich Heine, in which the tyrant's own servants kill him, must have shocked parishioners. Not only was the pastor quoting a poem in which servants murdered their king; he was quoting a Jewish author whose works had been forbidden and burned.[2]

Here, as in all his sermons after Hitler's reign began, Paul Schneider shows his radical obedience to God. He had placed his hand on the plow, and there was no looking back (Luke 9:61-62).

[2] The infamous burning of books took place on May 10, 1933, in Berlin. Other such fires followed in other cities. Heinrich Heine had written that "where people burn books, they will end by burning human beings." http://en.wikipedia.org/wiki/Nazi_book _burnings; accessed July 16, 2012.

A Sermon about Giving Thanks
in the Third Reich

October 3, 1937

Dickenshied, Germany

> The eyes of all wait upon thee; and thou givest them their meat in due season. Thou openest thine hand, and satisfiest the desire of every living thing. The LORD is righteous in all his ways, and holy in all his works. The LORD is nigh unto all them that call upon him, to all that call upon him in truth. He will fulfil the desire of them that fear him: he also will hear their cry, and will save them. The LORD preserveth all them that love him: but all the wicked will he destroy. My mouth shall speak the praise of the LORD: and let all flesh bless his holy name for ever and ever.
>
> *Psalm 145:15-21 KJV*[3]

Dear Christian Friends,[4]

A thanksgiving feast even in this year of our church's hardship![5] This has always been for us in the church, in the village, and in the city an especially

[3] We should recall that the Old Testament was not an approved text in Nazi Germany and that using a psalm was allowing a Jewish word to be heard in an approving fashion. As he notes later in the sermon, the text was known and used by many Christians as a prayer at meals. It is worth noting that the Old Testament was out of favor in Nazi Germany, yet Confessing pastors did not avoid it in their preaching.

[4] The German is *Liebe Gemeinde,* or literally "Dear congregation"; it is the standard opening for sermons.

[5] The German word is *Kirchennot* without the possessive pronoun "our." I am inserting the pronoun because I believe that the pastor is talking as a pastor to his beleaguered congregations. It had been a very hard year for both pastor and members. They had seen their pastor arrested by the Gestapo twice, and they had lived with the growing tensions and

joyful festival; an occasion for thanking God for the harvest of the field and the visible blessings that God bestows upon our labor that fills our barns and cellars. This year is no different, and so we certainly do not want to allow the storms of distress that are raging over our beloved evangelical church[6] to rob or choke us of joy and gratitude. Even on this day we want to rejoice with the psalmist at God's benevolence and reign over the gifts that he once more has given us.[7]

How rich and kind[8] is our God in his giving! This is what the first verses of our psalm tell us, these verses that have become a table prayer for many families.[9] Today we want to pay special attention to two words from the text. Several times the little words "Thou" and "Thee" are capitalized, and yet for us these are such common sounds.[10] "The eyes of all wait upon thee; and thou givest them their meat in due season. Thou openest thine hand, and satisfiest the desire of every living thing." Behind the power in our arms at work, behind the moving force of nature and the

---

conflicts between parish and state. They knew their pastor to be outspoken and noncompromising; and most in the congregation loved him for it. Yet it was parishioners in Dickenschied who, after the service, informed the Gestapo that the pastor had returned illegally to preach and demanded his arrest. Albrecht Aichelin, *Paul Schneider: Ein radikales Glaubenszeugnis gegen die Gewaltherrschaft des Nationalsozialismus* (Gütersloh: Gütersloher Verlagshaus, 1994), p. 207 n. 128.

[6] Certainly here the pastor is referring to the embattled Confessing Church as a whole.

[7] As noted in the editor's introduction, the Nazis were eager to suggest that benevolence was the state's business and not God's. Here Schneider reminds his congregations that God and not the Nazi state is the benefactor to whom we owe our thanks and praise. Also, uniting himself and his congregation with the Jewish singer simply bypasses Nazi anti-Semitic propaganda.

[8] German *gütig* may mean benevolent, gracious, benign, affectionate, kindhearted, among other things. Once again he contrasts the loving-kindness of God with the harsh, hateful, and violent god of Nazism.

[9] Perhaps the grace Schneider refers to is *Danket dem Herrn, denn er ist freundlich, und seine Güte währet ewig,* which says, "Thank the Lord, for he is kind and his kindness endures forever." http://www.labbe.de/liederbaum/index.asp?themaid=28&titelid=185; accessed August 23, 2012.

[10] In German "thou" *(du)* and its various forms still serve as the familiar form of address and so do not sound old-fashioned. While one could translate these familiar pronouns with the more modern "you" and "your," something of the intimacy in the German is lost. That God relates to us as *du* rather than as *Sie* is a remarkable feature of our faith that we should try to retain. It is nice that English forms do come close to the German *du, dein,* and the verb ending *-est* so that we have something of the sounds of the German. I have followed Schneider's capitalization of these forms.

sprouting of the plants, behind all the mysterious blooming and growing, we see — invisible, to be sure, yet so alive and real — the personal and fatherly "Thou" of our living God and heavenly Father.[11] It is precisely this Thou, who according to his promises with Noah still gracefully holds firm and secure the laws of preservation governing a sinful world and sinful people. "So long as the earth stands, shall not cease sowing and harvest, frost and heat, summer and winter, day and night." Let us never rob God of this honor by running to hide behind natural laws or natural power, or behind laws and forces like "blood and soil," in order to flee this great and personal "Thou" of the living God who on this day of thanksgiving comes to us so fatherly, so warmly, and so intimately in his gifts![12]

A second little word appears in our text that expresses God's rich goodness toward us and that, by being repeated, finds emphasis: that little word "all." All eyes await thee; thou fillest all living things with delight. This includes the creatures that do not have our ability to reason, that in their animal instinct, as we put it, seek their food and await God's gifts. In their own way, these creatures can serve as models for us, as our Savior reminded us when he spoke of the carefree way the birds of the air find nourishment.[13] The hen that finds a drink of water lifts her small head up to heaven as if giving thanks, and in so doing reminds us reasonable men and women of the divine Giver from whom we too receive drink and food. By night carnivores search out their prey to satisfy their hunger. So too men rise early and go to their work and lay claim to income and nourishment. All, even evil and godless men, whether they know it and admit it and thank God for it or not, await God's open hand.[14] Even a Belshazzar, a godless, prideful ruler of Babylon, who sets himself above God and says in his pride and contempt, "Here is the great Babylon that I myself have built through my own power and for the honor of my own glory,"[15] re-

[11] Certainly Schneider's reference opposes Nazi Germanic paganism.

[12] Here Schneider takes direct aim at Nazi teaching, even using the Nazi words "blood and soil" *(Blut und Boden)*. Schneider is here on the offensive, suggesting that those who "hide behind" a scientific or Nazi view of creation are cowards avoiding the benevolent God of Christians and Jews.

[13] Matt. 6:26 and Luke 12:24.

[14] The pastor did not see Christian truth as relative. Even Nazis who rejected Christian claims were living under the God of Jesus Christ, who let his rain fall on the good and the evil alike (Matt. 5:45).

[15] Aichelin notes that here Schneider is freely quoting from the poem "Belshazzar" by the German Jewish writer Heinrich Heine (1797-1856). The quote may reference Belshazzar's prideful blaspheming of God during his banquet: "And blindly his audacity

ceived this power on loan from God, as he was soon to learn. So too, all who do not thank God for his gifts still receive them from the One who lets his sun rise in his goodness over the evil and the good, and who lets his rain fall on both the righteous and the unrighteous.[16]

But God's blessings are even much more than these gifts. Upon the gifts from our fields and acres he places also his benevolent word, as the laying of produce on our church altar symbolizes. Through the church he calls us into his house to worship him, so that we call in turn to him, the giver, through our prayers and pleadings. Only in the context of his holy and blessed word should the blessing of his gifts first be unlocked for us. Here we should, and indeed may, recognize that God as Father of our Lord Jesus Christ — and through him as our Father — gives us everything. And here we learn that God still upholds the world by his gracious ordinances — not because of our cleverness and worth but because the blood of his beloved Son cries out on our behalf to God in heaven from Golgotha's cross for mercy. Here God calls us through all his other gifts to the Gift of Gifts, even to Jesus Christ. Here Jesus Christ himself gives himself to us as the bread of souls unto eternal life.

Now[17] let us consider[18] the abundance of God's goodness in his gifts for our bodily needs through which he maintains us so that salvation and redemption in Jesus Christ are proclaimed and that many people may

---

carries him away; And he blasphemes the Divinity with sinful word. And he boasts defiantly, and he blasphemes wildly. The servants roar their approval" ("Und blindlings reißt der Mut ihn fort; Und er lästert die Gottheit mit sündigem Wort. Und er bürstet sich fresh, und lästert wild; Die Knechtenschar ihm Beifall brüllt"). The Nazis had burned books by Heine because of his Jewishness, yet he remained a popular poet. The poem and Schneider's implied reference to it are excellent examples of indirect attacks on Nazism in that in using an ancient example of dictators and their downfall one could indicate that the current example of this rebellion against God would not last forever. The entire poem reads like a mocking of Nazi rallies with Hitler's boasting. Aichelin cites the biblical reference as well (Dan. 5:30); Aichelin, *Paul Schneider*, p. 207 n. 127. These references to the poem, the poet, and the Old Testament would not have found favor with the Gestapo.

[16] Matt. 5:45.

[17] In the sense that now that we know that these gifts come from God we can use this knowledge to guard ourselves from the pride and arrogance of supposed self-sufficiency. Pride and boasting were hallmarks of Nazi rhetoric. The preacher continues this line of thought throughout this section of the sermon. The rhetorical question the sermon is answering is, "Where does this new German prosperity come from?" For the Nazis the answer was from German superiority, and for the preacher the answer is that of the psalmist and Christ: "Not from you but from God in his providential bounty."

[18] German *vermessen*, whose root meaning is to measure.

yet be blessed. Now we are safeguarded from misusing God's gifts in selfish greed or arrogant wastefulness and from our heart becoming hard and proud and self-assured like the farmer in the parable, that we might misjudge[19] ourselves and think our soul lives from these earthly gifts: eat, drink, dear soul, you have supply for many days.[20]

Now our prayer of thanksgiving attains at last a full, warm, heartfelt tone toward the heart of God, and we praise rightly God's rich and benevolent gifts when we say: "The eyes of all wait upon thee; and thou givest them their meat in due season. Thou openest thine hand, and satisfiest the desire of every living thing."[21]

The wealth of God's goodness in his gifts joins with the holiness and justice of his rule; and now we want to cry out: How holy and just is God in his governing! In the same way that God continues to maintain this world beneath the cross of his beloved Son by his providential rule, so too is the precious, innocent blood poured out for our sins our guarantee of the holiness and justice of divine providence. For the sake of this blood God's goodness in giving and taking, in granting and refusing, wills to bring us to repentance. "If they will not repent, then God has already drawn his bow."[22] Woe to those who in the face of God's mercy become worldly and forgetful of God! For the sake of his justice and holiness God has embedded failed harvests and expensive times, droughts and unfruitful years, poverty and sickness into his providential rule. These misfortunes are God raising his hand to warn us as individuals and as nations that we are to receive these gifts from the hand of the Most Holy and Just One in humility and repentance, seeking always his blessing.

Holy and just are all the ways of God even with the gift of his word. Let us not forget that on this day of thanksgiving, and let us consider it well! Worse than the rising cost of food for a people is the rising cost of God's word.[23] The truth that we have to fear this rising cost of hearing

[19] German *vermessen* from the Old High German *firmezzan:* to measure wrong due to arrogance. See Gerhard Wahrig, *Deutsches Wörterbuch* (Berlin: Bertelmanns, 1974), s.v. *vermessen.*

[20] Luke 12:13-21, my translation of the German text.

[21] Ps. 145:15-16 KJV. In the Luther translation we find *Speise* (food), which the King James translators render as "meat." The Luther translation ends with the phrase *nach deinem Wohlgefallen* (according to your pleasure), which the King James omits.

[22] Ps. 7:12, my translation of the German text.

[23] Germany had experienced hyperinflation during the postwar Weimar years. Although the economy was improving under the Nazis, hardship and anxiety continued. Here

101

God's word in Germany could dampen our joy and gratefulness now that so many evangelical pastors are suffering jail and persecution simply because they proclaimed God's word and God's will boldly and purely and without fear of displeasing the governing authorities.[24] This was also the case in Israel's time, of which we read that God's word was costly in the land. In the time of Elijah there was besides him no prophet of God in the country because the godless queen Jezebel and her equally godless husband Ahab had liquidated all the prophets in the country.[25] Those were not blessed or good times for Israel. They brought godless government, devastating war, poverty, and rising expenses.[26] But it is always the nation and its people who are to blame when such an expensive time of hearing God's word comes. Certainly we too have brought this period of the church's crisis[27] in Germany upon ourselves with our indifference and contempt of God's word. But woe to us if we are forbidden to plant and harvest God's word among the old and the young in our villages and congregations! What does it profit a man if he gains the whole world and thereby does great damage to his soul! Therefore, O Land, O Land, O Land — hear the Word of the Lord![28]

The holy and just rule of God diverges into two paths. A path of grace for serious men and women of prayer who fear God and in their times of need cry out to God and for whom God himself — the great Giver — is more precious than all his gifts and all his creatures, and a path of judgment for the godless. The Lord is near to all who call upon him, all who call upon him in seriousness.[29] If we sincerely want something from him and come with a God-fearing heart, he will hear us calling to him and

---

the pastor relates the cost of living with the living cost of being a Christian in Nazi Germany; a price he had paid through Gestapo arrests and which was just about to cost him his life in Buchenwald.

[24] Recall that the Confessing Church had just gone through a summer in which many pastors had been arrested, including Niemöller, who had formed the Pastors' Emergency League. Martin Niemöller would be imprisoned in the Sachsenhausen concentration camp in Oranienburg, outside of Berlin. Unlike Paul Schneider, he would survive.

[25] Once again the pastor links Hitler to tyrants in the Old Testament. The arrests of pastors (and perhaps the anti-Jewish measures) were emptying Germany of needed prophets.

[26] On September 1, 1939, Germany would invade Poland. The pastor clearly foresees the coming destruction of Germany through Hitler's aggressive war against humanity.

[27] German *Kirchennot*.

[28] Jer. 22:29.

[29] Perhaps here the preacher references the Nazi paganism on the one hand and the hypocritical references to God on the other hand that peppered Nazi speech.

we will experience his help. This pertains to our need for bread and God's word; for the needs[30] of daily existence that today press down especially hard on those who fear God and on our churches and congregations.[31] God is asking us if we have really and truly been brought to our knees in prayer by the distress in our churches, in our congregations, and in our schools.[32] When the government took away religious instruction from the schools and churches, were we as worried about our children's Christian instruction as we were happy to have them freer for work? How sad that there is not enough serious prayer on behalf of the congregation and the church and their Christian concerns! Why is this? I fear that many do not want God to lead them into a real need for daily bread for existence, or into the needs of the church and the need for God's Word.[33] So many turn aside into the paths of the world, into its crooked ways of hypocrisy, dishonesty, lies, and compromises with the current spirit of this world and its disobedience. But how will a person ever experience God's help if that person will not be pulled into the distressing needs of our day? It is impossible. And so he denies himself the direct experience of the living God and God's wonderful help.

Today we should be aware of the fact that confessing Jesus will carry a price and that for his sake we will come into much distress and danger, much shame and persecution. Happy the man who does not turn aside from these consequences. He will then see that God is a sure help in times of trouble who will come to our aid. He will come to know what God promises all who fear God: before they call out I will hear them; even before they cry out to me, I will answer them.[34] Be assured that in times of trouble one can be comforted knowing that "he who sits beneath the pro-

[30] The German word *Not* carries a wide range of meanings, but here has to do with dire threat by the Nazis to Christian existence.

[31] Once again the preacher indicates the Nazi pressure on Christians and the persecution of the churches.

[32] A major conflict existed because of attempts by Nazis to impose Nazi teaching on religion classes in the schools. Confessing pastors were urged to resist these efforts. See Aichelin, *Paul Schneider,* p. 137.

[33] The sentence stresses the need for Christians in Nazi Germany to risk their total dependence on God's mercy and providence, to take no thought about food or clothing or shelter or imprisonment when it comes to obeying God. Paul Schneider had entered into such a radical faith as he preached this sermon. Again, Schneider is repeating time and again the German word *Not* as a state of emergency, need, and danger. I have maintained his repetition of the word "need" to convey more literally the German text.

[34] Isa. 65:24.

tection of the Most High and beneath the shadow of the Almighty may say to the Lord: my confidence and my fortress, my God in whom I hope."[35] Yes, the man who is justified — he alone will be comforted even in his death and may say, "If I but have thee, I will ask nothing more of heaven or earth. If my body and soul languish, still, O God, art thou my heart's comfort and my portion."[36] The mercy and wonderful aid of God that help us through our troubles will be the experience of the congregation and church that do not draw back from persecution. In the middle of the storm, the words of the Lord hold true for the church that the gates of hell will not prevail.[37] The Lord will certainly show himself to be alive and real in her midst: "Behold, I am with you even to the end of the world."[38]

There would, however, be something lacking in God's holy and just governance if his paths were not also paths of justice for all the godless. When Belshazzar, the Babylonian ruler, had fully ripened in his godless, proud, and wasteful misuse of God's gifts, when he had drunk himself sick and mocked God by profaning the temple's holy vessels along with all the important men and their women and their concubines, when the fiery handwriting appeared on the wall of the king's banquet hall and he drew back in fear, instead of confessing that the time of judgment had come, "in that very night Belshazzar was murdered by his servants."[39] Just as over the rich landowner in the parable, so also over every farmer who neglects the sowing of God's kingdom as he tends to the sowing and filling of his barns there stands the hour of judgment: "You fool, this night your soul will be demanded of you!"[40]

Woe to those seducers who seduce a people, a nation, and our young people to fall away from the living God and his word that alone nourishes the soul for eternal life! Woe to those who allow themselves to be seduced — parents and children — because earthly needs were more important to them than eternal and divine bread of heaven. Woe to that generation of whom nothing better can be said than was said to the generation in Noah's time: they ate, they drank, they celebrated and made merry! Over them

[35] Ps. 91.
[36] Ps. 73.
[37] Matt. 16:18.
[38] Matt. 28:20.
[39] Here the pastor quotes the conclusion of Heine's poem "Belshazzar" almost verbatim. The German text reads "Belsatzar ward aber in selbiger Nacht / Von seinen Knechten umgebracht" (But Belshazzar was in that very night / by his servants killed).
[40] Luke 12:20.

now rests the judicial authority of God's final and eternal judgment. He who has ears, let him hear! You indifferent and secure and self-justified sinner, get up and seek your Savior!

Thanksgiving festival! We praise the richness of God's goodness in his gifts to us. We praise the justice and holiness of his providence. What then should our thanksgiving be? The last verse of our texts tells us: "My mouth shall speak the praise of the LORD." Not the mouth of other people, only the pastor's, for example, but rather your own mouth must confess your God as the Father of our Lord Jesus Christ, in this place and in front of this congregation, but also outside in the world too and in public, to those who want to hear it and to those who do not want to hear this, before this nation and state and all earthly authorities. "Let all flesh praise his holy name always and forever!"[41] This means that our praise and honor of God must not be hidden in a corner. If it is because of faith that today our path, dear congregation, is so attacked, as it openly is, since everyone is talking about your steadfastness and confession of faith, because they do not want the praise and confessing of God and his church to take place, then let this be an honor and an encouragement to continue on this path of a Confessing Church. Let this be our thanksgiving! Come, close the ranks!

> I sing in all eternity of the grace of the God of Mercy.
> He faithfully loves his people, forgives and has patience.
> My mouth will announce his faithfulness and truth
> That even our grandchildren will find the God whom we found.
> Yes, his mercy rises and will rise forever,
> And his truth will remain steadfast in heaven.[42] Amen.

[41] Ps. 145:21.
[42] An eighteenth-century hymn based on Ps. 89 (http://www.f-bier.de/eg_part/biblische_gesaenge/pdf/eg622.pdf); accessed July 16, 2012.

JULIUS VON JAN

O Land, Land, Land:
Hear the Word of the Lord!

If for no other reason than the sermon he preached the Sunday after the terrible pogrom against German Jews termed *Kristallnacht*, Julius von Jan (1897-1964) belongs in the annals of heroic Christian witnesses in Nazi Germany. Following his sermon on November 16, 1938, he was severely beaten by a group of some five hundred Nazi thugs, and dragged to the city hall, where he was tried and then thrown into jail.[1] A few days later, the SA plastered his parsonage with the sign *Judenknecht* (Jew servant).[2]

Julius von Jan, whose father was a pastor, was born in Schweindorf, Germany, and was the fourth of seven children.[3] After attending the *Volkschule* from 1902 to 1905, he spent six years at a Latin high school and then completed three years in advanced seminars. Like a number of preachers in this collection, he volunteered for military service when the First World War broke out. From 1915 to 1917 he served on both the eastern and western fronts. Wounded in April 1917, he was taken prisoner by the British, and remained in captivity until the end of 1919. He recalled that the time he spent as a prisoner was life changing. He helped other prisoners cope with the hardships of captivity and dealt with his own bitter disappointment at Germany's losing the war and the fall of the Kaiser Reich. Upon his return to Germany he began his theological studies in Tübingen. He passed his first theological examination in 1923. From then until the completion of his second theological exam in 1925, he gained practical experience at churches in various parishes. After graduation he became pastor of a church in Herrentierbach. His marriage to Martha Munz was celebrated in 1927, and the couple had two children.

In 1935 he assumed the pastorate of a church in Oberlenningen whose pastor, a Reverend Rheinwald, had died of a heart attack after confrontations with the local Nazi Party leader and the village police. Von Jan ran into problems with the Nazis not long after Hitler came to power. He joined the Confessing Church, and as a Confessing pastor he considered it his Christian duty to alert his congregation to the deep conflicts between Nazism and Christianity and to advise them of the Nazi outrages and abuses. But even more than pointing out where the state was interfering with Christian practice and adopting a pagan worldview, he never tolerated the Nazi persecution of the Jews. He was also quick to stand up publicly for pastors who had been persecuted by the state or arrested. One of these was Martin Niemöller, who had been removed from the Berlin-Dahlem pulpit and thrown into a concentration camp.

Between 1933 and 1938 Julius von Jan had many confrontations with the Nazi authorities as well as with the "German Christians." Fortunately the majority of his congregation supported their pastor rather than the Nazis. Interestingly, he wrote in the parish newsletter that the explosion of the zeppelin *Hindenburg* was an indication that Germans needed to repent of sins and reject the political interpretation of Christianity offered by the German Christians.

When the local cultural minister demanded that all clergy who taught religion in the schools take a loyalty oath to Hitler, he joined other pastors in signing a statement indicating that they would not do so. He insisted that the German Evangelical Church take a stand on the matter. According to von Jan, God's word demanded far more loyalty that did a political system that he rejected.

When the Nazi pogrom against the Jews occurred in November 1938, von Jan was adamant that these sinful and disgraceful events had to be exposed for what they were. Silence was no option. He knew full well that speaking out in his sermon would endanger him and his family, and a few days after preaching the sermon, about five hundred Nazi supporters attacked him, leaving him severely wounded. He was dragged to a public hearing, where he was accused of being a traitor before being carried off to jail.[4]

This confrontation began a series of arrests, interrogations, and forced exile from his parish. On November 15, 1939, he was tried and found guilty of "misusing the pulpit" and "treachery" by a Nazi judge in a "special court" *(Sondergericht)* and sentenced to sixteen months imprisonment. These courts were not subject to civil law and were known for quick and severe sentencing. His crime was mixing politics and religion and thus endangering the public peace. After his release in May 1940, he preached in various churches, but in 1943 he was drafted into an artillery unit for political prisoners *(Strafkompanie)*, and served on the Russian front. He returned to Germany after falling ill. After a short time in an American prisoner of war camp, Julius von Jan returned to his home church, where church members greeted their pastor warmly.

After 1958 ill health, partially due to his war experience, limited his work. His last years were spent in a pietistic Moravian community *(Herrnhuter Brüdergemeine)*.[1]

The sermon that follows centers on the prophet's cry for justice and warning of God's wrath if offenders of God's love for his people do not repent and change their behavior. As many of our pastors note, God is not to be mocked. While things appear to be going in Hitler's direction and Germany seems invincible and the persecuted weak and worthless, God, not Hitler, is the ultimate reality of this world. Like other pastors profiled in this work, von Jan's courage and willingness to be persecuted for Christ and his truth are truly noteworthy.

[1] See the Wikipedia free encyclopedia entry on the "Moravian Church" for a good overview.

O Land, Land, Land:
Hear the Word of the Lord!

November 16, 1938
Day of National Atonement
Oberlenningen, Germany

O earth, earth, earth, hear the word of the LORD.

Jeremiah 22:29 KJV

The prophet calls out: O land, land! Hear the word of the Lord! If we hear only this little sentence, we will not understand what hard struggles and distresses provoked Jeremiah to utter this cry. He is standing among a people *(Volk)*[2] to whom the Lord has revealed himself throughout a long history as father and redeemer, as guide *(führer)*[3] and helper filled with power and grace and glory. But this people *(Volk)* of Israel, and especially its kings and its princes, trampled upon the law of God with their feet.[4] Jeremiah conducted a bitter battle against all this injustice[5] in the name of God and of

[2] As in each sermon, I place the German word *Volk* in parentheses to indicate the presence of this word in the German text. This common word was twisted by Nazi propaganda into a racial concept. How the preacher and the congregation heard this word in the sermon is impossible to know. Perhaps it carried no more significance than "people" or "nation," but perhaps it signaled a Christian use of a Nazi term to show that the Jewish people have a positive relationship with God that the Bible captures and that Nazi terminology distorts. Leaving the German word in the translation allows the reader to decide.

[3] Certainly reference to God as the Führer of the Jews was not lost on the congregation.

[4] This hermeneutic of presenting a negative image of Old Testament Israel and implying a parallel between the ancient people of Israel and contemporary Nazi Germany was common in sermons by Confessing pastors. In Christian interpretation of these passages there is always the understanding that even in disobedience God continued and continues to love the Jews. See, for example, the sermon by Karl Barth in this collection. Yet Israel's disobedience offers Germans a stark example and warning.

[5] German *Recht und Unrecht* (justice and injustice) had become urgent concepts

justice. For almost thirty years now he has been preaching the word of God to his people *(Volk)*. He contradicts the sermons filled with lies preached by those who announce salvation and victory in their nationalistic intoxication.[6] But he is not heard. The faithful man of God becomes more and more lonely. Then comes the great hour when God calls his prophet:

> Thus says the LORD: "Go down to the house of the king of Judah, and speak there this word, and say, . . . 'Thus says the LORD: Do justice and righteousness, and deliver from the hand of the oppressor him who has been robbed. And do no wrong or violence to the alien, the fatherless, and the widow, nor shed innocent blood in this place. For if you will indeed obey this word, then there shall enter the gates of this house kings who sit on the throne of David, riding in chariots and on horses, they, and their servants, and their people. But if you will not heed these words, I swear by myself, says the LORD, that this house shall become desolation. For thus says the LORD concerning the house of the king of Judah:
>
>> You are as Gilead to me,
>>> as the summit of Lebanon,
>> yet surely I will make you a desert,
>>> an uninhabited city.
>> I will prepare destroyers against you,
>>> each with his weapons;
>> and they shall cut down your choicest cedars,
>>> and cast them into the fire.
>
> And many nations will pass by this city, and every man will say to his neighbor, "Why has the LORD dealt thus with this great city?" And they will answer, "Because they forsook the covenant of the LORD their God, and worshiped other gods and served them.'"" (Jer. 22:2-9)[7]

---

following the horrible pogrom *(Kristallnacht)* against the Jews throughout the German Reich a few days before.

[6] This sentence contains two important Nazi terms, *Heil* and *Sieg,* that easily become the Nazi greeting *Sieg Heil.* Nazi Germany was intoxicated in these days with nationalism, hatred, and hubris.

[7] I have used the RSV translation of the passage. Although the pastor begins with verse 1 of the chapter, in the German text he cites the passage as verses 2-9. One can hardly imagine what these words must have sounded like on that day in Nazi Germany and the courage of the pastor to speak them.

The king hardened his heart against the word of God and was led into captivity by his enemy. His successor persecuted the prophet and died after a short reign. And the third king was at the helm only three months when he fell into the hands of the Babylonians! All this our chapter narrates. In a short period of time the reigns of three unrepentant kings were finished. In his deep pain over all this Jeremiah cries out to his people *(Volk):* O land, O land: hear the word of the Lord!

Why do you become unfaithful to the true God? Why do you no longer attend to his commands? Do you not see how things have gone for your kings because of this? O land, dear homeland; hear the word of the Lord!

In these days there is a questioning running through our people *(Volk):* "Where is the prophet in Germany who is being sent into the king's house to speak the word of God to him? Where is the man who calls out like Jeremiah: 'Do justice and righteousness, and deliver from the hand of the oppressor him who has been robbed. And do no wrong or violence to the alien, the fatherless, and the widow, nor shed innocent blood in this place'?"

God has sent us such men! They are today either in concentration camps or muzzled. But those who come to the houses of princes and there are able to do holy deeds are preachers of lies, as were the national enthusiasts in Jeremiah's day, and can only call out salvation and victory[8] but cannot proclaim the word of the Lord. The men of the church leadership, whom the newspapers have been writing about this past week, did speak the command of the Lord in a worship service clearly and did bow before God for our church and our people *(Volk)* because of the terrible and horrifying violation of God's commandments.[9] Everyone knows how they have been ridiculed as traitors to our nation *(Volk)*[10] and have lost their income — and painfully our bishops have not recognized their duty to side with these who have spoken the word of God.

If therefore today some *have to keep silent and others do not want*[11] to speak, then certainly we truly have every reason to observe a day of repentance, *a day of mourning* over our sins and the sins of the nation *(Volk)*.[12]

---

[8] German *Heil und Sieg;* perhaps this was a reference to the Nazi greeting *Sieg Heil.*

[9] I have been unable to find information on this incident.

[10] The German term is *Volksschädling.* This was a special term of hatred the Nazis applied to those who objected to their policies. See the entry in Cornelia Schmitz-Berning, *Vokabular des Nationalsozialismus* (Berlin: Walter de Gruyter, 2007), pp. 671-73.

[11] Italics throughout the sermon are in the original German text.

[12] As noted in the editor's introduction, the notion that Germans could sin was simply not part of the Nazi worldview. The Christian message challenges Nazi pride at every turn.

A crime has occurred in Paris. The murderer will receive his just punishment because he has sinned against the commandment of God.[13]

Along with our people *(Volk)*, we mourn the victim of this criminal act. But who would have thought that this one crime in Paris could be followed by so many crimes in Germany? Here we see the price we are paying for the great falling away from God and Christ, for the organized anti-Christianity.[14] Passions have been released, the laws of God jeered at, houses of God[15] that were sacred to others have been burned to the ground, property belonging to the foreigner plundered or destroyed, men who faithfully served our nation *(Volk)* and who fulfilled their duty in good conscience have been thrown into concentration camps simply because they belong to another race, and all this without anyone being held accountable![16] Even if the authorities do not admit their hand in this injustice, the healthy sensitivity of the people *(Volk)* feels the truth without any doubt — including where people do not dare speak of this.

And we as Christians see how this injustice burdens our people *(Volk)* before God and has to draw his punishment upon Germany. It is written: "Do not be fooled! God will not be ridiculed. What a person sows,

[13] The reference is to the murder of a German diplomat in Paris by a Polish Jew. The event gave Goebbels the excuse to ask Hitler's permission to use storm troopers against the Jews throughout Germany. The violence against the Jews throughout the Nazi Reich began on November 9; Matthew Hughes and Chris Mann, *Inside Hitler's Germany: Life under the Third Reich* (New York: MJF Books, 2000), p. 101.

[14] The German here is *Antichristentum,* an unusual word that captures the government-sanctioned attacks on Christianity that began soon after Hitler became chancellor. See the editor's introduction.

[15] The German word is *Gotteshäuser.* Pastor von Jan avoids using the word *Synagoge.* Perhaps because he wants his congregation to note that synagogues and churches are both houses of God, making it more difficult to segregate the worship of Jews from the worship of Christians. Nazis had no problem heaping scorn on synagogues, so a forceful reminder that these buildings were also sacred structures might have helped Christians in Germany connect with the horrors of the previous week.

[16] Notice the shift in tenses here. These synagogues belong to the past because they have been utterly destroyed by the Nazis. Also, the pastor laments the lack of justice in that no Nazi was being held accountable for criminal actions. Already Nazi Germany had passed from a state built on laws to one built on terror! Von Jan cites the respect Germans should have for German Jews: they served Germany in World War I and they did their duty to their country. Referring to German Jews as foreigners and members of another race illustrated the context in which the so-called Jewish question was discussed in Germany. Nazi race biology assigned Jews to an inferior race and to the status of alien residents in Germany. But even were that true, it does not justify the actions of *Kristallnacht.*

he will reap!" Yes, it is a horrifying seed of hatred that has been scattered upon the soil once more. What a horrible harvest will grow from this if God does not send our people *(Volk)* and us grace for sincere repentance.

But when we talk in this manner about God's judgment, we know that many are thinking to themselves: How can he talk today about God's judgment and punishment of Germany just when it looks like everything is improving and in this year ten million Germans have been brought into the Reich?[17] Here one clearly sees God's great blessing on Germany! True, God is showing us an amazing patience and mercy at the moment. But this is exactly why the words are true: O Land, Land, Land, hear the word of the Lord! Hear now at long last! Do you not know that God's goodness must lead to repentance? In the biblical chapter before us the prophet is commissioned by God to declare, "As I live, says the LORD, though Coniah the son of Jehoiakim, king of Judah, were the signet ring on my right hand, yet I would tear you off and give you into the hand of those who seek your life."[18] A person and a nation *(Volk)* can be elevated to the highest honors, but when their heart closes to God, it can suddenly be plunged into the depths. External good fortune and success all too easily lead us humans into an arrogance that can destroy all the blessings of God and thus end in a free fall. That is why the day of repentance is a day of mourning over our sins and the sins of our nation *(Volk)* that we confess before God, and this is a *day of prayer:* Lord, grant us and our nation *(Volk)* a renewed hearing of your word and a renewed respect for your laws! And begin with us! We love so much to go our own ways. We are so busy with many things and take so little time for the silence in which we may hear the Lord's word, be it in the house of God,[19] be it in our prayer closet.[20] That's why so many days pass without our having let God be our Lord, because in the morning we were not present to him to hear his orders. A Christian who fails to seek every morning this silence to hear his God endangers himself and harms God's affairs. For without the Lord's word we are all given over to demonic

---

[17] According to Nazi theory, Germany was not restricted to the borders following the First World War. Hitler was moving to restore Germany's prewar borders and thus bring "Germans" "home to the Reich" *(Heim ins Reich!)*

[18] Jer. 22:24-25 RSV.

[19] Note here the use of the same term used earlier to refer to the synagogue: house of God *(Gotteshaus),* rather than the German word for church, *Kirche,* a subtle but important linking of Christian and Jew.

[20] Matt. 6:6. The German is *Kämmerlein,* a little room. I follow the King James Version.

forces and all seductive voices of the underworld. When I sometimes ask in the youth group about how things stand with the daily reading of the Bible, only one or two from a dozen answer me. All the others go into their day without the Word of God. How might this be among us who are adults? Here, to be sure, is a great sin of us Christians. If only we were faithful in hearing the orders of our Lord for our day, then even the nonchurched people *(Volk)* would hear a witness to the Lord, and be spared many an evil step. Therefore, O Land, Land, Land, hear the word of the Lord!

Yet in closing we do not want to forget that for us Christians the Lord's word is more precious and clearer than for a Jeremiah. Because this word is fulfilled in Christ our Lord, who told us, "Repent, for the kingdom of heaven has come near." Through him our day of repentance becomes *a day of thanksgiving.* The world loves to ridicule repentance because it has no clue that authentic repentance is the gate to the happiest of lives, and not in the beyond but already here on earth. If I might be permitted, I would like to remind us of the story of the prodigal son, of his homecoming filled with deep repentance and the rich life that begins there at home for him because of his father's kindness. Everyone who has come home through this door of penance to his Lord knows how close the kingdom of heaven has indeed come. And if we have stood today with our people *(Volk)* before God repenting, then this confession of guilt of which people think they are not permitted to speak, has been at least for me today like the casting off of a great burden. Praise God! The truth has been spoken aloud before God and in God's name. Now the world may do to us whatever it wishes. We stand in God's hand. God is faithful. But you, O Land, Land, Land, hear the word of the Lord. Amen.[21]

[21] I believe these closing remarks capture the reason pastors and priests spoke out against Hitler's crimes knowing full well the punishment and suffering that could quickly come. Pastor von Jan has no illusion that his sermon will change the course of events, but he stands under holy obligation to preach the word "in season and out." As Bonhoeffer wrote in the essay on the church and "the Jewish question," there would come a time when the Christian would have no other choice but to "throw himself beneath the wheel" of the oppressor's instruments of death.

A Sermon about *Kristallnacht*

Helmut Gollwitzer (1908-93) was born in Bavaria and began his university studies in theology at Munich. Before his doctoral work under Karl Barth in Basel, Switzerland, he studied in Erlangen, Jena, and Bonn.[1] After finishing his studies in 1937, he joined the Confessing Church and became the pastor of the Berlin-Dahlem church following the arrest of their pastor, Martin Niemöller, in June 1937. Already at this time, Gollwitzer had made a name for himself as a theologian, and many considered him among "the most important preachers of the time."[2] Gollwitzer's sermons were no more sympathetic to the Nazis than Niemöller's had been, and it was not long before the Gestapo expelled him from Berlin and forbade him to speak anywhere in the Reich *(Reichsredeverbot)*.[3] He escaped these difficult restrictions by volunteering to serve as an army medic.[4]

Just as the war was ending, the Russians captured Gollwitzer, and he spent four years in a prison camp. His book about that experience became a best seller in Germany. In the following years he taught at the university in Bonn (1950-57) and then at the Free University in Berlin. Along with his university teaching, he continued preaching at the church in Berlin-Dahlem. Through his books, published sermons, and other writings Gollwitzer became a well-known critic of West German capitalism as the country rebuilt and experienced an economic boom. He was also critical of the Vietnam War, and he opposed the arms race between the West and the Soviet Union.

Writing about his views on preaching in 1990, Gollwitzer acknowledged that "in no other form of speech are things taken so seriously, is our whole existence so challenged, even put at risk. In no form of speech does our word itself so much take the form of action, of intervention in the history of the hearers, as in this."[5] Having learned to preach in the 1920s, he remained convinced of the "seriousness of the preacher's situation."[6] This certainly holds true for the sermon below. It was preached the Sunday after the *Kristallnacht* pogrom against the Jews of November 8-9, 1938. The sermon has not lost its power and, like the von Jan sermon on the same day, is clearly a prophetic voice calling Germans to repentance and reminding them that sin has terrible consequences. Maybe not today, maybe not tomorrow, but surely God's righteousness will judge Germany harshly for the sins of *Kristallnacht*. The question for the Christians in the congregation that morning was simple: On whose side will you be standing when the wrath of God comes like a destructive storm over the Third Reich? The sermon leaves each Christian a clear choice: either you side with the Nazis or you side with Christ and the Jews. From a note to the German text we know that even members of the congregation had lost loved ones in the Nazi violence of that night.

A Sermon about *Kristallnacht*

November 16, 1938
Day of Penance: Sunday Following Kristallnacht

Berlin-Dahlem, Germany

And he came into all the country about Jordan, preaching the baptism of repentance for the remission of sins; as it is written in the book of the words of Esaias the prophet, saying, The voice of one crying in the wilderness, Prepare ye the way of the Lord, make his paths straight. Every valley shall be filled, and every mountain and hill shall be brought low; and the crooked shall be made straight, and the rough ways shall be made smooth; and all flesh shall see the salvation of God. Then said he to the multitude that came forth to be baptized of him, O generation of vipers, who hath warned you to flee from the wrath to come? Bring forth therefore fruits worthy of repentance, and begin not to say within yourselves, We have Abraham to our father: for I say unto you, That God is able of these stones to raise up children unto Abraham. And now also the axe is laid unto the root of the trees: every tree therefore which bringeth not forth good fruit is hewn down, and cast into the fire. And the people asked him, saying, What shall we do then? He answereth and saith unto them, He that hath two coats, let him impart to him that hath none; and he that hath meat, let him do likewise. Then came also publicans to be baptized, and said unto him, Master, what shall we do? And he said unto them, Exact no more than that which is appointed you. And the soldiers likewise demanded of him, saying, And what shall we do? And he said unto them, Do violence to no man, neither accuse any falsely; and be content with your wages.

Luke 3:3-14 KJV

Dear Friends in Christ,[1]

Who then on this of all days still has a right to preach? Who then should be preaching repentance on such a day? Have not our mouths been muzzled on this very day? Can we do anything but fall silent? What good has all the preaching and the hearing of sermons done us and our people and our church? How, following all the years and centuries of preaching, have we come to this place where we find ourselves today and as we find ourselves today? What good has it done that God has allowed our people to have so much success? What good has the great gift of peace done that we received with such joy just two months ago,[2] so that today each of those Ten Commandments that we have just heard[3] has struck us like a hammer blow right in the face and has knocked us to the ground? What a short blink of an eye separates that report of peace and this Day of Repentance! Back then we told ourselves in this very place that the new peace opens a new space for repentance — and now, so few weeks later, how's it going?

How have we used this period of time? What do we expect God to do, if we come to him now singing, reading our Bibles, praying, preaching, and confessing our sins as if we can really count on his being here and on all this being more than empty religious activity? Our impertinence and presumption must make him sick. Why don't we at least just keep our mouths shut? Yes, that might be the right thing to do. What if we just sat here for an entire hour without saying a word, no singing, no speaking, just preparing ourselves silently for God's punishment, which we have already earned? And when that punishment becomes obvious and visible, we will know better than to go running around screaming and railing against it wondering, "How can God let something like this happen to us?" Yet how many of us will do just that and in our blindness not see the connection between that which God allows and that which we have done and brought upon ourselves? We really should prepare ourselves so that we can say when it comes upon us: "O Lord, our sins have earned us this" (Jer. 14:7).[4]

It's not as if I enjoy any of this, but rather it's that I cannot evade the

[1] German *Liebe Gemeinde*.

[2] A reference to the Munich agreement between Hitler and Chamberlain, September 29-30, 1938.

[3] It was a tradition to read the Ten Commandments aloud on this Sunday.

[4] Here again we note the insistence that sin carries serious consequences no matter how remote those may appear in the present moment.

task — that's the reason I am speaking like this to all of you.[5] And because you all are willing to hear, let us listen together to what another man said once in another time. Let's listen to what John the Baptist said to the people of his day. And as we do, we want to notice how he continues to speak to us today; for what he said to the people of his day applies just as much to us today on this Day of Penance. All of you certainly want God to come into your life, to care about our church and about this nation *(Volk),* just as He[6] cared about the Jewish nation *(Volk).* But what that means is that this nation *(Volk)* and this church will be addressed in the same manner — and not a bit differently — as were that people *(Volk)* and that church.[7] May each and every one of you who today takes the name of God on your lips find this acceptable![8]

Where the kingdom of God comes to people, there stands John the Baptist at the door, and he makes the door into the narrow gate with this frightening shout: "O generation of vipers, who has warned you to flee from the wrath to come?" The word "repentance" turns the door into the narrow gate, the most despised and yet the most important word of our time.[9] It is a time when no one wants to repent, and yet it is precisely in this unwillingness to repent that we find the secret to the misery of our time. Because ours is a time that cannot tolerate this word, the most vital thing linking people to each other lies broken and shattered:[10] the ability of a person to give another his rights, the ability to admit one's own error and one's own guilt; the ability to find the guilt in himself rather than in the other, to be gentle with the other but strict with oneself.

---

[5] Here we can see the freedom the text gives the preacher to speak an uncomfortable truth.

[6] In German the pronoun is capitalized.

[7] Here again the German word *Volk* has to be emphasized since it was a key word in Nazi vocabulary, having both racial and nationalistic meanings. To hear that God cares for the Jewish *Volk* on this Sunday after such horrible and violent events against the Jews by the German *Volk* would have certainly carried weight.

[8] The hypocrisy of praying to God in the name of Jesus the Jewish Messiah on the one hand and being indifferent or complaisant with the events of the pogrom on the other is beyond the pale. To pray to *this* God is to care for *this* people just as God does.

[9] Nazis ridiculed the weakness of Christians who had to repent or ask for forgiveness for actions they considered signs of weakness. Nazis never repented of anything, especially of hatred and violence against Jews.

[10] A direct reference to the broken windows and shattered glass of Jewish shops and synagogues following the night of rage and murder. *Kristallnacht* is translated as "the night of broken glass" in English.

Because these abilities are becoming more and more impossible for one person after another and God's standards are becoming unknown to the people — those standards by which we will all be measured — for this reason all real communion between people lies shattered.[11] They do not want to know that their groups do not oppose one another like black and white. Who cannot admit his guilt before God can no longer do so before men. Then begins the insanity, the insanity of persecution that must make the other person into the devil himself in order to make himself into a god.[12] Where repentance stops, inhumanity begins; there all common bonds shatter even while one tries to strengthen them through tenacious self-justification and self-pardon.

Out of the *desert*[13] comes this call for repentance: from that place where human standards and interests lose their validity, where they disappear from sight, as they will for each of us in our hour of death. Wherever people are caught up in their daily affairs, wherever they are encircled by their own desires, and wherever the standard for their own conduct is its tangible usefulness and personal success, this call of God must really sound like a call from the desert and its invitation like a summons into the desert. God calls us to a negation of life. Our age is not so mistaken when it sees in this word "repentance" something of the negation of life. Repentance wipes away everything we think important, it sweeps away ruthlessly our interests and considerations, and it dries up everything that we hoped to mention in our favor. This contradiction is not without reason; whoever repents denies his own life; whoever allowed himself to be baptized here in the Jordan by John, said in effect: I am a man or a woman who must be drowned. Here all noteworthy conduct is for naught: "My wounds stink and suppurate due to my foolishness. I walk bent over and bowed down, for my sins reach above my head; like a heavy burden they have become too much for me" (Ps. 38:6, 7, 5). Repentance is the terrible discovery that I live under a death sentence, and even worse, that I must say yes to this condemnation to death. I am convicted not only outwardly by the sentence itself but inwardly by my own guilt. This is what happens with repentance: my life is annihilated and destroyed not only outwardly but also inwardly. All my defensive weapons — both those pointing externally toward others

[11] Again, Gollwitzer is alluding to the terrible night. Along with shattered windows and lives of the Jews, Christianity lies shattered in Germany.

[12] The whole purpose of Nazi propaganda was to make the Jews into devils and the Nazis into gods.

[13] Italics in original.

and those pointing inwardly toward myself — have been lost. I have to confess: it is *right*,[14] everything is entirely right that now happens to me. And I will go much further and say that even more could come my way and everything that befalls me will be entirely right.

This is not an attitude that a person can acquire on his own; it is not a way of thinking that a person can choose one day and exchange leisurely for another the next. Only the resounding cry that calls out to us can bring us to this point. It is like an enemy guard crying out in the night when he has discovered a soldier crawling toward him. We have been spotted. Who would then be able to talk the matter over, who would be able not to freeze on the spot or keep from running away from this path that leads to ruin?

O generation of vipers[15] — this is how an entire people is addressed. A people *(Volk)* who according to everything we know about them was in no way whatsoever any worse than we are today.[16] They were a people *(Volk)* caught up in a justified war of self-determination from a foreign oppressor and a people that was trying eagerly and diligently to hear the divine law and to follow it. If John the Baptist were to raise the same cry today, he would most likely be denounced as a notorious traitor of the nation.[17] Surely he would find himself condemned by a unity front of the Evangelical Church as a shameful public enemy of the people, and all church connections to him would be severed. Maybe even in his day people were so outraged by [John] that they cried out: "How can a person today talk like old Jeremiah did hundreds of years ago? Maybe it was the right thing to do back then, but not today because we are a renewed people *(Volk)*."[18] What then does this old language about repentance have to do with us! It was a special grace of God for the people *(Volk)* that he did not allow Jeremiah's fate to befall John the Baptist. The whole nation *(Volk)* submitted to John's call, and they went out to him in the desert and were baptized. I am sure John's call for repentance seemed uninteresting to many in his day. It is so in every age to the person who exchanges the serious confession of sin and prayer for the national propaganda! Whoever considers himself a Christian and yet shares the outrage over this call to re-

[14] Italics in original.

[15] Italics in original.

[16] Comparing Germans to Jews like this would not have been well received by the authorities.

[17] As indeed would soon happen to many pastors like Gollwitzer, Schneider, Bonhoeffer, Barth, etc.

[18] Nazi "renewal" had no place for sin and repentance.

pentance should at least know that he has exchanged God's standard for the standard of the current political propaganda and has replaced the altar of divine justice with the altar of his own nation's self-justification.[19]

"You brood of vipers" means then: you hypocritical, poisonous, crawling worms! With these words an individual, a people *(Volk)*, a church is received at the entrance to God's kingdom *(Reich)*. He does not speak so to those who keep their distance but rather to those who have come out to him in the desert. These people who have a true desire to be baptized are addressed in this way and are welcomed with the news: God is disgusted at the very sight of you. Surely we today are familiar with the disgust we feel where evil is not simply evil but rather dresses itself up in a repulsive manner as morality, where base instincts, where hate and revenge, parade about as great and good things.[20] No ditch seems to be deep enough to distance us from such evil. But that is what is being said to those who come here in the desert: this is how God sees *us*.[21] It is exactly this disgust that God has for us. And in this way each of you is greeted at the entrance to the kingdom *(Reich)* of heaven. But is He[22] not right to do so? He would be equally justified even if this truth were hidden from us and if we could not test it out for ourselves. This is how a person shows that he has been called into the kingdom of heaven — he lets himself be talked to in this way. He knows that we look completely different to God than to ourselves, that we have been cast into the same ditch as all the others: you brood of vipers.

Yet it is not completely hidden from us. There are enough indications alerting us to the fact that the current fronts do not fall simply into categories of guilt and innocence, black and white. We have been trapped in the same great guilt and our faces also turn red with shame and we are afflicted by a common disgrace. It is inside us all; this truth that upright men and women can turn into horrible beasts is an indication of what lies hidden within each of us to a greater or lesser degree. All of us have done our part in this: one by[23] being a coward, another by comfortably stepping out of everyone's way, by passing by, by being silent, by closing our eyes, by laziness of heart that only notices another's need when it is openly

[19] This rhetorical net would catch "German Christians" and many pro-Nazi Christians.

[20] Nazi marches and rallies come to mind.

[21] Italics in original.

[22] Capitalized in the German.

[23] Notice the rhetorical power of this long sentence in which each of the nine indictments is introduced by the preposition "by" like the tolling of a bell.

apparent, by the damnable caution that lets itself be prevented from every good deed, by every disapproving glance and every threatening consequence, by the stupid hope that everything will get better on its own without our having to become courageously involved ourselves.[24] In all these ways we are exposed as the guilty people we are, as men and women who have just enough love left over for God and our neighbor to give away when there is no effort or annoyance involved.

"Who hath warned you to flee from the wrath to come?" Those who today are in great pain, those whose loved one is missing who otherwise would be with them here, those who today sigh under a heavy burden — all these must hear this question. Hearing this question shows the only way to bear this sorrow in a way that it might be a blessing. Because in this question we recognize in today's suffering the foreshadowing of the coming wrath. Not because in every individual case we can determine some guilt. But rather because in this question with its terror I recognize and confess whether or not I stand guilty or not guilty in all this. Have I come into this suffering for the sake of Christ or does it appear to have nothing to do with Christ? In any case, God has a charge against me, a more serious one than I ever imagined. He looks at me differently than I can look at myself. I can only see what is before me, but he sees into that part of my heart that I am unable to see. In repentance human beings see that which is coming: the wrath of God coming from disgust. What are all the other questions in comparison to this one: "Who warns us to flee the coming wrath?"

It is a good hour, may it be a blessing, when the blows of God's judgment startle each of us, our nation *(Volk),* and our church out of our peace and security like the clapping hands of the beaters startle the rabbit, when the terrible blows drive you, dear friend, dear people, dear church, out of your daily mundane routine into this terrifying question: "Where then might I flee that I might escape?" A good hour then, this hour of ours, because our question must not remain without an answer! In the Baptist's question we sense the amazement of those men and women who have come out to him apparently because they have been told to flee the coming wrath. Had they not been told to go out to him, they surely would not have come. Here with him lies the only possibility of escaping the wrath. Where he baptizes, the person is not only drowned and killed but also cleansed

[24] Certainly Christians in the congregation had done all these things in the hope that things would get better without their having to risk their comfort and safety.

and led into life. In baptism the frightening coming of the heavenly kingdom is transformed into great joy, the terrifying day of the Lord into a festival. The negation of life that belongs to repentance comes from a tremendous affirmation of life. Whoever repents negates his own life because he knows how it must disgust God. But that he is called to repentance comes from the fact that God will not allow this disgust to stand, that God has long ago affirmed this life that is disgusting to him: thus it is that God has loved this brood of vipers and he has given his only begotten Son, so that all who believe in him will not be lost but will have eternal life.

So it is that the negating no of repentance comes from the most hopeful yes. In baptism we find death and resurrection, no and yes, fear and joy, hell and heaven — all tied up together. That is why it is a "baptism of repentance for the forgiveness of sins." With the forgiveness of sin a life-saving wall is erected between your present suffering and misery as the foreshadowing of the coming wrath and the wrath itself. The connection between your former life and the coming wrath is destroyed: "The noose is loose; free the goose!"[25]

Two questions dominate John's call to repentance. The first has to do with the fleeing from the coming wrath, a question whose purpose is to flush us out time and again. But then we may answer with gratitude, "God himself has told us to flee this coming wrath; he himself has pointed us to the one John points toward, to the Lamb who takes away the sins of the world, to the crucified Lord of whom Paul says, 'So praise God for his love toward us, that Christ has died for us while we were still sinners. So we will be even more safeguarded from the wrath, having been justified through his blood'" (Rom. 5:8f.).[26]

The second question raises a concern that only now arises: "*What then should we do?*"[27] In answer John the Baptist places your neighbor right before your eyes just at the moment of forgiveness. The unwillingness to repent destroys the bridge leading to your neighbor. Repentance rebuilds this bridge. This neighbor does not excel in any way that would cause the world to find him worthy of help — nowhere is it said that he deserves our help. Nowhere are we told that between him and you there is a common bond of race or a people *(Volk)* or special interests or class or

[25] German: *Strick entzwei, wir sind frei.* My English rendition aims for rhyme and meaning. The literal meaning is "Rope in two, we are free."
[26] Here I have translated the German text of Scripture.
[27] Italics in the German.

sympathy.[28] He can only point to one thing, and it is that one thing that makes that person your neighbor — he lacks what you have. You have two cloaks, he has none; you have something to eat, he has nothing left to eat; you have protection, he has lost all protection; you have honor, honor has been taken away from him; you have a family and friends, he is completely alone; you still have some money, his is all gone; you have a roof over your head, he is homeless.[29] In addition to all this, he has been left to your mercy, left to your greed (see yourself in the example of the tax collector!), and left to your sense of power (see yourself today in the example of the soldier!).

So now the Baptizer dismisses us after our baptism, after the eradication of the divine repulsion and anger. He lets us go now as men and women for whom God has done a marvelous thing. He lets us go now back to our lives, and he shows us where God is waiting for us: in the poor neighbor. In a most practical way God says to us, "Divide what you have, and let him who has nothing enjoy your bounty just as you do." John means to tell us that things don't have to be any longer the way they were or that the old game has to begin again or that this national day of repentance has no value or that the unfruitful tree has to remain without fruit. He means to tell us that if today pain and fear are real and if God's word has told us anything, then today many things could be different. But will they be? Will the biblical warnings that today press upon us and come so near have more power than in the past? These warnings that are so practical, these warnings that point to such everyday things and uncomfortable things: Be hospitable without complaining! Bless those who persecute you! Do not be lazy in doing what you must do! Speak for all who are speechless and speak up for the cause of all who have been abandoned!

God wants to see deeds. But he damns them when we think we can flee the coming wrath through them. But he wants to see deeds, good works by those who have fled divine wrath with the help of Christ. If he does not see such deeds, it might well be that he will let everything sink away from us that he has given us; it might well be that this national day of repentance

[28] Questioning the importance of race in Nazi Germany on that day must have sounded like a thunderclap. Here Gollwitzer strikes against every pretense of Nazism's superiority to the Jew.

[29] On this Sunday it would have been shockingly clear that Gollwitzer meant the Jews without his having used the word. Gollwitzer here echoed Bonhoeffer's essay "The Church and the Jewish Question" (see editor's introduction). This is a powerful example of a biblical text addressing the present crisis.

might be his final offer. Now just outside this church our neighbor[30] is waiting for us — waiting for us in his need and lack of protection, disgraced, hungry, hunted, and driven by fear for his very existence. That is the one who is waiting to see if today this Christian congregation has really observed this national day of penance. Jesus Christ himself is waiting to see.

Amen.

[30] Again, on this Sunday in Nazi Germany, everyone in the congregation knew that the neighbor in need was their "Jewish" neighbor.

HELMUT GOLLWITZER

....

A Sermon about Faith as War Begins

Not only in Nazi Germany but also during the Cold War years, Helmut
Gollwitzer appears to have been a very popular preacher. His name was
known during the Third Reich in Confessing Church circles, and Karl Barth
published many of his sermons and Bible studies in *Theologische Existenz
heute*. Through this publication, Gollwitzer was able to speak to Christians
far beyond the local parish in Berlin-Dahlem.[1] In these sermons, as in sermons by Barth, Bonhoeffer, and others, the demands of the gospel became
sharp and radical. Each sermon ended with a choice on the part of the congregation — obedience to Christ or to the state.

The following sermon was preached just three days after Germany in-
vaded Poland. Gollwitzer had the task of preaching to a congregation whose
main concerns now were the war and the dangers war brings. Certainly there
was great anxiety for fathers and sons and brothers who would soon be
caught up in the hostilities. For Confessing Church pastors, preaching turned
from the threats to Christianity by Nazi paganism and "German Christian"
heresy to the tasks of pastors. Just as Isaiah could utter words of judgment on
one occasion and words of comfort on another, so too preachers in Germany
had to shift emphasis as the situation moved from internal political and
theological matters to matters of war. The sermon began with a pastoral
tone but soon developed sharp edges.

Where then was the God of peace on this September morning? From
the first words of the sermon it was clear that the preacher's task on this
Sunday was to find a way to fill the gap between the words of faith and the
words of war. The text from Isaiah has to do with the Lord's saving his peo-

[1] On Barth's important journal see the editor's introduction.

ple in times of great distress by lifting them up and carrying them. The New Testament text from Matthew's Gospel centers on Jesus rescuing the drowning Peter and his reprimanding the disciple, "O you of little faith, why did you doubt?" Here too there is a lifting up in a moment of great distress. The congregation must have just recited the Apostles' Creed, for the pastor began by recalling the first words of the creed, "I believe in God, the Father Almighty." It is this link between faith in the creed and in the gospel that Gollwitzer used as a springboard into his message on the third day of war, a message of the Lord's presence in great distress.

A Sermon about Faith as War Begins

September 3, 1939

Berlin-Dahlem, Germany

In all their affliction he was afflicted, and the angel of his presence saved them: in his love and in his pity he redeemed them; and he bare them, and carried them all the days of old.

Isaiah 3:9 KJV

And immediately Jesus stretched forth his hand, and caught him, and said unto him, O thou of little faith, wherefore didst thou doubt?

Matthew 14:31 KJV

Dear Friends in Christ,[2]

Once again today we have repeated the words: "I believe in God, the Father Almighty." This creedal statement that we have just finished hearing lays out for us what faith means on this particular day; on this day when what we have long feared and seen coming has been imposed upon us in an unavoidable way.[3] There seems to be a contradiction between the creed and this day, between this watchword of faith and all that we feel in our hearts

[2] German *Liebe Gemeinde.*
[3] These words indicate that this war is not the will of the German people but of a dictatorial authority that has forced Germany into a war. The German verb *verhängen* means both to impose and to inflict as in a punishment. While the Nazis would claim that Germany was forced into the war by its enemies, Gollwitzer implies that it is the German government that has inflicted war on its citizens.

and what we see written on the sober faces of people we meet.[4] Only the children seem not to sense this contradiction. When we walk through our beloved Dahlem, we see them playing on playgrounds as if nothing has happened. They appear to know far less than we know, we who still carry the vivid memory of those years from 1914 to 1918.[5]

Could it be that children know more than we do? In any case, they are both a picture and a sign of what we too can do if we really mean it when we say, "I believe in God Almighty." "Unless you become as little children, you cannot enter the kingdom of heaven."[6] After all is said and done, the kingdom of heaven is when someone can say to us, "I do believe in God the Father." When a heart has become steadfast through grace, when a person can say, "I know that my redeemer lives," "I lie down and sleep in complete peace; for you alone, O LORD, help me so that I dwell secure" (Ps. 4:9).[7] When these words live in a person's heart, then the kingdom of heaven has begun and a person has entered it. But the kingdom of heaven is far more than this. Its reality and what it contains are beyond compare. But it begins so small: in the very heart of the man or woman who can say "Father" to God.

How then do we enter this heavenly kingdom? In no other way than through becoming children, in no other way than through being born again, in no other way than through the Holy Spirit. That's what Jesus tells Nicodemus in their evening conversation. That is certainly timely advice for today. For there can be no doubt that the Almighty who loves us as a Father, who wants the best for us, has sent us these days so that they might serve for the best, that is, for our entering into the kingdom. There can be no doubt that he means well with us and has our best in mind so that we do learn to pray for the Holy Spirit. To all earthly appearances that does

[4] The description of Berlin on September 9 by William Shirer in *The Rise and Fall of the Third Reich* confirms what Gollwitzer says here. The streets were filled with fearful and anxious people rather than the jubilant throngs that welcomed war in 1914 (Shirer, *The Rise and Fall of the Third Reich* [New York: Simon and Schuster, 1960], pp. 597-98).

[5] Unlike Nazi glorification of war in general and the nationalistic manipulation of the "Great War," Gollwitzer offers a far more sober and realistic assessment. This is certainly not the kind of prowar rhetoric the Nazis would want.

[6] The German *Himmelreich* contains the same word as in Hitler's Third Reich. The contrasts between the two realms is far easier to note in German than in English, with our tendency to translate *Reich* as "kingdom" in religious contexts and to keep it as "Reich" or "empire" in its political sense.

[7] The reference to Ps. 4:9 is in the German text; in English Bibles the verse is Ps. 4:8. I have translated the German text here rather than quoting an English version of the passage.

not seem like much. But it is the greatest thing if only we can pray rightly. For then all things are secure. It is to that place that these days are now driving us.

To be sure, in these days many pagan prayers are being lifted up to God in many countries and in many churches, weak-winged prayers that barely reach the church ceiling. To pray rightly means not only to pray for God's protection and power, to pray rightly is no insecure groping in the fog. *To pray like the heathen*[8] is to pray for God when we are at a loss, to call for his help for human plans and wishes just as we might press an ally into our service.[9] To pray like pagans is to pray full of self-confidence and without repentance.

To pray rightly[10] — when we learn to do that, then these days provide us a tremendous service — to pray rightly means first of all to call upon him whom we know as Father. We do not know what the dark womb of the future conceals.[11] We worry ourselves sick trying to cut through this darkness; but still we do not know what is coming. But there is One who knows exactly. He knows what we will experience in this coming year, what Christmas 1939 will be like for us; he knows what will happen to our sons and our brothers. These things he already knows. And him we do know. He is not nameless fate or some fickle demon. He is the God of truth who has told us that we may call him "Father," and who beckons us to be confident that "we should believe that he is our true Father and we his true children to the end that we in all confidence and assurance may go to him with our requests just as children bring their needs to their earthly father." Our prayers are beset by surging uncertainties; they toss like a ship on a raging ocean. But of one thing we may be certain: steadfast above our prayers stands the guiding star of this Father who calls to us and who has revealed himself to us. It is to him we call out, and for this reason alone there is certainty in all our prayers. And still another thing is sure: we know a Christian prayer by the presence of repentance that it contains, a turning around.

In the coming days there will be a lot of cheap faith in God offered up, and there will be much pagan faith in God even in our Christian churches. But truly the only person who can trust completely in God is the

[8] Italics in the German text.
[9] Nazi speech called often on God to bless Nazi ways.
[10] Italics in the German text.
[11] German *der dunkle Schoß der Zukunft*.

person who can bow before him. The only person who may make the fourth petition of the Lord's Prayer — the request for daily bread that includes peace as well — is the person who acknowledges at the same time: We have not earned this day's bread but rather this war with all its horrors. We have each and every one of us brought all this upon ourselves and we richly, richly deserve the consequences.[12] Only that person may make the fourth petition who in the same breath makes the fifth: "And forgive us our guilt!"[13] If I may name but one sin, we have become very hardhearted.[14] We all must accuse ourselves of having brought so much misery upon ourselves by allowing so much evil to happen while we watched unmoved, and now this evil threatens us.[15] With hearts unmoved and with only the thought of what is good for us and our nation *(Volk)*, we have witnessed how other nations *(Völker)* have experienced that very thing that now has come upon us, and indeed we have only asked how it might benefit us and not what God wills and blesses. We have been cowardly[16] and have only wanted to save our own lives. And today God is teaching us in the clearest of ways that no man can secure his own existence and that it is good to trust only in him and not to want to secure our existence through sinful acts and omissions that God has forbidden. We have often preferred our life to God's blessing; we have wanted to maintain our existence even against God; and now we are in danger of really losing

[12] To Nazis these remarks would be high treason. Instead of proclaiming the righteousness of Germany's cause, as so many preachers did in 1914, Gollwitzer attributes it to sin and lack of faith.

[13] The German text of the Lord's Prayer has *Schuld,* which means guilt as well as debt.

[14] Gollwitzer may well have in mind the new morality of cruelty that the Nazis valued. Schmitz-Berning (in *Vokabular des Nationalsozialismus* [Berlin: Walter de Gruyter, 2007], pp. 294-95) has a lengthy discussion of hardness under the entry of *hart, Härte.* She cites the study by F. G. Kneisel, whose work on the way German vocabulary had changed since the First World War appeared in 1940. Her discussion and the citation from Kneisel demonstrate that under National Socialism historically negative terms like "hard," "intolerant," and "fanatical" were transformed into positive attributes while formerly positive ones like "considerate" and "patient" became negative terms.

[15] Certainly one need only think of the persecution of German Jews by the Nazis and the heartless passivity of Christians in the years from 1933 to 1941. Now that the war had begun, the persecution would intensify and escalate into the horrible "final solution" of gas ovens and extermination camps. And the Nazi temple would be pulled down by its own sinfulness and Germany left in ruins.

[16] To infer that Germans were less than heroic let alone cowardly was certainly taking one's life in one's hands.

132

everything that we have won by unrighteous means: our high-handed and unjustly secured life.[17]

We have participated in the hatred and the mutual condemnation that reign in the life of each individual and in the life of all the peoples in the world *(Völker)*. We were all too ready to answer injustice with injustice and only looked to secure our own right and our own advantages while being indifferent to the rights and honor of the other person.[18] Now the fruit that had to grow from that is visible. Woe to us if we are terrified by the fruit and not its cause — which is us. Woe to us if the affliction of war does not move people in every nation to reflection and confession of guilt. To pray rightly is to pray with a repentant heart. Entering the kingdom of heaven is only possible through conversion. Whoever asks for help has to say: Lord, we do not deserve it. "We bow before you with our petition, counting not on our righteousness but on your great mercy" (Dan. 9:18b).[19]

To pray rightly therefore is to pray in every circumstance for *God's* will to be done in all these things. There are a number of permissible petitions that we may make, although they carry no promise of fulfillment: that our life may be spared, that peace will soon be restored, that no great political shame befall our people — all these we *may* include in our prayers. But we *should* plead deeply and fervently for that which God has promised.[20] He has promised that those who flee to him in repentance and trust will receive a steadfast heart. Those who flee to him in repentance and trust will not find the many forms of temptation overwhelming. "You will overcome," he tells us. He has promised that he will not be silent. He will let us hear him, if we truly flee to him. He has promised to give us the "end for which we wait."[21] That's why the outcome of all this will be good, if we but believe.

And finally, on our own behalf, on our church's behalf, on our nation's behalf, and on behalf of all for whom we care — we may gratefully acknowledge: "He took them up and carried them all the days of old."[22] A verse from a hymn describes the abiding experience of all who rightly pray

[17] A radically different interpretation of Germany's economic and political development since 1933.

[18] Again one is struck by Gollwitzer's allusion to the stripping of rights and honor from German Jews that had taken place in Germany since 1933.

[19] My translation of the German.

[20] Italics in this paragraph are in the German text.

[21] Jer. 29:11.

[22] Isa. 63:9.

for the Holy Spirit: "The Lord is good. No harm is so great that he has not both the power and will to protect us. If we be surrounded by the protective womb of eternal love, then we may recline in quiet peace. That is his protection that we may rest peacefully here. The Lord is good."[23]
Amen.

[23] From the hymn *Der Herr ist gut* by Johann Jakob Rambach (1693-1735). The German text reads: "Der Herr ist gut. Kein Elend ist so groß, er hat so Kraft als Neigung, uns zu schützen. Umschließet uns der ewgen Liebe Schoß, so können wir im stillen Frieden sitzen. Das macht ein Schutz, dass man hier sicher ruht. Der Herr ist gut." Gollwitzer quotes the fourth of nine verses. Each verse begins with "The Lord is good." (http://www.liederdatenbank .de/song/1291.) Accessed August 9, 2012.

GERHARD EBELING

A Sermon for a Victim of *Aktion T4*

Gerhard Ebeling (1912-2001) studied theology under Rudolf Bultmann and Emil Brunner, among others. Dietrich Bonhoeffer, however, was one of his teachers at the underground seminary in Finkenwalde, and this training certainly must have had a powerful effect on his thinking and preaching. After the war he was professor first of church history and then later of systematic theology in Tübingen. He later became a professor in Zurich, where he had received his theology degree in 1938.[1]

In 1995 Ebeling published a collection of sermons from the Third Reich, from which the sermon here is taken. In the foreword he explains that he first preached for a group of Confessing Christians whose church had been split by the Church Struggle, with the pastor, a member of the extreme Thuringian "German Christians," continuing in the pulpit. Ebeling conducted worship in a tiny space apart from the sanctuary for those members who stood with the Confessing Church.[2] He titled the collection *Sermons of an Illegal*, because he was not the legal pastor of the Confessing group nor had the recognized church ordained him, but rather the "illegal" Confessing Synod of Berlin-Brandenburg.[3]

After the start of the war Ebeling was drafted into the army as a medic. Surprisingly, he was still able to serve occasionally as pastor throughout the war until his unit fled the burning city of Berlin on April 20, 1945.[4]

As he explains in the foreword to the sermon collection, Ebeling decided to publish the sermons in the small volume because one of the sermons had been published separately and he thought there might be interest in the others as well.[5] The particular sermon he refers to deals with the horrible aspect of Nazism that judged the lives of certain individuals to be useless and disposable. In a sinister program first known as *Aktion T4*,

135

which later extended beyond the initial six institutions to concentration camps in the East, the Nazis systematically murdered some 100,000 people from 1940 on.[6] Here too, as in so many instances, we notice the terrible abuse of language by the Nazis. The transport of patients was overseen by the General Welfare Transport Society (Gemeinnützige Transportgesellschaft), while the group in charge of the actual killing in the gas chambers was called the General Welfare Foundation for Institutional Care (Gemeinnützige Stiftung für Anstaltspflege).[7]

The Nazis targeted individuals whose existence they considered "unworthy of life" or "unfit for life," depending on how one translates the infamous German phrase lebensunwertes Leben. In a nihilistic Darwinian society like the Third Reich, there is a hierarchy of life that places certain types at the top and others at the bottom of the values ladder. To be sure, the healthy Aryan was at the top of the pyramid and Jews at the bottom. But close to the bottom the Nazis ranked people who were greatly dependent on the care of others. In a world where love had no meaning, the notion of caring for the helpless and those with special needs carried no worth or merit; the mentally and physically challenged were viewed as only a drain on society. But as Hitler had said in 1929, Germany was still dominated by a "modern sentimental humanitarianism" in which the "weak" lived at the expense of the strong.[8]

Even Hitler, however, understood that Germans would never tolerate such a program of forced "euthanasia" and that such a venture should be placed on hold until war came. The mass murder of those unwanted human beings in Nazi society was conducted in secret and with much euphemistic cover (p. 383). Targeted patients were simply transported to one of the six killing facilities, and there they were gassed in showers (pp. 385, 391). Once the target of seventy thousand murders by gas had been achieved, Hitler ordered that patients be killed "by starvation and lethal medication" rather than by gassing (p. 402).

In sharp contrast to the murder of Jews, there were protests over the killing of helpless Germans. In spite of efforts to keep the whole program secret, word began to leak out. Family members were not satisfied with the fake death certificates listing false causes of death. Clergy too became suspicious, and some made inquiries (p. 399). In December 1940 Pope Pius XII condemned the policy, while in Munster Bishop von Galen's outspoken and courageous sermons publicly sounded the alarm that the government was murdering the poor and the sick (p. 402; see von Galen's sermon below).

In June 1940 a couple who belonged to another congregation in

Berlin came to Pastor Ebeling with the news that their son, Günter Rott-man, born 1906, had been killed by the government. They told him that their son had been a patient for some time in a Berlin hospital but then had been transported without their knowledge to an institution near Lenz, Austria, where he had died suddenly on June 23, 1940.

The government had sent them the urn with his ashes. They asked the pastor to preach their son's memorial service, which Ebeling was eager to do. In preparation for the service, Ebeling made numerous inquiries in Berlin concerning other such cases. Soon he was aware that this murderous activity was widespread. His contacts in the Confessing Church assured him that it was preparing a statement that would be sent to the *Reichskanzlei*, the headquarters of the Nazi government.[9]

In the memorial sermon Ebeling used Jesus' welcoming of the "little ones" of society as the command to view every human person as God's beloved child and not as disposable and inconvenient waste material. He also raised the challenging question of where God might have been in this tragedy. The answer came indirectly at the sermon's conclusion.

A Sermon for a Victim of *Aktion T4*

July 17, 1940

Berlin-Hermsdorf, Germany

Take heed that ye despise not one of these little ones; for I say unto you, That in heaven their angels do always behold the face of my Father which is in heaven.

Matthew 18:10 KJV

The darkness of this hour in which you must surrender the ashes of your son and brother to the earth is enormous. When one who is old and has lived a full life dies, the pain is lessened because that life was able to mature and then is gathered in like sheaves at the proper time. If one sacrifices one's life in devoted service as a mother or in a profession or as a soldier, knowing that the death was meaningful helps us get past the sadness. If one dies after a long illness or even unexpectedly suddenly yet in our presence, so that we may give that person love until the end and have communion with him — which today is so seldom — Christian communion in a common preparation for dying through prayer and reception of Holy Communion,[1] then there goes forth from such moments of leave-taking at the deathbed a peace that transfigures the darkness of death.

But none of these mitigating circumstances apply to the loss that has struck you so suddenly and unexpectedly like an annihilating stroke of lightning out of a clear sky. And the note they wrote that this death has spared your dear son a lifelong stay in an institution and that this knowledge should comfort you has not helped but rather it has darkened all the more this death so far from home about which you have learned no details.

[1] A clear reference to the Nazi paganism of the time but perhaps also to war casualties.

That then is the depth of the darkness, the challenging: Was this death God's will? And if it is according to the prophet's word: Does misfortune come to a city that the Lord has not caused (Amos 3:6)? — then here God's will and God's action are so dark, so black like the most sinister night! How then has he hidden himself so incomprehensibly in this inscrutable event — inscrutable as much to our earthly eyes as to the eyes of faith?

What life then has been lost with this death? This son was given to you as your firstborn child and was for you a sign of friendship with our God who blesses us and creates life. You brought him to be baptized so that his life might not be founded on his own powers but rather on rebirth based on God's grace. You knew the joy with him one has with a gifted person who lives not for self alone with his gifts and abilities but who rather feels the compulsion to sacrifice himself in the service of an idea, in service to others. So he was an early enthusiast for the new political movement[2] and indeed sacrificed a part of his health in this zeal. And then with the illness came much suffering for you.[3] But with the suffering deepened the love — the love like God's love that burns for the lost and leaves the ninety-nine for the sake of the one lost sheep in order to take that one on the arm and to care for it and to rejoice over it. So special is God's love that this love does not love those who are worthy of it but rather those who have special need of it.[4] Authentic parental love reflects this divine love. So these years filled with sorrow and pain were filled for you with rich testing of this parental love and finally these same years were filled with great comfort too as you and your son hoped that everything would be good again. But then came so suddenly the parting without the possibility of a final farewell, a frightening, torturous sixteen days of uncertainty about where your ill son was being kept, then the harsh communication of the death some four days previously, and finally the receipt of the ashes as the only visible remains of that life you have carried with so much love and sacrifice, with so much sorrow and hope.

[2] Recall that the Nazis referred to Nazism as the "Movement."

[3] Ebeling offers no details regarding this illness. Obviously the family knew them and there was no need to offer more information in the sermon. From the context, however, one might suppose that the young man suffered some kind of mental breakdown. Whatever the illness may have been, it rendered the young man "unfit for life" according to Nazi philosophy and therefore made his murder legal.

[4] Here Ebeling uses the German word *würdig* (worthy). The Nazis turned such people into unworthy and useless human beings who did not meet Nazi standards for worthwhile life. It is tragically ironic that the victim initially supported Nazism.

But we have not gathered to speculate over what has happened but to let God's word be spoken into our darkness and speculations, God's word of comfort from Jesus himself as recorded in the eighteenth chapter of Matthew's Gospel: "Take heed that ye despise not one of these little ones; for I say unto you, That in heaven their angels do always behold the face of my Father which is in heaven."[5] This challenges us: let go once and for all your speculating and hear what Jesus Christ thinks of this. Close your eyes with their view of things and let yourselves be shown how Jesus Christ sees this matter. Don't work yourselves to death worrying how you should come to terms with this but hear how Jesus will deal with it.

"Little ones" in the sense that Jesus means includes everyone who has no worth in the eyes of the world, whom the world pushes aside, from whom people walk away, about whom no one inquires. "Little" are the helpless children, "little" are the helpless widows and orphans, "little" too are the ones whom the world despises for the sake of its own belief,[6] "little" too are Jesus' disciples, "little" are the Christians, who follow their Lord; then Jesus himself was held to be small and regarded as nothing, one led like a sheep to slaughter. This then is a very large family; the children and those with no rights and the sick and the Christians and Jesus himself, he, our brother, who has made all of us "little ones" brothers.

Well, I don't need to speak much about that, how the world despises these "little ones." Your deceased son could sing a lament about it. And many of us gathered here could too. Yet I am compelled to speak and testify: that Jesus stands on the side of these little ones, for us little ones: "Do not despise one of these little ones." Jesus stands up for the life of the weak, the sick, and the vulnerable.[7] Not only with words and expressions of sympathy but with action. He healed the sick, he gave love and companionship to the despised and rejected sinners. Like the Old Testament prophets, he called "injustice" "injustice," "wrong" "wrong," and "sin" "sin." And his calling such things by name he passed on to his disciples, to Christians, to the church as our mission. So we must testify today to this work of Christ in the midst of our world so that we never despise one of the little ones, that we do not abandon those Christ has accepted and for whom he died. We are

[5] KJV.

[6] A clear reference to Jews and the unworthy ones according to Nazi belief.

[7] This phrase keeps the word "life" front and center for it was "life unworthy of life" that had caused the boy's murder. By linking the weak, the sick (for the son was "sick"), and the vulnerable with the noun "life," Ebeling attacks again this evil aspect of Nazi faith and action. There is no question on whose side Jesus is.

rather to stand with the sick and the weak and those without rights to the end that through the word of Christ even this son who was despised by the world and who lies here before us as ashes in an urn will be great and appear in a new light.

In order that we really might share with certainty and joy this new way of seeing the world through Christ's eyes that makes the little things great and the great things small, Jesus Christ tells us further something simply wonderful: "in heaven their angels do always behold the face of my Father which is in heaven."[8] That means that each one is esteemed individually by God as he is for who he is. Each one who welcomes God's mercy has access to the Father and the protection of the Father and peace with the Father. The angels, the Scriptures say, are "all ministering spirits, sent forth to minister for them who shall be heirs of salvation."[9] They are God's invisible servants who must serve even us little ones, and every need of ours that they see they show to God and every tear we shed they carry to God.

God cares for little ones and he grieves when the little ones are despised. Be sure that he does not tolerate the rejection of the little ones. He vows that he stands with the little ones of our time. And if we fail to see his concern for the little ones, the weak, and the sick in the world, then know that he has good reasons for this so that he might all the more beautifully reveal his allegiance with these little ones in the resurrection of the dead. If God does not despise the child, and the sick, and those without rights, how much less does he despise this dead son and his ashes. If Christ, his only Son, has been raised from the dead as we believe, then we too will live with him — in a life that will place all darkness in the light of God's incorruptible truth, in the clarification of the last judgment. We await this. And if we really believe, we even look forward to it. Amen

[8] KJV.

[9] In the German text the quotation (Heb. 1:14) is a statement and not a question as in the King James Version. I use the KJV wording but leave the punctuation as in the German text.

A Sermon about the Parable of the Great Banquet

Rudolf Bultmann (1884-1976) is primarily known for his scholarly work in New Testament studies, not for his sermons. Along with Karl Barth, he ranks as one of the two giants of twentieth-century Protestant theology.[1] From 1921 until his retirement in 1951, Bultmann taught New Testament at the university in Marburg.[1] He was born in the north German town of Wiefelstede, where his father was a Lutheran pastor. There were four children in the family, three boys and one girl. One of Rudolf's brothers was killed in the First World War, and the other did not survive imprisonment in a Nazi concentration camp.

After graduating from a German humanistic high school in 1903, where he concentrated on religious studies and classical Greek, Bultmann studied theology at Tübingen and Berlin before finishing at Marburg in 1910. He became a member of the Marburg faculty in 1921, and taught there until his retirement in 1951. Friedrich Schleiermacher, the nineteenth-century Romantic theologian, influenced his thinking, as did Martin Heidegger, a fellow member of the faculty at Marburg for several years. In his theology Bultmann reflects Heidegger's existentialism in philosophy.

Soon after joining the university in Marburg, Bultmann published *Die Geschichte der synoptischen Tradition* (1921).[2] This work was much discussed in Germany and later, after its translation into English, had a great influence on New Testament studies in the United States. In this work, Bultmann advances the idea that the interpreter of New Testament docu-

---

[1] Had Dietrich Bonhoeffer survived the war, he too would undoubtedly be included with Barth and Bultmann.
[2] Published in English as *History of the Synoptic Tradition* (Harper, 1963).

ments must take into account the original form the Christian message took in order to separate the form from the essence of the gospel. The outer form is cultural and cultures come and go, but the gospel's essence is timeless and appropriate for every age. In this way, the church may still find a hearing among modern men and women who cannot accept primitive ways of communicating.[3] Later, in his work on the historical Jesus, entitled simply *Jesus* (1926), Bultmann applied form criticism to the ministry of Jesus, and suggested that we must learn to separate the eternal truth of the gospel from the mythological worldview in which the message has come to us.[2] Here there is a subtle advance from discussion of forms to discussion of myths. Understandably, suggesting that myth was a part of Christianity caused much controversy.

In 1941 Bultmann presented his massive work *The Gospel of John*. Here Bultmann applies his method of interpretation to the entire Gospel and advances the idea that the author depended on a so-called Signs Gospel.[3] Along with this lengthy commentary on John, Bultmann gave a lecture that same year called "New Testament and Mythology." These lectures, given to the Society for Evangelical Theology, provoked "a raging controversy among churchmen and biblical scholars in his call that the New Testament message be distinguished from its 'mythology' in order for the timeless good news to be intelligible for modern man."[4]

For our purposes, however, his opening lecture of the summer semester in May 1933 provides a rare glimpse of his use of theology to address the politics of the hour. The title of the lecture was "The Task of Theology in the Present Situation."[5] He began by saying, "Ladies and gentlemen! I have made it a point never to speak about current politics in my lectures, and I think I also shall not do so in the future." But the new government and the enthusiastic way so many Germans were embracing it compelled the theology professor to offer his personal thoughts on the job of German theologians in Hitler's Germany. After insisting that for Christians God is always the "creator" who stands outside of time and history, he cautioned against identifying events in time and history too closely with God's will. Christians were to acknowledge that a part of creation entails being members of a nation, but this did not mean allowing oneself to be carried away beyond any ability to criticize political leaders when laws failed to reflect the obligation to love the neighbor. One example that he cited for his students was the growing popularity of defaming people who had different views. He concluded the lecture with these words: "As a Christian, I must deplore the injustice that is also being done precisely to German Jews by means of such defamation."

Although generally not a political activist, as noted in the lecture above, Bultmann was adamantly opposed to Nazism. Not surprisingly, he was a member of the Confessing Church. In 1933 he joined other Marburg theologians in signing a statement against the expulsion of pastors with Jewish heritage from church offices, and two years later he wrote a public letter objecting to Hitler's order that university professors of theology could not participate in the Church Struggle.[6]

Although many remember Bultmann the theologian, our emphasis is on Bultmann the preacher who preached many sermons "in Hitler's shadow" for the university community at Marburg. It is from a collection of the wartime Marburg sermons that the sermon offered here is taken. While most Americans recognize Bultmann's impact on theology, this sermon reveals his pastoral side. He was not lecturing from a university lectern but preaching God's word from a pulpit, and he was doing so in a time of crisis and danger. Although theologians will continue to read and debate his theology, his sermons deserve attention as well, for they reveal a master preacher. His Marburg sermons invite us to hear a Christian whose intellectual interests never overshadowed his concern for those who gathered for worship and to hear the "good news" of Christ in the Third Reich. We should notice the comment about his not having time to select an appropriate text for the occasion and then decide if the text at hand does not indeed speak to the current situation.

The sermon in this collection was preached in Marburg on the Sunday that Germany attacked the Soviet Union.

A Sermon about the Parable
of the Great Banquet

June 22, 1941

Marburg, Germany

Then said he unto him, A certain man made a great supper, and bade many: And sent his servant at supper time to say to them that were bidden, Come; for all things are now ready. And they all with one consent began to make excuse. The first said unto him, I have bought a piece of ground, and I must needs go and see it: I pray thee have me excused. And another said, I have bought five yoke of oxen, and I go to prove them: I pray thee have me excused. And another said, I have married a wife, and therefore I cannot come. So that servant came, and shewed his lord these things. Then the master of the house being angry said to his servant, Go out quickly into the streets and lanes of the city, and bring in hither the poor, and the maimed, and the halt, and the blind. And the servant said, Lord, it is done as thou hast commanded, and yet there is room. And the lord said unto the servant, Go out into the highways and hedges, and compel them to come in, that my house may be filled. For I say unto you, That none of those men which were bidden shall taste of my supper.

Luke 14:16-24 KJV

Dear Friends in Christ,[4]

All of us are deeply shaken and moved by the news we heard this morning.[5] Events have taken a new turn and we are now at war with Russia! With divided hearts we sang our processional hymn:

> Hallelujah, beautiful morning,
> More beautiful than we can imagine!
> This morning I have no worries. . . .

For if we try to forget our worldly concerns here in God's house or to surrender them to God, can we really forget the great worry that today burdens us all? If I had known earlier on what day I would have to deliver this sermon, then a long period of reflection would have been required to decide which text to choose, which text would be right for this day, for this hour. But now the choice has been removed from me for I had earlier chosen the text of the Gospel for this Sunday, and perhaps it contains just the right word for today. We intend to try in all calmness to consider what it wants to say to us.

There was a tradition in Jesus' country when he told this story that we need to understand if we are to really comprehend this text. When a well-to-do man wanted to arrange a large, festive banquet, he would first send around a tentative invitation with no exact mention of the day or hour of the feast. The invited guests were simply informed not to plan anything for the near future. And then when the day arrived, a second invitation went out, saying, "Now it is time! Come, for everything is ready!"

According to custom, the rich man in our story had invited many guests, and of course they had accepted the invitation, for who would allow a banquet to pass them by? But they had accepted the invitation casually because, as we see, they did not keep themselves ready to attend at a moment's notice. They did not arrange their time and their business with the expectation that the host's messenger would come soon to invite them for the particular day but rather went about their daily work as if there were no need to expect the call to the banquet. Indeed, they probably had completely forgotten about the invitation. And now that the messenger comes, they are all caught up in things that appear to them at the moment

---

[4] The German is *Liebe Gemeinde,* literally "Dear congregation."
[5] The German invasion of Russia began that morning.

to be more important than the invitation. One just bought a piece of land and has to assay it to see how he can make the best use of it. Another has just bought oxen and has to see to them. Still a third has just married and is thus prevented from coming. And others too, who are not exactly mentioned, have this or that preventing their coming. In short, not one of the invited guests has time now; not one is coming to the banquet. No wonder that the host becomes angry! Fine, then! Let them stay away! There will be others who are more than happy to come to a banquet! So he sends his messenger out again and has the poor and the lame who otherwise have to beg their food brought from the streets and lanes. And when he sees that there is room for others, he has vagabonds brought in from country paths and fields.

I

The story is a parable. What does it teach? One thing is very clear: the rich man's invitation to his banquet depicts God's call inviting people to his kingdom.[6] The invited guests — both the first ones and the latter ones, along with those who are compelled to come — are the people to whom God's call goes out. And those who hear the parable are asked if things will be for them as they were for the first ones invited who did not keep themselves ready and thus lost the joy of the banquet. The tone of the parable is clearly not comforting and encouraging as if we were to think primarily about those who were not invited at all but were later called. The tone is rather serious and threatening, as the ending makes clear, "For I say unto you, That none of those men which were bidden shall taste of my supper!"[7]

Against the backdrop of Jesus' own time, the parable is quite easy to understand. The ones first invited are the pious leaders of the Jewish people *(Volk)* to whom his call for repentance was so often directed, against whom his anger was so often kindled. It is those who for so long have known of God and God's call, who for so long have said, "yes, yes!" and who, now that Jesus has come and told them "now is the time!" close their

[6] The German word for "kingdom" is *Reich*. Did Christians hear the word as a challenge to Hitler's *Reich*? God's *Reich* and Hitler's *Reich* locked in conflict?

[7] Here I follow the KJV translation since Bultmann is quoting directly from the German scriptures, but I leave Bultmann's exclamation point.

ears to his call, and from whom he turns away and goes to the "tax collectors and sinners," who respond to his voice.

If Jesus is speaking to us now through this parable, then we too are challenged to consider if we belong to the first invitees who have known God's call for a long time and who have accepted his invitation, but who, when matters become serious, when the word now goes out, choose rather to tend to our personal business and reject God's call.

We can hardly neglect to apply this to our own nation *(Volk)* as a whole. We recall that it was once touched by God's call; it was invited by God when the gospel was proclaimed to our ancestors, to the old Germanic tribes. And then again it was touched by God's call in the sixteenth century when Luther's preaching let the gospel ring out. We have to think about those days when Germany was a Christian country.[8] Don't the churches that belong in every village scene and the monasteries and cathedrals that tower above our cities witness to this? Doesn't the Christian education provided to our youth in schools and churches testify to this?[9] Don't the Christian traditions that permeated our national customs *(Volksleben)* testify to it — the holidays, baptisms, and church funerals?[10] Still, churches belong to every village and city scene; still, church bells ring out on Sunday over houses and fields. And I do not want to discuss how now there are villages whose center no longer is the church. But I do have to ask one thing: How many churches are filled Sunday after Sunday with prayerful worshipers?[11] How many fellow Germans[12] let themselves be drawn by the ringing of those bells to the house of God? For how many people are the great cathedrals of our cities no longer sanctuaries where God's word speaks to

[8] A remarkable statement about how far Germany had decayed morally since the beginning of the Third Reich. The church buildings remained in every German city and village, but Christian faith and morality had disappeared.

[9] Teaching religion in German schools boasted a long tradition, but the Nazis sought to transform religious instruction into Nazi propaganda and to distort the Christian message. Many confessing pastors, Schneider and Busch (see below) in particular, conducted running battles with the Nazis over the church's authority to teach children and youth the basics of the faith.

[10] Notice the past tense here. Bultmann is mentioning what was obvious by 1941. Under Hitler and Nazism Christian traditions were far less prevalent than before 1933.

[11] One thinks of the churches filled with Nazi flags and swastikas. See note 7 on the Bonhoeffer sermon.

[12] Here Bultmann uses the Nazi term *Volksgenosse*. See repeated use of the word in von Galen's sermon and the essay in Cornelia Schmitz-Berning, *Vokabular des Nationalsozialismus* (Berlin: Walter de Gruyter, 2007).

them but only works of art where the Germanic spirit has been erected?[13] What has come of the Christian instruction given to our youth? Who feels bound today by Christian morality? We all know that Germany today no longer is a Christian country, that church life is only a remnant, and that many wish and hope that even this remnant will disappear.

What is the reason for this? Is it not that for us all, without exception, the affairs of daily life were more important than God's call? That the striving for profit, power, and pleasure was more powerful than the question: How am I holding myself in readiness for God? That the pleasure from technical progress, from athletic accomplishments and such, was greater than the joy from God's word? Is it not the case, briefly put, that the readiness for God's call was lost?

II

But then one could ask, "What should we hold ourselves in readiness for?" When then did the second call come to us, the one saying, "Come, for all is ready"? Hasn't that one failed to materialize? This question leads us to consider that always, whenever a nation *(Volk)* turns away from the church, the individuals are guilty. It is always to the individual that the second invitation goes out, that call: "Come, for everything is ready!" And this is always when the individual least expects it, when it is most uncomfortable for him, so that he really wants most of all to close his ears.

Just as in the time of Jesus his appearance was God's call — uncomfortable and tossed to the wind by crowds of people *(Volk)* — so this call of his rings out since that day everywhere again and again, and in that call he himself meets us everywhere again and again. Where does he meet us? Where did we perhaps not see him nor hear his call? Here Jesus has anticipated our question. For this is his word to those who failed to see him:

"For I was a hungered, and ye gave me no meat:
I was thirsty, and ye gave me no drink:
I was a stranger, and ye took me not in:
naked, and ye clothed me not: sick, and in prison, and ye
    visited me not. . . .

[13] The German is *deutscher Geist* (German spirit).

Inasmuch as ye did it not to one of the least of these, ye
did it not to me."

(Matt. 25:42-43, 45)[14]

So it is that always and everywhere our brother's need requires our sympathy and helping hand, there he meets us, there his call sounds for us.

Here we have to think again about the history of our nation (Volk). Certainly the church has attempted to the best of its ability to help in times of need, for example, in the work of the "home missions."[15] But it is now quite clear: if everyone calling himself Christian had had open eyes and an open heart for social need, for the growing needs of industrial workers, for the housing needs, etc., if a willingness to sacrifice and a joyfulness in doing without excesses had really been alive among us, then the contempt for the church and indeed the hatred against it never would have grown to the terrifying degree that is currently the case. The judgment would not have come about that condemns Christianity for having done little or nothing at all to make the world better!

But we do not want to linger in the past and think about what was neglected. Our complaints and accusations need to be a wake-up call for the present and should call us to think so that today we do open our eyes and offer a hand, so that we do hear God's call — each in his situation. And we need to begin by asking ourselves where it is in our daily life that God's call meets us. If we think only of the great needs, then we are less likely to notice the individual small needs requiring our help. And all the great needs grow really out of little ones, or better, from the fact that in our blindness we in the beginning failed to see the little needs.

Just where God's call meets each individual, you and me, in the course of our everyday life, at work, in the hustle and bustle of daily affairs, I cannot tell you, nor should I even try. For that is the secret of the encounter with Jesus, that he meets us always disguised in different forms; that is

[14] KJV translation following Bultmann's poetic formatting.

[15] The German is *die Innere Mission* and refers to the evangelical home missions that Johann Wichem began in 1848 to bring a Christian rebirth to Germany and other countries. See the entry under *Innere Mission* in Wikipedia: http://en.wikipedia.org/wiki/Inner_mission (accessed July 17, 2012). The Nazis severely restricted the mission's ability to provide services in favor of the Nazi social service called *Winterhilfswerk* that was begun in 1933. Restricting what the church was permitted to provide aided the propaganda that Christians were more talk than action. On the *Winterhilfswerk*, see the entry in Schmitz-Berning, *Vokabular des Nationalsozialismus*.

the secret of God's call, that it always sounds new, where and when one least expects it. I can only urge that each is prepared to hear the call, that each is ready to listen to it.

The folktale of the poor and the rich with which we are all familiar certainly knows that encounters with God often are improbable and that whoever is not prepared for them misses them to his own detriment. The folktale relates how God once wandered the earth as a simple wanderer and was looking for lodging for the night. He knocked at the door of a rich man and requested shelter for the night. The rich man saw the unimpressive wanderer at his door — he did not exactly appear as if he could pay well — and he turned him away with all sorts of excuses; it just wasn't convenient. Then God knocked at the door of a poor man and found a friendly reception. As the folktale later explains, the rich man had punished himself while the poor man received a rich blessing.

Indeed, joyfulness and goodness, patience and willingness to sacrifice belong to the readiness that is required of us — eyes open for whatever the hour may demand of us. Disguised comes God, comes Jesus to us. And if we fail to notice the encounter, then the moment is lost to us forever and we have deprived ourselves of that hour's blessing. For this reason we should make room in our restless and often hectic life for hours of quiet and reflection in order to examine ourselves and ponder the questions: What have I neglected? Who needs my help? Who longs to hear a kind word from me? We should not be consumed by the noise of the day, in our daily work with its cares, its joys and sufferings! We should not forget to notice what God wants to tell us here and there!

To be sure, God's call is very uncomfortable as a rule. When we ought to help, it seldom is convenient. Due to pressing work, one simply has not time! One is supposed to give all the time and does not have enough for oneself. It is true: there is more need than all of us together can meet. But have we always done what we could? Have we at least had a friendly glance, a good word when someone approached us? Or is it always nothing more than a bother when someone wants something of us?

III

But it is not only the needs of our fellow human beings in which God's call comes to us. It can be also our own need, our own fate, which hits us and shakes us. As long as life is moving along according to our plans and wishes, when it brings enticing tasks that match our strength exactly or brings success and joy to our work, our world seems to shine by its own light and to be illuminated from within. But we easily forget that the light that brightens our path falls in truth from outside on to our world as the light of God's goodness — like the sun's light upon the earth. And just as the sun's light can be covered by clouds when it goes down, so too can our world lie in darkness, this world of happy work and prideful success.

Then our world can become sinister and our activity and all human activity can become strange. When such a fate befalls us, this way for one and differently for another, then God is meeting us in the circumstance. But will we recognize him in the covering of darkness? Will we hear his call in the chilling silence of loneliness? Or do we fall then into doubt or in dull indifference and so rob ourselves of the blessing of our experience? "By their anguish God draws people through the darkness to himself" (Agnes Günther).[16] We should reflect on how uncertain the luster and happiness of our life are and should be ready in happy times for God's call that calls[17] us into the darkness — into the darkness to himself.

And haven't we perhaps learned that such a calling from God — uncomfortable and disturbing as it was — became a blessing for us? That through this we were torn from a life of routine and saved from torpidity and lethargy? And that our life received new drive, that it — either through our own need or seeing the need of another — received new depth so that we knew at last what it meant to be alive? And that we enjoyed the delight that was given us in a deeper and more grateful manner, and that we were drawn closer to our own families in new ways? And that in difficult days we were more patient and could draw blessings from hard times? How easily we sink into the monotony of everyday life; how easily we become deadened by the bustling activity of the world so that we become indifferent even to our own lives! Or how easily we are excited by things that merit no excitement! God's call, highly disturbing and uncomfortable, shakes us up, calls us back to our proper life, and gives us again the right sense of proportion for the things and activities we engage in.

To be ready now for the moment that is always the decisive moment?

[16] Agnes Günther (1863-1911) was the author of *Die Heilige und ihr Narr* (*The Saint and Her Fool*), a popular novel published in 1913. A film based on the novel was made in 1935. http://de.wikipedia.org/wiki/Die_Heilige_und_ihr_Narr and http://de.wikipedia.org/wiki/Agnes_G%C3%BCnther; accessed July 17, 2012.

[17] The repetitious translation reflects the German repetition of "call" as noun and verb. I have elected to be faithful to Bultmann's German: *der Ruf; rufen*.

The Christian faith is not something that lets us rest. It is not simply the possession of the conviction of certain teachings that one can make one's own once and for all. Rather the Christian faith is an attitude of the will. It is only alive in us when it continually proves itself in new ways. It does not suffice to have decided for faith in God once in the past, but rather this decision for faith has to be implemented anew time and time again whenever he encounters us, when his call meets us. Always again it remains true: Now! Through his encounters God puts us to the test. To be ready for his call, that demands from us that we keep an inner detachment from everything that has a claim on us, from our work and cares, from joys and sorrows; that nothing *entirely*[18] claims us, lest we become blind for his encounter and deaf to his call.

IV

And now we have come to our main point. To be ready for God's call means to be ready for the fact that our life or earthly work with its worries and plans, its sufferings and joys, is not the ultimate concern. What then does God's invitation mean? It is a call to something higher, something in the future, to something transcendent. It is the call from our world into his world! To be sure, sometimes things go badly for us here; the shabbiness and needs of our life press down upon us and we yearn for something more and are ready to hear the call into another world where sorrow and tears no longer exist. But God's call demands more! It demands that in good and bad times we are deeply aware of the fact that our world cannot give us ultimate satisfaction. His call demands that we decide between our world and his world, between the present and the future, between the immanent and the transcendent. Do we really want *him,* or do we want *our* world and *him* only occasionally for the transfiguration and improvement of *our* world? Is then what we plan and do here, what we construct and build with our worry and effort, what gives us joy one day and sorrow the next, really meant to be our highest and ultimate concern? To be that for which we live and die? Or don't we know a higher life? Are we ready to think seriously about eternity and to place our work and worry in the light of eternity and before the eternal judgment?

Indeed, do we know a higher life? Do we know anything about the

[18] Italics in the German text.

future and the beyond? We must confess, if we are honest with ourselves, that we do not *know* it, that we *know*[19] nothing of it. What we are acquainted with and what we know as fact — all that is nothing more than our life up to now, our life in this world, our life of earthly fate, the life of our plans and designs. But *that* means, to be exact, to count on eternity: to view this life we know so well as nothing more than preparatory, unfulfilled, and unfulfillable in our readiness for a future, fulfilled, and authentic life that God wants to give us. If we wanted to imagine, we could only sketch the images of our wishes and dreams. But it is just these images that we have to abandon. To be ready for God's future means to go into the darkness comforted and ready, ready for that which God has planned for our future.

But this future of God does not meet us only at the end of our days; rather, whoever hears his call is permitted always and again to experience something of it, how God makes it purer and stronger, quieter and more cheerful; how God answers the prayer:

Make me simple, profound, detached,
tender and still in Your peace![20]

But whoever has such readiness for God's call in his life will also find the readiness for God's final call that calls him away from this known life of ours into that unknown darkness. The greatest disturbance of our life is that this call will come to us. For how many people is this call the most unwelcomed of all! For how few does this call come at the right time! And who would, if he could, not ask for a delay so that he still could put things in order! But of course, when this call comes, one can't excuse oneself; it simply cannot be ignored. But then everything will depend on whether this call is the call *of God* calling us to himself or whether it is the eerie call of fate calling us into nothingness.[21] Then the question arises whether we are ready, whether we have learned in life to be ready for God's call.

We have not spoken of fate directly, in which we are standing at this

[19] Bultmann is using two different verbs that translate as "know." The first is to know by personal acquaintance *(kennen)*, and the second is to know intellectually *(wissen)*. I translated these verbs in the following sentence to make this distinction clear, but then lost the simplicity of the German.

[20] From the hymn "God Is Present" ("Gott ist gegenwärtig"; text at http://www .liederdatenbank.de/song/219; accessed August 9, 2012).

[21] Nazi atheism rejected a final judgment or afterlife.

time and whose eerie greatness just today again has been brought to mind. Is it necessary to speak of it explicitly? Whoever has understood what the demand for readiness means that our parable urges, he will also know what this demand means especially today. We all probably will know even without this parable that we have to be ready in word and deed, in quiet and bravery for that which is coming upon us. Our parable urges even more that we be ready for that which *God* wants to say to us through that which is coming upon us. It teaches us to seek firm ground on which alone we can find authentic quiet and bravery, on which we can gain the inner freedom from everything that this earthly future can bring: good and evil, victory and sacrifice — the inner freedom that we gain when we are ready for God's future and peacefully hold to Him.[22]

[22] This is the only place in the text where the pronoun for God is capitalized.

A Sermon about *Aktion T4*

August von Galen (1878-1946) was born in the northern German city of Oldenburg to a noble, Catholic family. He received his early education from the Jesuits in Austria. After being ordained to the priesthood, in 1904 in Munster, he served as the parish priest of St. Lambert Church. Soon, however, he was in Berlin, where he remained from 1906 to 1920. In the very Protestant Berlin, he ministered to the poor and worked to maintain the Catholic minority.[1]

He was a zealous German patriot during the First World War and distrusted the Weimar Republic during its short lifetime. In the Weimar years he spoke against the growing "godlessness of Germany," a theme he would later return to in Nazi Germany. In the same year that Hitler became chancellor, von Galen became the bishop of Munster. Von Galen was a patriotic, conservative, and well-educated German who certainly stood to the right of the political center. He shared the complaints of Germans after the war, so it is not surprising that he, along with many Christians in Germany, initially hoped that Hitler would be the leader a defeated and suffering nation needed.[2]

It was just over a year into the Third Reich, however, that the bishop began to oppose Nazi policies and tactics. On Easter Sunday 1934, he began to speak out against the anti-Semitic hatred and political tyranny of the new government. As the Nazi attacks took direct aim at the bishop, he became even more outspoken. Having access to Hitler, Bishop von Galen complained to the führer when the government violated the 1933 concordat with the Vatican. In November 1936, after the Nazis began removing crucifixes from all Catholic schools, the bishop denounced this intrusion into the church's domain so strongly that German Catholics engaged in a public protest. The objections that followed were so surprising and strong that the order was rescinded and Catholic schools soon had crucifixes on their walls again.[3]

Bishop von Galen now began to preach powerful sermons against the Nazis in response to the actions of the Gestapo in general, and in particular to the seizing of church property (just prior to preaching the sermon in this collection, the bishop read an announcement to the congregation outlining in detail recent Gestapo closings of religious houses in his dioceses). These facilities not only housed religious but also provided shelter for homeless individuals.[4]

In three sermons in July and August of 1941, the bishop confronted directly particular crimes of Nazism. On July 13 he told his congregation that, given the lawlessness of the Gestapo, no German was safe from being "taken one day from his home, deprived of his liberty, and locked up in the cellars or concentration camps of the Gestapo."[5] In a second sermon on July 20, he encouraged Catholic Christians to "stand firm," knowing that in Nazi Germany they were "not the hammer, but the anvil," and that their faith and "obedience to God, and loyalty to conscience" may require their very lives.[6] The sermon from August 3 addressed head-on the horrors of the T4 killings that were coming to the bishop's personal attention.[1] He warned that this horrible practice endangered every German, especially wounded soldiers and the elderly whose lives the authorities could well view as "unproductive" and thus useless. He expanded his verbal assault to include Nazi violations of the Ten Commandments and warned his congregation not to have contact with such anti-Christian, immoral people. As many in our collection did, he then prophetically warned Germans of God's coming judgment on the nation for such hateful practices.

The Nazi leaders were so outraged by the three sermons that many called for the bishop's execution "for treason," but Hitler let him live for fear that his death would spark outright revolt in Munster.[7] Instead of execution, the bishop lived under house arrest for the remainder of the war.[8]

After these three sermons, von Galen's opposition became less outspoken. The war was beginning to bear down on the German homeland, and the members of his flock needed a pastor more than a prophet.[9]

In the footnotes I have included comments by the Gestapo about the congregation's response to the bishop's sermon.

[1] See the editor's introduction and the introduction to Gerhard Ebeling's sermon.

A Sermon about *Aktion T4*

August 3, 1941

St. Lambert Church, Munster

And when he drew near, seeing the city, he wept over it, saying: If thou also hadst known, and that in this thy day, the things that are to thy peace; but now they are hidden from thy eyes. For the days shall come upon thee, and thy enemies shall cast a trench about thee, and compass thee round, and straiten thee on every side, And beat thee flat to the ground, and thy children who are in thee: and they shall not leave in thee a stone upon a stone: because thou hast not known the time of thy visitation. And entering into the temple, he began to cast out them that sold therein, and them that bought. Saying to them: It is written: My house is the house of prayer. But you have made it a den of thieves.

Luke 19:41-46 Douay-Rheims 1899 American Edition

As Jesus neared Jerusalem and saw the city, he wept over it.

Luke 19:41[2]

Dear members of our diocese! Our Sunday Gospel reports a shocking event. Jesus weeps! The Son of God weeps! Whoever cries is suffering pain, either pain in the body or in the heart. At the moment Jesus was not suffering yet in his body, and yet he wept. How great the pain in the soul of this bravest of men must have been, that he wept! Why did he weep? He wept

[2] Unless otherwise noted, biblical translations are mine from the German text.

over Jerusalem, over the holy city of God, the capital city of his people *(Volk)*, this city so precious to him. He wept over its inhabitants, his fellow countrymen,[3] because they did not want to recognize what alone could turn away the punishment foreseen by his omnipotence and predetermined by his divine justice: "If you would but recognize what things serve to give you peace!" Why don't the inhabitants of Jerusalem recognize it? Not long before Jesus had declared, "Jerusalem, Jerusalem, how often I wanted to gather your children as a hen gathers her chicks under her wings, but you did not want it!" (Luke 13:34). You did not want it! I, your king, your God, I *wanted!* But *you* did not want it.[4]

How secure, how sheltered, how protected the tiny chick is beneath the wings of the hen! She warms, she nourishes, she protects it. That's how I wanted to protect and guard you against every trouble. I wanted to! You did not! That's why Jesus weeps, that's why this strongest of men[5] weeps, that's why God weeps. Because of the foolishness, because of the injustice, because of the crime of *"not wanting."*[6] And over the evil[7] too that has to come from what his omniscience sees approaching, from what his justice has to impose when man sets his "not wanting" against God's commandments, against all the warnings of his own conscience, against all the loving invitations of godly friends and the best father: "If you had only recognized, even today, on this day, what serves to give you peace! But you did

[3] German *Volksgenossen*. This was a word that had fallen out of use in the nineteenth century but returned under Nazism with racial overtones. Loosely, the term meant fellow members of a cultural or national group. In the Third Reich it assumed racial overtones. Because of their "racial impurity," Jews could not be *Volksgenossen*. See the detailed discussion under *Volksgenosse, Volksgenossin,* in Cornelia Schmitz-Berning, *Vokabular des Nationalsozialismus* (Berlin: Walter de Gruyter, 2007), pp. 660-64. The bishop is using the term to underscore that these are Germans and they enjoy full rights as citizens. I do not think that he is making any comment about racial purity, but readers may differ on this. He may also be stressing that Catholics in Germany are Germans too. He will use this word many times in the course of the sermon. I cite each occurrence because of its importance in Nazi Germany and to underscore its ironic use by the bishop.

[4] According to the notes on the German text, the bishop underscored these two words. Unless otherwise noted, the italics in the translation follows the bishop's underscoring in the German text.

[5] The German noun is the noun *der Mann,* meaning simply male as opposed to female.

[6] The German is *über das Verbrechen des Nichtwollens,* where "not wanting" becomes a noun.

[7] The German is *das Unheil* as opposed to *das Heil* or "well-being" God in Christ offers.

not want it." It is something terrible, it is some injustice never heard of before;[8] it is the advent of ruin itself[9] when man[10] sets his will against God's will![11] I wanted, but you did not want. That's why Jesus weeps over Jerusalem.

Devout Christians! In the pastoral letter from the German bishops that was read in all Catholic churches in Germany on July 6 of this year, we read, among other things, "Certainly according to Catholic moral teaching there are positive commands that do not obligate us when doing so might involve great difficulties. But there are also sacred duties of conscience from which no one can free us, that we must fulfill, cost what it may, even our own life: never and under no circumstance outside of war and justified self-defense is a human being[12] permitted to kill an innocent person."[13] Yet on July 6 I had cause to add the following commentary to the words of the joint pastoral letter:[14]

For months now we have been hearing reports that on orders from Berlin, patients who have been sick for a long time and perhaps appear incurable have been forcefully taken away from mental hospitals.[15] On a regular basis the patient's family soon receives word that the sick person has died, that the body was cremated, and that the ashes can be delivered to them.[16] Generally there is the near certain suspicion that these numerous and unexpected deaths of mentally ill persons did not come about naturally but were intentionally caused and that people are thereby following the teaching that one may annihilate "unworthy life." This means, of course, the killing of innocent human beings when one thinks their lives no longer have value for the nation (Volk) and state. This is a terrifying teaching that

[8] Human beings owe God justice, and to go against God's will is to commit injustice.

[9] The German is a compound noun, Verderbenbringendes, which adds force to the idea.

[10] Here the German is der Mensch, the inclusive noun indicating a human being.

[11] The bishop, like Schneider, von Jan, and others, reminds Christians in Germany that God will not be mocked and ignored forever. The hubris and evil of Nazi criminals will bring destruction to the nation. In 1941 the war was going well for Germany and the Nazis must have found such warnings ludicrous.

[12] The German is again der Mensch.

[13] The German is ein Unschuldiger.

[14] It is difficult to determine from the German text where the quoted comment ends.

[15] The German is Heil- und Pfleglanstalten, rendered as "mental hospitals." This was the infamous Aktion T4.

[16] "Loud cries of 'boo'" (Gestapo report).

attempts to justify the murder of the innocent, and that fundamentally gives free rein to the violent killing of invalids who are no longer able to work, of cripples and of the incurably ill, and of our enfeebled elderly!

As I have learned from reliable sources, even now they are making lists of such patients in the mental hospitals in Westphalia, of so-called "unproductive" fellow countrymen[17] who will be transported away in a short time and killed. Already this week the first transport has left the institution in Marienthal-Munster!

German men and women! Paragraph 211 still has legal force in the Reich's Legal Code: "Whoever intentionally kills a human being[18] and has done so with forethought, will suffer the death penalty because of the homicide."[19] No doubt it is to shield those who are intentionally killing those poor people — our family members — from this legal punishment that they are transporting certain patients from their home[20] to a distant hospital. Any one of a number of illnesses is then listed as the cause of death.[21] Because the body is immediately cremated, neither the family nor the police can later determine whether the listed illness had really been present.

I have been assured that people in the Reich Ministry of the Interior and in the office of Reich Chief Health Leader Dr. Coniti[22] make no secret of this, that in reality a large number of the mentally ill in Germany have already been intentionally killed. The *RStGB*[23] provides in §139: "Who ever receives credible information of the intent . . . to commit a crime against life and neglects to inform the authorities or the endangered person in due time . . . will be . . . punished."

When I learned of the plan to transport the sick from Marienthal in order to kill them, I filed a written complaint on July 28 with the public

[17] German *Volksgenossen.*

[18] German *"ein Mensch."*

[19] The bishop references German civil law as the ethical and legal code of conduct even in Nazi Germany. Of course, Nazi policy always trumped civil law.

[20] The German word is *Heimat* and here implies that the unfortunate were taken from their home to one of the distant death centers: Bernburg, Brandenburg, Grafneck, Hadamar, Hartheim, or Sonnenstein. See Michael Burleigh, *The Third Reich: A New History* (New York: Hill and Wang, 2000), p. 391.

[21] A checklist of some sixty causes of death was provided. See Burleigh, *The Third Reich,* p. 394.

[22] The Nazi office is *Reichsgesundheitsführer.*

[23] *RStGB* = *das Reichstrafgesetzbuch,* the Reich Legal Code the bishop earlier referred to.

prosecutor's office in the district court of Munster that reads as follows: [the text is omitted from the sermon's published text].[24]

I have no information about any response from the public prosecutor's office or the police.

Already on July 26 I had filed an objection with the Westphalia provincial administration that has authority over the institutions entrusted with *the care* and *healing* of the sick. It did no good! The first transport filled with innocent human beings condemned to death has already departed![25] And as I now hear, already eight hundred patients have been transported away[26] from the mental hospital in Warstein.

So we have to assume that the poor, defenseless patients will sooner or later be killed. Why? Not because they have committed a capital crime, or — for example — have attacked their attendant or caregiver so that he had to use force against them to save his own life. Those are cases in which, along with the killing of armed enemies of the country in a just war, the use of even deadly force is justified and often necessary. No, it is not because of such reasons that those unfortunate patients have to die, but rather because they have become "worthless life" according to the judgment of some office, according to some expert opinion in some agency. And because according to this expert opinion these people belong to the "unproductive" fellow countrymen.[27] Someone determines that they can no longer produce goods, that they are like old machines that no longer run, that they are like an old horse that has become incurably lame, that they are like a cow that no longer gives milk. What does one do with such a machine? It is scrapped. What does one do with a lame horse, with such unproductive cattle?

No, I refuse to extend the comparison to its logical conclusion — no matter how fruitful its warrant and illuminating power!

We are not talking here about machines; it has nothing to do with

[24] The text is found in Clemens August Graf von Galen, *Akten, Briefe und Predigten, 1933-1946*, ed. Konrad Repgen, Veröffentlichungen der Kommission für Zeitgeschichte, Reihe A: Quellen: Band 42 (Mainz: Matthias-Grünewald-Verlag, 1988), #341, pp. 874-83.

[25] The German editor notes that sisters traveling with the innocent victims reported that these transports had more than one hundred patients and the first destination was hospitals in Weilmunster and Scheuern, and from there they were transported to the "death facility" *(Vernichtungsanstalt)* Hadamar. Von Galen, *Akten, Briefe und Predigten 1933-1946*, p. 877 n. 5.

[26] I have chosen to translate *abtransportieren* literally to capture the sinister idea of "transport" that we know so well from the Holocaust.

[27] German *Volksgenossen.*

horses or cows, whose only purpose is serving people, to produce goods for people! You can whip them or slaughter them, when they no longer fulfill this purpose. No, here we are dealing with human beings, our fellow human beings, our brothers and sisters! Poor men and women, sick men and women, unproductive men and women if you like! But have they forfeited their right to life[28] because of that? Do you, do I, have the right to live only so long as we are productive, only so long as we are viewed as productive by others?

When this basic principle is set up and used to allow the killing of our "unproductive" fellow human beings,[29] then woe to us all when we become old and weak with age! If one is allowed to kill our unproductive fellow human beings, then woe to our invalids who have used, sacrificed, and exhausted their strength and their healthy bones! If one can violently liquidate our unproductive fellow men and women, then woe to our brave soldiers who return to their homeland terribly injured, crippled, and invalid![30] If we ever concede that people have the right to kill "unproductive" fellow human beings — even if at the moment it affects only the defenseless mentally ill — then *categorically the murder* of every unproductive human being (thus the terminally ill, the cripples no longer able to work, the invalids due to work or war), then the murder of each one of us is permitted when we become old and weak. Then a secret edict needs only to order that the procedures carried out on the mentally ill may be extended to other "unproductive" people, that these procedures can be used also on people with incurable lung diseases, feeble with age, invalid due to age, or on severely wounded soldiers. Then none of us can be sure of our own life.[31] Some agency can put any of us on the list of the "unproductive," whose life has been judged now to be "worthless life." And not one police officer will protect you, and not one court will punish or sentence the murderer to the appropriate punishment! Who then can still place trust in his physician? Perhaps he will report his patient as "unproductive" and get the instruction to kill him. We cannot imagine the brutalization of morality, the mutual suspicion even within families that will be introduced if this horrible model is tolerated, accepted, and fol-

[28] German *das Recht auf das Leben,* a term with which we too are familiar.
[29] The German is *Mitmenschen* = a fellow human being. In this section of the sermon the bishop uses the term *Mitmenschen* four times and *Menschen* twice. Thus six times the humanity of the victims is emphasized with no reference to national identity.
[30] A most reasonable fear in Nazi Germany.
[31] Loud shouts of "boo" in the church (Gestapo report).

lowed. Woe to all people, woe to our German nation *(Volk),* if the sacred commandment of God that "thou shalt not kill," this commandment that the Lord communicated in the midst of thunder and lightning on Sinai, this commandment that God as creator has written on the conscience of human beings from the beginning, is not only violated but tolerated and practiced without any punishment!

I want to cite an example of something that is happening right now. In Marienthal there was a fifty-five-year-old man, a farmer from the rural community of Munsterlandes — I could even mention his name — who has suffered from mental disturbances for years now and whom therefore they entrusted to the provincial mental hospital in Marienthal for *care.* He was not completely insane; he could receive visitors and was always delighted when relatives came. Just fourteen days ago he had a visit from his wife and from one of his sons who is a soldier and was home on leave from the front. The son is really devoted to his sick father. Thus it was hard to say good-bye. Who knows if the son will ever return to see his father because he can be killed in battle for his fellow countrymen.[32] The son, the soldier, will most likely never see his father again on earth because his father has been put on the list of the unproductive.[33] A relative who wished to visit the father this week in Marienthal was turned away with the information that the patient had been transported away by order of the council of ministers for defense. They could not say where. In a few days the family will be notified.

How will this notification read? Again, as in so many cases, that the man has died and that the body has been cremated, that the ashes will be delivered if a certain fee is paid?[34] Then the soldier who is on the battle-field and is risking his life for his German fellow countrymen[35] will not see his father again on earth because his German fellow countrymen[36] at home[37] have killed him!

[32] German *Volksgenossen.*

[33] "Loud boos from the congregation" (Gestapo report).

[34] Here the editor has noted that the bishop issued an order on August 12, 1941, that pastors report all cases of Catholic funerals where the body has been cremated, supplying the name, the cause of death, the place, and the date of death. Von Galen, *Akten, Briefe und Predigten 1933-1946,* p. 879 n. 6.

[35] German *deutsche Volksgenossen.* It is interesting that here and in the next sentence the bishop uses the adjective "German" to emphasize his point.

[36] German *Volksgenossen.*

[37] German *Heimat,* a word that has many meanings, all of which connote a place of safety and peace. It is the "home" you can always return to and be "at home."

These facts that I have just mentioned are true. I can give the name of the sick man, of his wife, of his son the soldier, and I can tell you where they live.

"Thou shalt not kill!" God wrote this commandment on the conscience of human beings long before a penal code authorized punishment for murder, long before a prosecutor and court investigated a murder and punished a murderer. Cain, who killed his brother Abel, was a murderer long before there were states and courts. And he confessed, pressured by the accusation of his conscience: "Greater is my iniquity than any forgiveness I might find! Anyone finding me will kill me, the murderer" (Gen. 4:13).

"Thou shalt not kill!" This commandment of God, the only Lord[38] who has the right to determine life and death, was written on the hearts of men from the beginning, long before God communicated his moral law to the children of Israel on Mount Sinai with those succinct and short sentences chiseled in stone, which are recorded for us in the sacred Scriptures, that we as children learned by heart from the catechism.[39]

"I am the Lord, your God!" So begins this unalterable law. "Thou shalt have no strange gods next to me." The one transcendent, omnipotent, omniscient, eternal, and just God gave these commandments. Our creator and judge. Out of love for us he wrote these laws on our hearts and communicated them to us, for they correspond to the needs of our God-created nature; they are the unavoidable norms of a reasonable, divinely pleasing, salutary, and holy human and communal life.

God, our father, intends with these laws to gather us his children as a hen gathers chicks under her wings. If we humans follow these commands, these invitations, this call of God, then we will be cared for, protected, preserved from calamity, protected against threatening ruin like the chick under the hen's wings.

"Jerusalem, Jerusalem, how often I wanted to gather your children as the hen gathers her chicks under her wings. But you did not want it!" Is that to become true again in our German fatherland, in our Westphalia home,[40] in our city of Munster? How is it in Germany, how is it here with

[38] The German is *Herr*. As in English, the German word for "lord" has several connotations: lord, Lord, master, gentleman, etc.

[39] Perhaps with the repetition here of common morality the bishop is reminding his congregation that this natural law and this commandment are so deeply imbedded in the consciences and minds of Christians that no one can ever say, "We did not know this was happening and we did not know that it was wrong."

[40] The home is *Heimat*.

us, this obedience to the divine commandments? The eighth commandment: "Thou shalt not give false witness, thou shalt not lie!" How many times is this brashly, even publicly, violated!

The seventh commandment: "Thou shalt not take possession of another's goods!" Whose possessions are still secure after the high-handed and inconsiderate dispossession of property belonging to our brothers and sisters in Catholic religious orders? Whose property is protected if these possessions are not returned that were illegally confiscated?

The sixth commandment: "Thou shalt not commit adultery!" Just consider the directive and the reassurance contained in that notorious open letter from Rudolf Hess, who has in the meanwhile disappeared, that was published in all the newspapers about free sex and unmarried maternity.[41] And indeed, look at what we can glean, observe, and experience concerning this point right here in Munster in terms of shamelessness and vulgarity! What shameless clothing the youth have had to accustom themselves to. Preparation for future adultery! For this destroys modesty, the protective wall of chastity.

Now we come to the fifth commandment: "Thou shalt not kill" — this is set aside and violated right in front of the very people obligated to protect civil order and human life. And this is due to an exception made for the legal killing of innocent people, albeit sick, fellow human beings, simply because they are "unproductive" and can no longer produce goods.

How are things going regarding our obedience to the fourth commandment, which demands we honor and obey our parents and those in authority? The authority of parents has already been terribly eroded and will be even more shaken by all these orders that have been laid upon young people and that are contrary to their parents' will.[42] Do we believe that sincere respect and conscientious obedience of the *national* authorities will long remain if they continue to violate the commandments of the highest authority, the commandments of God, if they fight against and

[41] The German editor notes that the letter by Hess was published on December 23, 1939, and was addressed to a German mother. It approved the conception of children outside of marriage as permitted and praiseworthy in times of war. Von Galen, *Akten, Briefe und Predigten 1933-1946*, p. 880.

[42] Here the bishop is making reference to the Nazi encroachment of parental authority through the *Gleichschaltung* of young people in organizations like the Hitler Youth and League of Young German Girls. Hitler said early on that once he had possession of the youth, there would be no way to stop the Nazi movement. Protestant pastors too resisted the growing influence of the Nazi Party over young people (Schneider and Busch offer examples).

even attempt to destroy faith in the one, true, transcendent God, the Lord of heaven and earth?[43]

Following the first three commandments disappeared long ago in the public arena in Germany and in Munster. How many have disgraced Sundays and feast days and have eluded worship services! How God's name is taken in vain, dishonored, and blasphemed! And the first commandment, "You shall not have other gods besides me!" Instead of the one true God they have made idols of their own pleasing, so that they might bow down to them: nature or the state or the nation *(das Volk)* or the race.[44] And how many people there are whose god is really their "stomach," as Saint Paul tells us (Phil. 3:19); whose god is their own well-being for which they sacrifice everything, even honor and conscience, for sensual pleasure and the greed for money and power. Then they might try even to assume authority to make themselves lord of life and death over fellow human beings.

"As Jesus neared Jerusalem and saw the city, he wept over it and said, 'If only you would recognize, even today, on this day, what makes for peace! But now it is hidden from your eyes. Behold, the days will come when your enemy dashes you to the ground, you and your children, and no stone will be left on top of another, because you did not recognize the days of your visitation.'"[45]

With his physical eyes Jesus saw that day only the walls and towers of the city of Jerusalem, but divine omniscience saw deeper, recognized how things stood internally with the city and its inhabitants: "Jerusalem, how often I wanted to gather your children as the hen gathers her chicks under her wings, but you would not have it!" That is the great pain that pressed on Jesus' heart, that drew his tears. I wanted the best for you. But *you* would not have it! Jesus sees the sinfulness, the horrible, the criminal, and the harbinger of ruin of this *not wanting!* The little human, the fragile creature, places his created will against God's will![46] Jerusalem and its in-

---

[43] A reference to Nazi atheism and hatred of Christianity as discussed in the editor's introduction.

[44] These indeed are the idols of Nazism.

[45] Again we note the Christian warning that God will not let Germany's crimes go unpunished. As 1945 demonstrated, God's punishment for sin is not metaphor.

[46] The German with its emphasis on the "tininess" of humans appears to mock Nazi self-importance and hubris: "Der kleine Mensch, das hinfällige Geschöpf, stellt seinen Willen gegen Gottes Willen!" Here in a nutshell is a large part of Christian rhetorical response to Nazi rhetoric. Using Israel as an example, the implication for Nazi Germany is clear.

habitants, his chosen and preferred people *(Volk)*, place their will against God's will! Foolishly and criminally he mocks God's will! That's why Jesus weeps over the detestable sin and over the unavoidable punishment. God is not mocked!

Christians of Munster! Did God in his omniscience at that time see only Jerusalem and its people *(Volk)*? Did he weep only over Jerusalem? Are the people *(Volk)* of Israel the only people *(Volk)* that God surrounded with a father's care and a mother's love, protected and drew to himself?[47] And are they the only ones who would not have it? That rejected God's truth? That cast God's law away and thus fell into ruin?

Did Jesus, the omniscient God, at that time also look upon our German nation *(Volk)*? Upon our regions of Westphalia, our region of Munster, and our region of the Lower Rhine? And did he also weep over us? Cry over Munster? For a thousand years he has instructed our forefathers and us with his truth, led us by his law, nourished us by his grace, gathered us as a hen gathers her chicks under her wings. Did the omniscient God see at that time that he would have to speak his judgment over us too: "You would not have it. See, your house will become desolate"? How terrible that would be![48]

Oh, my Christians! I hope there is still time. But it is high time! That we recognize, even today, on this day, what makes for peace, what alone can save us, what alone can keep us from God's judgment: that we wholeheartedly and without curtailment accept God's revealed truth and confess[49] it with our lives; that we make God's commandments the guideline of our life and take seriously the saying: better to die than sin; that we with prayer and genuine penance plead for God's forgiveness and mercy for us, our city, our country, and our dear German people *(Volk)*!

But whoever wants to challenge God's tribunal, whoever mocks our faith, whoever despises God's laws, whoever makes common cause with those who alienate our youth from Christianity, whoever robs and casts out members of our religious orders, whoever makes common cause with those who hand over our innocent human beings, our brothers and sisters,

[47] This positive statement of God's love and care for Israel ran counter to Nazi hatred and persecution of the Jews. Also, Nazis would detest any comparison of themselves to Jews.

[48] The warning that God's punishment for sin is no harmless metaphor. Germany in 1945 gave stark witness to God's wrath.

[49] The word is *bekennen* = to acknowledge or confess, and is found in the Confessing Church *(die Bekennende Kirche)*.

to death; with those we will avoid all close association and we will withdraw ourselves and our families from their influence lest they infect us with their godless thinking and acting, so that we too do not become guilty and thus fall prey to the punishment that the just God has to impose and will impose on all who, like the thankless city of Jerusalem, did not want what God wants.

O God, let us all recognize today, on this very day, before it is too late, what makes for peace!

O Sacred Heart of Jesus, sorrowful to the point of tears over the blindness and the misdeeds of people, help us by your grace always to strive for that which pleases you, and to renounce that which displeases you, so that we remain in your love and find rest for our souls. Amen.

Let us pray for the poor sick people threatened with death and for our banished members of religious orders, for all who suffer need, for our soldiers, for our nation *(Volk)* and for our fatherland and for our führer.

The Way of True Faith

Wilhelm Busch (1897-1966) was born in Elberfeld to Wilhelm and Johanna Busch.[1] His father was a pastor. His mother came from a Swabian pietistic family. After finishing high school, Wilhelm served as an officer in the First World War. After the war he studied theology at Tübingen, and following his marriage to Emilie Müller, he served as a pastor in a mining district in the Ruhr area of Germany. He spent many years (1929-62) as pastor to youth in the city of Essen, where he was active in the Weigle House, a youth ministry begun by his predecessor Pastor Wilhelm Weigle.

The Nazis arrested him many times because his work with Christian youth and with the Confessing Church kept him in conflict with Nazi ideology. Throughout the Nazi era he worked diligently to provide young Germans with the basics of Christianity as a means of keeping them from falling victim to the new worldview. The tug-of-war between the pastor and the authorities, who orchestrated attempts to tempt young men and women from church activities, proved to be a constant and dangerous struggle. The Nazis did everything in their power to pull young Christians out of church activities and force them into the Hitler Youth. If the youth did not enter willingly, then the Nazis were more than prepared to help them do so through beatings and street attacks.[2] One example from the early days of the Third Reich is characteristic. After the Hitler Youth had forcefully occupied two Catholic youth homes, Busch and his youth knew that the Weigle House was next on their list. For some time, more than 100 young men stood guard to protect the property from the Nazis.[3] When they did attack the house, they were not prepared for Christians to fight back. After this incident, the local police promised to protect the property from further attacks. Yet for some time to come, young men stood guard to protect the property from the Nazis.[1]

The youth pastor had so many interrogations with the Gestapo that for his twenty-fifth interview he wore a black suit with a flower bouton-niere. When one of the Gestapo asked in amazement what he thought he was doing, he said he was celebrating their twenty-fifth anniversary.[4] Per-haps he was so interesting to the Gestapo because the ideological battle for the minds of young Germans was vital to the Nazification *(Gleich-schaltung)* of the culture. It was expected that young boys between the ages of fourteen and eighteen would be members of the *Hitler Jugend* while young girls of the same age would belong to the *Bund Deutscher Mädel (BDM)*.[2] In his ministry he worked night and day to prevent the youth who came to the Weigle House from being engulfed by the new paganism.

In his book on Wilhelm Busch's ministry during the Third Reich, Ulrich Parzany relates the findings of a Gestapo agent who worked his way into a meeting at the Weigle House of Confessing Church members on June 18, 1935. The agent's report to his superiors indicates that the theme of Busch's presentation was "The Youth Question." Here the pastor said, as quoted by the Gestapo agent, that the youth were in more danger than ever before. Just two days before, a young person who had participated in programs at the Weigle House had had a book of the Hitler Youth taken from him. Pastor Busch related that the content of the volume was nothing but Hitler Youth songs and dirty jokes that were so vulgar that the pastor could not relate them. Then the pastor told of a letter he had received from a father after his daughter returned from a meeting of the *BDM*. The fa-ther's letter made it clear to Busch that German young people were in grave danger of succumbing to Nazi paganism, and the pastor feared that young boys and girls could not be left alone anymore in such a toxic atmo-sphere. According to Busch, the Nazis were trying everything imaginable to separate the young from the Christian gospel, and even prayer before meals was being strictly forbidden at events.[5] No wonder he was often in-terrogated by the secret police!

Busch's ongoing battle with the Nazis over the right of the church to

[1] Ulrich Parzany, *Im Einsatz für Jesus: Programm und Praxis des Pfarrers Wilhelm Busch* (Neukirchen-Vluyn: Aussaat Verlag, 1995), p. 151. One should note that police pro-tection was more the exception than the rule in Nazi Germany. Each parish, village, city, and town had its own experience with all things Nazi. More freedom here, less freedom there. Some pastors arrested, others simply reprimanded.

[2] In English, "Hitler Youth" and "League of German Girls."

teach and influence young Christians reminds us of the courage of count-less pastors who continued to work in their congregations to maintain the integrity of the gospel and the faith. It is too easy in our day to overlook the danger then of simply proclaiming the basics of Christianity. To mention sin, for example, was frowned upon by the political powers, for the Ger-manic race did not believe in such outdated concepts. To mention faith in Jesus was to remind Germans of their need for salvation that comes to them from a Jew. As I have often mentioned in this volume and as the ser-mons themselves make clear, speaking the language of faith was daring.

After the war, Wilhelm Busch admitted his personal guilt at not pro-testing the Nazi persecution of the Jews. He said what so many must have felt: "Naturally we did something here and there. But we did not scream out as we should have screamed. That was a murder of many millions. I want to say that now quite openly. And if I talk about my little experiences, then it is like a number with a minus sign in front. How a person of my gen-eration can live without forgiveness of sins is beyond me."[6] Following his retirement in 1962, Busch continued to preach and remained very active until his death on June 20, 1966. A number of his sermons and biblical med-itations appeared in print. He did write one book, *Gospel Freedom: My Expe-riences with the Secret Police (Freiheit aus dem Evangelium: Meine Erlebnisse mit der Geheimen Staatspolizei)*, about his interrogations by the Gestapo.

The Way of True Faith

February 22, 1944

Essen, Germany

If he be the King of Israel, let him now come down from the cross, and we will believe him.

Matthew 27:42b KJV

"God my creator, who gives songs of praise in the night" we read in Job 35:10.[3] The Bible certainly has a lot to say about such blessed hours of the night. In the night Job wrestled with the Lord until he blessed him. In the night Lot was led out of Sodom. In the night the Lord opened the secrets of the future for Daniel (Dan. 2:19). In the night Nicodemus talked with the Lord. And in the night Jesus searched for the face of his Father.

But one of the most beautiful hours of the night has to do with Abraham. God had promised him a son. But now Abraham had grown old. And the son was not there. And then God led him one night outside his tent. A man alone with God in the stillness of the night. Above the sleeping earth the stars flame. And then God says, "Do you see the stars? Can you count them? So will be your seed." And then it says so beautifully, "Abraham believed the Lord. And the Lord reckoned it as righteousness."[4] If only we had such faith! The people beneath Jesus' cross also talked of faith. But they had no inkling of true faith. I would like to point out to you[5] a few things in contrast to their foolish mocking.

[3] The pastor has omitted the first part of the verse that reads in full, "But none says, 'Where is God my Maker, who gives songs in the night'" (RSV). I follow the German punctuation that does not indicate the omission.

[4] Gal. 3:6. My translation of the German text.

[5] The German here is the familiar plural *euch.*

The Way of True Faith

1. How True Faith Originates

As the Son of God was hanging on the cross, his enemies called out, "Climb down now and we will believe you." They had a very clear idea of how faith originates, namely, through miracles and success. If Jesus pulls off the miracle and climbs down from the cross — they say — then we can all believe!

Jesus did not answer them. Why not? Was he unable to do this miracle? But of course he could!

But — and now I have to say something, something that cannot be said clearly enough — faith in miracles and success is just the exact opposite of true faith. Everyone who knows sacred Scripture knows that the Antichrist will come at the end of time. And you need to read in Revelation 13 for yourselves to see how he will bring people to believe in him: through gigantic successes, through miracles that he does.

True faith originates very differently. It originates through the working of the Holy Spirit in our hearts. This Holy Spirit — yes, with what might I compare his working? It is like a light in the night's darkness so that one recognizes with sudden terror one's own darkness, lost state,[6] and guilt. He[7] is like a strong wind that pulls us to the savior. He is like a floodlight that lets all its light fall upon the crucified so that one knows, "Even me, even me he redeems there." He is like the sun in spring before which the old, evil, dead nature must yield so that joy and peace might enter. Through the work of the Holy Spirit, for whom we are all permitted to ask, true faith originates.

2. How True Faith Gets Its Bearings

The mockers standing beneath the cross were thinking this way: "Faith gets its bearings by our own wishes." They reasoned like this: "When a savior comes, then he will have to be a great king and wonder-worker." And so they said beneath the cross, "If you climb down now from the cross, then we will believe you! Then you really are just like we imagined."

---

[6] The German here is simply *Verlorenheit,* which I am tempted to translate as "lostness."

[7] The Holy Spirit.

That's how most people do this. They use their wishes to get their bearings in the faith. They think up a god for themselves who has to suit them in every way. If he does not, if he for example does not bring the son home from the battlefield or if he does not protect the house from the air raids — in short, if he does not climb down from the cross — then they have no use for faith. And just remember, the mockers beneath the cross were scripture scholars. They should have known that true faith does not use our wishes to get its bearings but rather *the Bible*.[8] Had they taken their Bible seriously, they would have known that the savior does not redeem us with power, pomp, and force but rather with suffering and dying. That's the way it is proclaimed already and everywhere even in the Old Testament. Then one is not offended by the cross because one has read, "He has been wounded for our misdeeds and slain because of our sins . . . through his wounds we are healed" (Isa. 53).[9] Then one does not take offense when the Lord leads us into suffering. For it says in the Bible, "We have to enter the kingdom of God through much affliction" (Acts 14:22).[10]

When the great battle over faith erupted in the Middle Ages, Luther, the man of God, stood one day before the Diet of Worms. All the worldly and spiritual power imaginable was assembled there in great splendor. And then he was ordered to take back everything that he had written. And how did he answer? "One must show me in the Bible where I have erred. Then I will retract it. Otherwise, no."

True faith gets its bearings from the Bible. And therefore it holds to this book with great passion. And it says, "If your word is no longer valid, on what then should faith rest?" "Not for a thousand worlds would I let go of your word!"[11]

3. What True Faith Dares

Oh, how these mockers are still standing beneath the cross! As long as the Lord fed people, healed the sick, he was okay. But when his path goes into

[8] Italics in original.

[9] Here I translate the German.

[10] I translate the German text here.

[11] A verse from a hymn by Ludwig Zinzendorf. Full text at http://www.christ-im -dialog.de/index.php?option=com_content&task=view&id=1666&Itemid=53 (accessed August 24, 2010).

the darkness of suffering, they say: "That is going too far! We aren't going any farther. Climb down and we will walk with you again!"

When I was a small child, an older cousin wanted me to accompany him into a cave in Württemberg. When we arrived at the cave's entrance, we lit our candles. And then we went inside. But after only a short while it became eerie for me. This darkness! And that dripping of water — and then — yes, I turned around and left him alone.

How many behave like this with Jesus. For a period of time he is okay. But when things head into the dark, into the dying of the old man, into the shattering of our wishes and hopes, then one says: "That is going too far. I am turning around."

True faith, however, goes with the savior even into the darkness. Thus we read of Abraham (Heb. 2:8):[12] "By faith Abraham was obedient when he was called to go out . . . and he went out and did not know where he was to go."[13] He went with Jesus into the darkness and the unknown. And one day the command came that he should sacrifice his only son on Mount Moriah. He did not scream: "That's going too far!" but rather he went comforted by faith along this dark path that led ultimately to light.

So true faith does not say: "Climb down from the cross, and then I will believe in you," but rather:

I will go with you to the cross,
So that I might live with you,
Who have risen from the dead.[14]

[12] The citation should be Heb. 11:8.
[13] I translate the German.
[14] Unknown source. Most likely a hymn.

A Sermon about the Loyalty Oath to Adolf Hitler

An important aspect of Hitler's vision for the Third Reich was the unity of all "Germans" in one great empire. The slogan *Heim ins Reich*[1] captured perfectly the idea that all "ethnic Germans" should live in one unified country. To realize this dream Hitler had to ignore existing national borders, but that presented no problem for him. Through talks if possible and force if necessary, Hitler meant to expand the German Reich and so to undo what history had done to divide "Germans" from each other.

On February 12, 1938, the German chancellor met with Austrian Chancellor Kurt von Schuschnigg. Hitler quickly made it clear to his interlocutor that he was in no mood for negotiation or compromise, insisting that he was on a "historic mission" whose completion had been appointed by "Providence."[1] The Austrian was given an ultimatum: either the Austrian government approve annexation *(Anschluss)* or German troops would march into the country. Schuschnigg, who loved his country and was no Nazi sympathizer, resigned. Soon thereafter he and his wife were arrested and placed in a concentration camp.[2] The path then was quickly cleared for the annexation. Austria ceased to exist as an independent nation and in March 1938 became a part of the Third Reich and was renamed *Ostmark*.[3]

The vast majority of Germans in the homeland were jubilant, as were the majority of Austrians. Photographs of Hitler's triumphant reception in Vienna and of Viennese Nazis humiliating the city's Jews testify to the depth of Nazi sentiment in Austria, while at the same time dispelling any illusion that Austria had been taken over against the country's will.

For Germans Hitler had gained a major victory without guns or tanks,

[1] German for "[Come] home into Reich."

although German military force certainly added weight to his demands. Any German sitting on the fence waiting for Hitler to fail had to realize that now was the time to show Nazi colors. The intoxication of Nazi victory spread even into the ranks of Christians.

Soon pastors too found themselves caught up in the afterglow of the *Anschluss*. Doctor Friedrich Werner, a "German Christian" and president of the Evangelical *Oberkirchenrat* (EOK)[2] of the Evangelical Church of the Old Prussian Union,[4] came up with the idea that an appropriate gesture for Hitler's birthday (April 20) would be for all pastors to swear an oath of loyalty to their führer, just as military officers did.[5] Those who refused would be dismissed from their pastorates.[6] The first to swear the oath were pastors in Thuringia,[7] which is not surprising because in this part of Germany the German Christian movement was the strongest.

For pastors in the Confessing Church, however, the matter of the oath was far more complicated. Although many of the Confessing Church clergy had celebrated the *Anschluss* as patriotic citizens,[8] this requirement asked for more than love of country; it demanded personal allegiance to an earthly ruler. The wording was: "I swear that I will be faithful and obedient to Adolf Hitler, the Führer of the German Reich and German people *(Volk)*, and will observe the laws and will conscientiously fulfill my official duties, so help me God." And the punishment was that "Whoever refuses to render the oath is to be dismissed."[9] Christians are to obey the appointed authorities and the laws of the land, yet their ultimate loyalty is to God, not men (Acts 5:29). Could pastors then in good conscience and as faithful Christians do what was being required without violating their ordination vows?

For Dietrich Bonhoeffer and other pastors who had by now been declared "illegal," the oath was not required since they had pretty much fallen out of official sight. But for pastors who were ordained prior to 1933, it was a firm expectation.[10] For some pastors whose status was also "illegal," the way was cleared to return to favor with church authorities through reexamination and the swearing of the loyalty oath.[11]

Interestingly, the oath controversy was not just an internal German affair, for news of the requirement spread abroad. On May 17 a story in the London *Times* reported that "10,000 pastors of the Protestant Church" had to decide before the month's end "between dismissal or taking the oath."

[2] *Oberkirchenrat* was the upper consistory and was a governmental office (see http://en.wikipedia.org/wiki/Consistory; accessed July 17, 2012).

The demand, as the paper's Berlin correspondent explained, presented "a grave conflict" for Confessing Church pastors who were being required to profess "obedience" to a church "they do not recognize."[12]

As the Confessing pastors wrestled over the oath requirement, the Confessing Church Synod in the Old Prussian Union said pastors could add their own understanding of the oath's meaning as a way to mitigate the radical nature of its text.[13] Although most pastors ended up taking the oath, those who did not were often viewed as going out of their way to confront the government over an issue that did not warrant risk.[14] For Karl Barth and Dietrich Bonhoeffer, however, the thought of Confessing Church pastors swearing an oath to Adolf Hitler was betraying the gospel. Both men were in absolute agreement that for a pastor to swear the oath was simply shameful.[15] In November Barth lost his teaching position in Bonn for refusing to swear a similar oath required of university faculty, and the university authorities replaced him with a German Christian.[16]

It is ironic that Hitler appears to have been indifferent to this entire affair. In August Martin Bormann expressed his view to regional party leaders (*Gauleiter*) that the oath was a church matter and it mattered little to him whether a pastor took it or not, since the only oaths that were binding were those ordered directly by the Nazi Party or the Nazi state.[17] Pastors, however, did not know this as the controversy was raging, and the threat of dismissal loomed large. In the end, most pastors did take the oath.[18] Although this particular crisis passed, the Confessing Church had confronted a direct question of loyalty to the Nazi state, and in the eyes of the minority the majority had betrayed the gospel.

Regardless of one's view about what was the right path for Confessing pastors to take in the matter, Christians were confronted with a question as old as the gospel: What do Christians owe to the state? How does one decide? It was in this spirit that a sermon was written for pastors of the Old Prussian Union to use in their congregations. To what extent the sermon answers the question at hand is a matter for readers to decide. But the sermon, as the text shows, brings the oath controversy into conversation with Jesus' reply to the question of the Pharisees about paying the tax. Each reader must decide whether or not the sermon offers the proper guidance.

An explanation for the unusual means of helping pastors reach a decision in the matter precedes the sermon proper. I could find no record of how many pastors, if any, preached the suggested text.

A Sermon about the
Loyalty Oath to Adolf Hitler

August 21, 1938

In accordance with the decision of the Sixth Prussian Confessing Synod in its second meeting, we are sending our brothers a "Sermon concerning Oaths." We intend to offer the best help in this situation by not placing a meditation in your hands but rather the example of a complete sermon manuscript. We do so because what is said here is of the greatest importance, as will be clear.

The brothers who wish to use this sermon verbatim from the pulpit may do so in this one extraordinary situation. Of course, those pastors who want to deliver a sermon on this matter in their own words are free to do so. We would only ask the brothers urgently that they not leave anything unsaid that must be said if we do not wish to appear untrustworthy to our congregations.

This following sermon is intended for the first Sunday after Trinity, August 21, 1938.

> Render therefore unto Caesar the things which are Caesar's;
> and unto God the things that are God's.
>
> *Matthew 22:21 KJV*

Dear Friends in Christ,

This is the biblical text that the church of Jesus Christ has always invoked whenever we have been accused of hostility to the state because of the confession of faith our Lord requires of us. In a report of martyrdom from the year 180, we read that when a female Christian was ordered to render divine homage to Caesar, she rejected this unreasonable demand with the words, "We render honor to Caesar as Caesar but fear we render to God alone." Our fathers in the faith invoked this text in the time of the Reformation. We ourselves have bound ourselves in *these years of the Church Struggle,*[3] in which state and church here in Germany have fallen in opposition to one another. We want to listen to this text in the matter of the *loyalty oath* which, as you know, we pastors are being compelled to swear. What does the Lord say in this text? There is in his reply the answer to a temptation-filled question put to him by the Pharisees in order to entrap him, "Tell us, what do you think: Is it right that one pays tax to Caesar or not?" They intended to trap him with this question. If he were to say yes, they would accuse him of doing homage to the foreign rule of the Roman Caesar and of betraying his own people *(Volk).* But were he to say no, they would accuse him of rising up against Caesar and of being an enemy of the state.[4] All of you know this story well, how the Lord sees through their hypocrisy and has them show him the coin in question that has the image and inscription of Caesar on it. Then he rejects the temptation with the words, "Give then to Caesar what is Caesar's and to God what is God's." We have to hear these words in the simple and unambiguous manner in which he spoke them and avoid succumbing to this temptation by making the answer of our Lord Christ into a twofold reply with a double meaning. It is simply not the case that with this answer a division is made between the area over which Caesar has authority and the area over which God is Lord. It is simply not the case that here the state receives its own area of authority in which God has nothing to say and that the church receives that province for itself in which it might satisfy its religious requirements. And it is certainly not the case that, as one hears again and again today, the state enjoys power over affairs of this life while the church must be satisfied with what is left over, namely, the afterlife. Not true! If one so twists the Lord's word, then what results is our having to surrender any obedience to God in any area of our earthly life and leave to him nothing but the authority over heavenly affairs. In truth, the Lord's answer summons us to complete obedience to the first commandment. This is valid in all matters pertaining to this life and the afterlife, for the state and the church, for the hour of wor-

[3] All italics in the sermon are in the German text.
[4] Being an "enemy of the people" *(Staatsfeind)* was a deadly serious matter in Nazi Germany and could lead to one's arrest or execution. Surely this German word would have echoed loudly throughout any church where this sermon was preached.

ship and for the hours of our daily lives *until death*.[5] If we are to give to the state what belongs to the state, then it is because even here we are to obey God according to whose merciful ordering of matters the secular authority is allowed to conduct stately affairs. This simply means that we should not and are forbidden to give to the state what is not allowed the state and that the state itself must render to God what is God's, for God is and remains Lord and Judge over the rulers and the ruled. Our Lord shattered the temptation and won the victory[6] in our place — for we have elsewhere fallen to temptation. And in this victory we take comfort. He alone has given God across the board the honor that is due God and the honor we deprive him of. So he was the one crucified in our place and who for us has risen from the dead. Let us take comfort in the fact alone that he advocates for us in every temptation so that we do not succumb and undergo eternal death.

What then does the Lord's answer mean for us who are confronted with the question whether or not we should swear the loyalty oath to Adolf Hitler that is being demanded of us? Does a government oath belong to those things that secular authority may demand of its subjects? We read in the Sermon on the Mount, "But I say unto you, Swear not at all; neither by heaven; for it is God's throne: Nor by the earth; for it is his footstool: neither by Jerusalem; for it is the city of the great King. Neither shalt thou swear by thy head, because thou canst not make one hair white or black. But let your communication be, Yea, yea; nay, nay: for whatsoever is more than these cometh of evil."[7]

The confessional statements of our church have understood this word of our Lord to mean that a Christian may not swear an oath on his own behalf but that he may swear an oath when required by state authorities. And this is so because the world exists under the rule of falsehood to such an extent that the state is permitted to erect a dam against falsehood with oaths in order to *control* lying. According to this recognition in Holy Scripture as witnessed to by the confession of the Reformation, we have from the former explained that we are prepared to swear a politically mandated loyalty oath insofar as the oath is not against God and if the state demands it of us. But now we heard this demand not from the mouth of the state but from the

---

[5] These words are highlighted in the German text and are quoted from the text of the Hitler oath under discussion. Nazis were expected to be "loyal/faithful until death."

[6] The German word for victory is *der Sieg* and, along with *das Volk*, was a highly charged word in Nazi language and worldview.

[7] Matt. 5:34-37 KJV.

law gazette of a church body that has no ecclesiastical authority and is bound neither to Scripture nor to the confessions and therefore cannot and must not be recognized by us. Still more, this church body gave the oath an interpretation in which it was said that it binds us to more than God's Word demands. As a result, a storm of resistance broke out among our clergy. More than 2,000 pastors refused to swear the oath under such circumstances, although threats were made that anyone not swearing the oath would be removed from his pastorate. Faced with this opposition, the illegitimate ecclesiastical body dropped its interpretation of the oath but obviously without expressly recanting it. Indeed, things went so far that pastors were allowed to give a written explanation of their understanding of the oath's meaning prior to swearing it. In this explanation they could declare that after swearing to the oath they would continue to be bound to their ordination oath, that they did not recognize the false church authority, and that they must continue to obey God rather than men. I will now read to you the instructions concerning the oath that the Sixth Confessing Synod of the Evangelical Church of the Old Prussian Union decided upon:

1. God's word binds the pastor to daily love in all life's relationships and to obedience to the authorities while in the pastoral office in which God has placed him. The oath to be sworn to the Führer Adolf Hitler calls upon God, and this recognizes the earnestness of responsibility toward God to be faithful and obedient. Thus there is justification for the oath.

2. The decisive factor about the obligation for us Christians is the fact that we are swearing before God who is the Father of our Lord Jesus Christ. As with every calling upon God, so too with this oath it is clear that we cannot promise anything or confirm anything or seek his help in anything that is contrary to his revealed will.

3. The duties of a pastor are set forth in the ordination oath. This binds the pastor to the word of God alone that is given in Holy Scripture and is witnessed to in the church's confessions. Therefore there is no Lord other than the Lord Jesus Christ for the ordained servant of the Word in the practice of his office. Thus the duties of the pastor's office assumed in the oath of ordination are neither expanded nor reduced in the oath of the secular authorities. Insofar as the pastor has certain public functions that are recognized by the state, he merely swears before the secular authorities to fulfill the duties of the office that flow from this office.

4. The use of the state's legal code for administrators[8] for pastors and the recognition of a church leadership that is not tied to the confession and the constitution of the church are not allowed by the swearing of this oath because they contradict the pastoral duties sworn to by pastors in their oath of ordination.

This explanation of the oath has been received by the other side, and the pastors wishing to swear the oath may add this qualification to the record of their taking the oath.[9] Also, our question as to whether the state really is demanding this oath of us has been clarified enough that we, based on certain facts and pieces of information, have come to the conclusion that the state does want this of us even though the state itself has not expressly said so. And thus it is that almost all pastors who earlier had been unable to render the oath because of their conscience being bound to God's Word have gone on to swear the oath or have said they are ready to do so. Perhaps someone, when reading the explanation of the oath that the pastors have given, might think that is sufficient. In this matter the pastors have wanted only to give the state what belongs to the state and God what belongs to God. But the awesome urgency that we must bring to our congregation is simply this: despite the clarification, we are still confronted with the question whether or not we really would be allowed to swear this oath. No matter how hard we have tried to get an answer to this question from the state itself, we have been unable to do so. The clarification that we are giving assumes the position that the oath is required without however appropriating this position. Is our action really clear-cut for the state and our people (*Volk*) if we swear the oath along with the qualifying statement that the seriousness of an oath allows? The state demands unconditional and unreserved obedience from the scores of people who take an oath. Un-

[8] The German here is *Beamtenrecht* and has to do with the official status of pastors in Germany as state administrators or officials. German pastors still receive their salary from the state because they are officials of the state. This relationship made it difficult for German pastors to stand up to the Nazis because their livelihood was at risk. Bonhoeffer and other pastors in the Finkenwalde illegal seminary had lost financial support from the government. At this point in the sermon, a distinction is being drawn between the work of pastors and other government workers when it comes to how the Nazi administrative code is to be applied.

[9] This may well mean that the forces wishing to compel pastors to swear the Hitler oath had agreed to pastors qualifying their actions. It appears that having as many pastors as possible swear the Hitler oath was more important than having them actually agree to its content.

conditional and unreserved obedience we owe only to God, whose law binds us in life and death. Now we have rendered the oath with the reservation that regarding the führer and Caesar we must obey God more than men in the appropriate circumstances.

But then one could ask whether this matter between the authorities and ourselves had to be brought out in the daylight before we would be allowed to swear the oath. But regardless of this, point four of the oath's regulations threatens us with dismissal from our pastoral office, and this remains in force. Have we perhaps paid too much attention to point four, which the hostile spirit brought into the church, rather than look only at the text of sacred Scripture and ask the Holy Spirit that he lead us to simple and clear obedience in the matter of the oath? How are we going to feel if a small group of pastors, just a handful, says to us, "Dear brothers, we cannot swear the oath now. May God help us! Amen!" And then if these brothers are really released from their office and service in the church?! And what do we intend to say, if the brothers who follow us into the pastoral office no longer have the opportunity to provide such an explanation, as we were permitted to do? In church matters it is not enough if one individual keeps his conscience safe, for it is written, "Who seeks to keep his life will lose it." Does this not stand written above the Confessing Church because she did not look to God's command and promise alone but with great distress and much skill sought a compromising way out? Again, in this matter of the oath, can we withdraw from the command to render to Caesar what is Caesar's? We have to lay the distress and guilt of this matter on your conscience too.[10] We neither want to nor can we justify ourselves, and we know of only one real and sure comfort, namely, that the God who is Lord also over such things as the swearing of oaths, this God who alone has the power to bind or loose, who forgives sins, will have his mercy win the victory over all human distress, guilt, confusion, and conscientious fear. We want to ask the Lord who took our place, suffered temptation, and won the victory to help us be obedient to his Word in rendering to the state what we truly owe it. May he guard us from the oath bringing us into a false obligation in which we do not dare to say and to risk what we owe God in obedience to his Word. Even if scores take the matter of an oath lightly and are not much bothered in their conscience, if they have sworn the oath three or four or five times, still we want to take this matter seriously, for we are swearing the oath calling upon the name of God. We have

[10] Here the preacher is addressing his congregation directly.

always acknowledged our obligation to the authorities and we have confirmed this in the oath, and so we want to say openly in this hour how we understand the obligation contained in the oath. We do not understand our having sworn loyalty, obedience, and heeding of the law to mean the same thing that the totalitarian claim of the new worldview understands by these.[11] God's Word has total claim on our allegiance and obedience. With God's Word we pray for the authorities, especially for the Führer and Chancellor.[12] God's Word allows us to ask that God keep and bless those in authority in matters that serve to further the authentic well-being of our nation *(Volk)*. God's Word allows us to pray that God will not render to the authorities anything that is contrary to God's Word. God's Word allows us to ask that our secular authorities refrain from doing what contradicts God's Word. We do not assume responsibility for those laws that oppose the gospel when we swear the oath since we made the oath in the presence of the Holy Spirit. We want to say this clearly so that we do not appear to be dishonorable or sneaky to the authorities. And also in order that we do not become untrustworthy to our congregations. It is clearly not hostility to the state[13] and not disloyalty or insubordination that bring us to say this but rather service and obedience to those matters that servants of God's Word are called and required to do. It is our prayer that our word will find the ear of those to whom we wish to render what is due them for the sake of the Lord Jesus Christ. It is our prayer that he might enable us and everyone who bows to God's grace in Christ to render to him in all things that which is his. But there is nothing at all that does not belong to him. Amen.

[11] This sentence contains explicit Nazi language: *Totalitätsanspruch* and *neue Weltanschauung*. The claim of totalitarian authority over all life in Nazi Germany and the new way of viewing the world were radically hostile to Christianity. When pastors swore allegiance to state authorities, it did not mean they would accept anything that was in clear opposition to the Christian faith.

[12] In German all nouns are capitalized. Here I have capitalized both "Führer" and "Chancellor" because the reference is clearly to Adolf Hitler and not just to any "führer" (leader) or "chancellor"; only Hitler assumed both titles, as far as I know.

[13] German *Staatsfeindschaft*. Hostility to anything the Nazi state wanted was tantamount to treason.

Notes

Note to the Preface

1. Edith Stein, *Aus der Tiefe leben: Ein Textbrevier,* ed. Waltraud Herbstrith (Regensburg: Topos plus Verlagsgemeinschaft, 2006), p. 36.

Notes to the Introduction

1. Victoria J. Barnett, "The Role of the Churches: Compliance and Confrontation," in *The Holocaust and the Christian World: Reflections on the Past Challenges for the Future,* ed. Carol Rittner, Stephen D. Smith, and Irena Steinfeldt (New York: Continuum, 2000), p. 57.

2. Klaus Scholder, *The Churches and the Third Reich,* vol. 1, *Preliminary History and the Time of Illusions, 1918-1932,* trans. John Bowden (Philadelphia: Fortress, 1987-88), p. 222.

3. Berlin Proclamation to the German Nation, February 1, 1933, at http://www.hitler.org/speeches/02-01-33.html (accessed August 9, 2012).

4. Scholder, *Churches,* p. 22.

5. Stuttgart speech of February 15, 1933, at http://www.hitler.org/speeches/02-15-33.html.

6. Scholder, *Churches,* p. 223.

7. Scholder, *Churches,* p. 224.

8. Scholder, *Churches,* p. 223.

9. Eberhard Bethge, *Dietrich Bonhoeffer: Eine Biographie,* 8th ed. (Gütersloh: Chr. Kaiser/Gütersloher Verlagshaus, 1994), p. 305.

10. Richard Steigmann-Gail, *The Holy Reich: Nazi Conceptions of Christianity, 1919-1945* (New York: Cambridge University Press, 2003), p. 14.

11. Niklot Beste, *Der Kirchenkampf in Mecklenburg von 1933 bis 1945: Ge-*

schichte, Dokumente, Erinnerungen (Göttingen: Vandenhoeck & Ruprecht, 1975), p. 83.

12. Beste, *Kirchenkampf,* p. 84.

13. Beste, *Kirchenkampf,* p. 86.

14. Wilhelm Rott, "Was ist positives Christentum?" *Evangelische Kirchenarchive,* Berlin, Bestand 50/4888, pp. 1-73. Page numbers to Rott's essay are placed in the text. This essay also is available as *Was ist positives Christentum?* (Neuwied: Heuser, 1937).

15. Victor Klemperer, *The Language of the Third Reich: LTI — Lingua Tertii Imperii; A Philologist's Notebook,* trans. Martin Bradley (New York: Continuum Impacts, 2006), pp. 104-5.

16. Klemperer, *Language,* pp. 105-6.

17. Klemperer, *Language* p. 108.

18. Klemperer, *Language,* p. 114.

19. Cornelia Schmitz-Berning, *Vokabular des Nationalsozialismus* (Berlin: Walter de Gruyter, 2007), p. 276.

20. Klemperer, *Language,* p. 110.

21. Quoted in Schmitz-Berning, *Vokabular des Nationalsozialismus,* p. 276.

22. Klaus P. Fischer, *The History of an Obsession: German Judeophobia and the Holocaust* (New York: Continuum, 2001), pp. 376-77.

23. Michael Burleigh, *The Third Reich: A New History* (New York: Hill and Wang, 2000), p. 5.

24. Burleigh, *The Third Reich,* p. 260.

25. J. S. Conway, *The Nazi Persecution of the Churches: 1933-1945* (Vancouver: Regent College Publishing, 1968), pp. 364-65.

26. Burleigh, *The Third Reich,* p. 260.

27. Schmitz-Berning, *Vokabular des Nationalsozialismus,* p. 642.

28. Harwood L. Childs, ed. and trans., *The Nazi Primer: Official Handbook for Schooling the Hitler Youth* (New York: Harper, 1938), p. 5. Page references have been placed in the text.

29. Klemperer, *Language,* p. 167.

30. Klemperer, *Language,* p. 178.

31. Klemperer, *Language,* p. 179.

32. Walter Klemperer, *LTI: Notizbuch eines Philologen,* 17th ed. (Leipzig: Reclam Verlag, 1998), pp. 26-27.

33. Klemperer, *Language,* p. 133.

34. Burleigh, *The Third Reich,* pp. 72-73.

35. Eberhard Röhm and Jörg Thierfelder, *Evangelische Kirche zwischen Kreuz und Hakenkreuz: Bilder und Texte einer Ausstellung,* 4th ed. (Stuttgart: Calwer Verlag, 1990), pp. 78-79.

36. Dietrich Klagges, *Das Urevangelium Jesu: Der deutsche Glaube* (Leipzig: Armem-Verlag, 1933), p. 110.

37. Klagges, *Das Urevangelium Jesu,* p. 163.

38. Klagges, *Das Urevangelium Jesu,* p. 165.

39. Susannah Heschel, "When Jesus Was an Aryan: The Protestant Church and Antisemitic Propaganda," in *Betrayal: German Churches and the Holocaust,* ed. Robert P. Ericksen and Susannah Heschel (Minneapolis: Fortress, 1999), p. 72.

40. Heschel, "Aryan," p. 73.

41. Burleigh, *The Third Reich,* pp. 255-56.

42. Burleigh, *The Third Reich,* p. 382.

43. Schmitz-Berning, *Vokabular des Nationalsozialismus,* pp. 380-83.

44. http://en.wikipedia.org/wiki/Action_T4 (accessed May 16, 2012).

45. Burleigh, *The Third Reich,* p. 400.

46. Burleigh, *The Third Reich,* p. 398.

47. Burleigh, *The Third Reich,* p. 259.

48. Burleigh, *The Third Reich,* p. 256.

49. Scholder, *Churches,* p. 189.

50. Scholder, *Churches,* p. 195.

51. Scholder, *Churches,* p. 194.

52. Klaus Scholder, *Die Kirchen und das Dritte Reich, Band 1: Vorgeschichte mit und Zeit der Illusionen 1918-1934* (Frankfurt: Propyläen, 1977), p. 247.

53. Scholder, *Churches,* p. 195.

54. Peter Matheson, ed., *The Third Reich and the Christian Churches* (Grand Rapids: Eerdmans, 1981), p. 5.

55. Burleigh, *The Third Reich,* p. 257.

56. Conway, *Persecution,* pp. 11-12.

57. Scholder, *Churches,* p. 207.

58. Scholder, *Churches,* p. 208.

59. Röhm and Thierfelder, *Kreuz,* p. 25.

60. Scholder, *Churches,* p. 209.

61. Conway, *Persecution,* p. 58.

62. Conway, *Persecution,* p. 56.

63. Röhm and Thierfelder, *Kreuz,* p. 39.

64. William L. Shirer, *The Rise and Fall of the Third Reich* (New York: Simon and Schuster, 1960), p. 236.

65. Ian Kehrshaw, *Hitler, 1889-1936: Hubris* (New York: Norton, 1998), pp. 251-52.

66. Scholder, *Churches,* p. 545.

67. Kurt Dietrich Schmidt, ed., *Die Bekenntnisse und grundsätzlichen Äußerungen zur Kirchenfrage des Jahres 1933* (Göttingen: Vandenhoeck & Ruprecht, 1934), p. 91.

68. Schmidt, *Bekenntnisse,* p. 92.

69. Ferdinand Schlingensiepen, *Dietrich Bonhoeffer, 1906-1945: Eine Biographie* (Munich: C. H. Beck, 2006), p. 180.

70. Schmidt, *Bekenntnisse*, pp. 107-8, translation mine. There were two versions of the Bethel Confession, one in August that Bonhoeffer contributed to, and the final version in November that Niemöller had published. Bonhoeffer considered the second version too weak for his signature and did not sign it (Geffrey B. Kelly and F. Burton Nelson, eds., *A Testament to Freedom: The Essential Writings of Dietrich Bonhoeffer* [San Francisco: HarperCollins, 1995], p. 544). Yet in reference to Luther, the two versions did not differ (http://www.lutheranwiki.org/Bethel_Confession; accessed August 23, 2012).

71. Burleigh, *The Third Reich*, pp. 154-55.

72. Burleigh, *The Third Reich*, p. 252.

73. Röhm and Thierfelder, *Kreuz*, pp. 28-29.

74. Schmitz-Berning, *Vokabular des Nationalsozialismus*, p. 277.

75. Schmitz-Berning, *Vokabular des Nationalsozialismus*, p. 278.

76. Schmitz-Berning, *Vokabular des Nationalsozialismus*, p. 278, translation mine.

77. Conway, *Persecution*, p. 34.

78. Conway, *Persecution*, p. 35.

79. Conway, *Persecution*, p. 35.

80. Conway, *Persecution*, p. 35.

81. Conway, *Persecution*, pp. 38-42.

82. Conway, *Persecution*, pp. 38-44.

83. Schmitz-Berning, *Vokabular des Nationalsozialismus*, p. 60.

84. Röhm and Thierfelder, *Kreuz*, p. 154.

85. Röhm and Thierfelder, *Kreuz*, p. 48.

86. Schmidt, *Bekenntnisse*, p. 185.

87. Schmidt, *Bekenntnisse*, p. 185.

88. Schmidt, *Bekenntnisse*, p. 189.

89. Schmidt, *Bekenntnisse*, p. 190.

90. Heinz Zahrnt, *Die Sache mit Gott: Die protestantische Theologie im 20. Jahrhundert*, 3rd ed. (Munich: Piper, 1996), p. 23.

91. Zahrnt, *Sache*, p. 26.

92. Zahrnt, *Sache*, p. 9.

93. Zahrnt, *Sache*, p. 39.

94. Alan Richardson, ed., *A Dictionary of Christian Theology* (Philadelphia: Westminster, 1969), pp. 191-94.

95. Karl Barth, *The Epistle to the Romans*, trans. Edwyn C. Hoskyns (New York: Oxford University Press, 1968), p. 56.

96. Barth, *Epistle to the Romans*, pp. 50-51.

97. Hartmut Genest, *Karl Barth und die Predigt: Darstellung und Deutung von Predigtwerk und Predigtlehre Karl Barths* (Neukirchen-Vluyn: Neukirchener, 1995), p. 137.

98. The lectures are available in English: Karl Barth, *Homiletics*, trans. Geoffrey W. Bromiley and Donald E. Daniels (Louisville: Westminster/John Knox, 1991).

99. Karl Barth, *Homiletik: Wesen und Vorbereitung der Predigt* (Zurich: TVZ, 1966), p. 98.

100. Barth, *Homiletik*, p. 94.

101. Barth, *Homiletik*, p. 95.

102. Röhm and Thierfelder, *Kreuz*, p. 48.

103. Zahrnt, *Sache*, p. 59.

104. Karl Barth, "Theologische Existenz heute!" in *Theologische Existenz heute*, ed. Karl Barth, vol. 1 (Munich: Chr. Kaiser Verlag, 1933), pp. 4-5.

105. Regrettably, I have been unable to locate any of Lackmann's sermons.

106. On Lackmann see http://de.wikipedia.org/wiki/Max_Lackmann; in English, http://en.wikipedia.org/wiki/Max_Lackmann.

107. Max Lackmann, "Herr, wohin sollen wir gehen? Ein Wort eines theologiestudenten an seine Kommilitionen," in *Theologische Existenz heute* (Munich: Ch. Kaiser Verlag, 1934), p. 5. Page references to this essay have been placed in the text.

108. Helmut Gollwitzer, *The Way to Life: Sermons in a Time of World Crisis*, trans. David Cairns (Edinburgh: T. & T. Clark, 1980), p. xii.

109. Schlingensiepen, *Dietrich Bonhoeffer*, p. 143.

110. Schlingensiepen, *Dietrich Bonhoeffer*, p. 143.

111. Kelly and Nelson, *A Testament to Freedom*, p. 132.

112. Kelly and Nelson, *A Testament to Freedom*, p. 132.

113. Kelly and Nelson, *A Testament to Freedom*, p. 132.

114. Schlingensiepen, *Dietrich Bonhoeffer*, p. 143.

115. Schlingensiepen, *Dietrich Bonhoeffer*, p. 143.

116. Eberhard Bethge, Renate Bethge, and Christian Gremmels, *Dietrich Bonhoeffer: A Life in Pictures*, trans. John Kabitz (Philadelphia: Fortress, 1986), p. 229.

117. Ian Kershaw, *Hitler, the Germans, and the Final Solution* (New Haven: Yale University Press, 2008), p. 180.

118. Kershaw, *Hitler*, p. 181.

119. Kershaw, *Hitler*, p. 182.

120. Clyde E. Fant, *Bonhoeffer: Worldly Preaching* (Nashville: Thomas Nelson, 1975), p. 7.

121. Dietrich Bonhoeffer, *Predigten, Auslegungen, Meditationen*, vol. 1, *1925-1935*, ed. Otto Dudzus (Munich: Kaiser, 1998), p. 13.

122. Eberhard Bethge, *Dietrich Bonhoeffer*, p. 506.

123. Fant, *Bonhoeffer*, p. 130.

124. Scholder, *Churches*, p. 581.

125. Kelley and Nelson, *A Testament to Freedom*, p. 544.

126. Röhm and Thierfelder, *Kreuz*, pp. 58-59.

127. Zahrnt, *Sache*, p. 73.

128. Röhm and Thierfelder, *Kreuz*, p. 59.

129. Conway, *Persecution*, p. 84.

130. Röhm and Thierfelder, *Kreuz*, p. 58.

131. Schlingensiepen, *Dietrich Bonhoeffer*, p. 181.

132. Conway, *Persecution*, p. 84.

133. Klemperer, *Language*, pp. 219-20.

134. Schmitz-Berning, *Vokabular des Nationalsozialismus*, pp. 204-5. References to this work have been placed in the ensuing text.

135. Wilhelm Niemöller, *Aus dem Leben eines Bekenntnispfarrers* (Bielefeld: Ludwig Bechauf Verlag, 1961), p. 45. References to this work have been placed in the ensuing text.

136. Günther Harder and Wilhelm Niemöller, eds., *Die Stunde der Versuchung: Gemeinden im Kirchenkampf 1933-1945: Selbstzeugnisse* (Munich: Chr. Kaiser Verlag, 1963), p. 79.

137. Harder and Niemöller, *Versuchung*, p. 79.

138. Harder and Niemöller, *Versuchung*, p. 80.

139. Harder and Niemöller, *Versuchung*, p. 82.

140. Harder and Niemöller, *Versuchung*, p. 83.

141. Albrecht Aichelin, *Paul Schneider: Ein radikales Glaubenszeugnis gegen die Gewaltherrschaft des Nationalsozialismus* (Gütersloh: Chr. Kaiser/Gütersloher Verlagshaus, 1994), p. 99.

142. Aichelin, *Paul Schneider*, p. 99.

143. Aichelin, *Paul Schneider*, p. 100.

144. Aichelin, *Paul Schneider*, p. 212.

Notes to Dietrich Bonhoeffer, Gideon

1. Ferdinand Schlingensiepen, *Dietrich Bonhoeffer, 1906-1945: Eine Biographie* (Munich: C. H. Beck, 2006), p. 21.

2. Schlingensiepen, *Dietrich Bonhoeffer*, p. 30.

3. Geffrey B. Kelly and F. Burton Nelson, eds., *A Testament to Freedom: The Essential Writings of Dietrich Bonhoeffer* (San Francisco: HarperCollins, 1995), p. 11.

4. Schlingensiepen, *Dietrich Bonhoeffer*, p. 90.

5. Schlingensiepen, *Dietrich Bonhoeffer*, p. 418.

6. Eberhard Bethge, *Dietrich Bonhoeffer: Eine Biographie*, 8th ed. (Gütersloh: Chr. Kaiser/Gütersloher Verlagshaus, 1994), p. 784.

7. Kelly and Nelson, *A Testament to Freedom*, p. 37.

8. Kelly and Nelson, *A Testament to Freedom*, p. 37.

9. Kelly and Nelson, *A Testament to Freedom*, p. 18.

10. Kelly and Nelson, *A Testament to Freedom*, p. 20.

Notes to Karl Barth,
A Sermon about Jesus as a Jew

1. James B. Torrance, "Karl Barth," in *The Encyclopedia of Religion,* vol. 2, editor in chief James Lindsey (New York: Thomas/Gale, 2005), p. 789.

2. Torrance, "Karl Barth," p. 789.

3. Torrance, "Karl Barth," p. 790.

4. Torrance, "Karl Barth," p. 790.

5. Victoria J. Barnett, *For the Soul of the People: Protestant Protest against Hitler* (New York: Oxford University Press, 1992), p. 156.

6. Torrance, "Karl Barth," p. 791.

7. Eberhard Busch, *Unter dem Bogen des einen Bundes: Karl Barth und die Juden 1933-1945* (Neukirchen-Vluyn: Neukirchener Verlag, 1996), p. 165.

8. Eberhard Busch, *Karl Barth: His Life from Letters and Autobiographical Texts,* trans. John Bowden (Philadelphia: Fortress, 1976), pp. 234-35, italics in original.

Notes to Paul Schneider,
Christ Crossing the Stormy Lake and Jesus' Glory

1. Albrecht Aichelin, *Paul Schneider: Ein radikales Glaubenszeugnis gegen die Gewaltherrschaft des Nationalsozialismus* (Gütersloh: Chr. Kaiser/Gütersloher Verlagshaus, 1994), p. 1. Page references have been placed in the following text.

2. Rudolf Wentorf, *Der Fall des Pfarrers Paul Schneider: Eine biographische Dokumentation* (Neukirchen-Vluyn: Neukirchener Verlag, 1989), p. 98.

3. Aichelin, *Paul Schneider,* p. 75.

Notes to Martin Niemöller, A Sermon about the
Relevance of Christianity in Nazi Germany

1. Unless otherwise noted, the biographical information is from the United States Holocaust Memorial Museum. "Martin Niemöller: Biography," *Holocaust Encyclopedia;* http://www.ushmm.org/wlc/en/; accessed August 12, 2010.

2. http://www.spartacus.schoolnet.co.uk/GERniemoller.htm; accessed May 25, 2012.

3. *Holocaust Encyclopedia,* n.p.

4. http://www.spartacus.schoolnet.co.uk/GERniemoller.htm; accessed May 25, 2012.

5. http://en.wikipedia.org/wiki/Martin_Niem%C3%B6ller; accessed May 25, 2012.

6. http://en.wikipedia.org/wiki/First_they_came.

Notes to Paul Schneider,
A Sermon about Giving Thanks in the Third Reich

1. This summary of events leading up to Paul Schneider's final arrest is taken from Aichelin Albrecht, *Paul Schneider: Ein radikales Glaubenszeugnis gegen die Gewaltherrschaft des Nationalsozialismus* (Gütersloh: Gütersloher Verlagshaus, 1994), pp. 192-98, 206-7.

2. Rudolf Wentorf, *Der Fall des Pfarrers Paul Schneider: Eine biographische Dokumentation* (Neukirchen-Vluyn, 1989), p. 175.

3. Wentorf, *Schneider*, p. 187.

4. Paul Schneider, *Der Prediger von Buchenwald*, ed. Margarete Schneider (Neuhausen/Stuttgart: Hänssler, 1995), p. 140.

5. Trence Prittie, *Germans against Hitler* (Boston: Little, Brown, 1964), pp. 117-19.

6. J. S. Conway, *The Nazi Persecution of the Churches: 1933-1945* (Vancouver: Regent College Publishing, 1968), p. 209.

Notes to Julius von Jan,
O Land, Land, Land: Hear the Word of the Lord!

1. Ferdinand Schlingensiepen, *Dietrich Bonhoeffer, 1906-1945: Eine Biographie* (Munich: C. H. Beck, 2006), p. 232.

2. Eberhard Röhm and Jörg Thierfelder, *Evangelische Kirche zwischen Kreuz und Hakenkreuz: Bilder und Texte einer Ausstellung*, 4th ed. (Stuttgart: Calwer Verlag, 1990), p. 128.

3. http://www.bautz.de/bbkl/j/jan_j.shtml. Unless otherwise noted, biographical information comes from the online entry of the *Biographische-Bibliographisches KIRCHENLEXIKON* of the Verlag Traugott Bautz (www.bautz.de/bbkl); accessed August 19, 2009.

4. J. S. Conway, *The Nazi Persecution of the Churches: 1933-1945* (Vancouver: Regent College Publishing, 1968), p. 376.

Notes to Helmut Gollwitzer, A Sermon about *Kristallnacht*

1. http://en.wikipedia.org/wiki/Helmut_Gollwitzer; accessed August 9, 2010. Unless otherwise noted, the biographical information comes from the Wikipedia article.

2. Wilhelm Niemöller, *Aus dem Leben eines Bekenntnispfarrers* (Bielefeld: Ludwig Bechauf Verlag, 1961), p. 211.

3. Niemöller, *Leben*, p. 234.

4. http://www.independent.co.uk/news/people/obituary-helmut-gollwitzer-1512367.html.

5. Helmut Gollwitzer, *The Way to Life: Sermons in a Time of World Crisis,* trans. David Cairns (Edinburgh: T. & T. Clark, 1981), p. xi.

6. Gollwitzer, *The Way to Life,* p. xi.

Notes to Gerhard Ebeling, A Sermon for a Victim of *Aktion T4*

1. "Gerhard Ebeling," in Wikipedia, July 28, 2006. The information in this overview of Ebeling's life is based on the Wikipedia entry unless otherwise noted.

2. Gerhard Ebeling, *Predigten eines "Illegalen": 1939-1945* (Tübingen: J. C. B. Mohr [Paul Siebeck], 1995), p. iv.

3. Ebeling, *Predigten eines "Illegalen,"* p. iv.

4. Ebeling, *Predigten eines "Illegalen,"* p. v.

5. Ebeling, *Predigten eines "Illegalen,"* p. v.

6. J. S. Conway, *The Nazi Persecution of the Churches: 1933-1945* (Vancouver: Regent College Publishing, 1968), p. 267.

7. Conway, *Persecution,* p. 268.

8. Michael Burleigh, *The Third Reich: A New History* (New York: Hill and Wang, 2000), p. 382. Page references to this work have been placed in the following text.

9. Ebeling, *Predigten eines "Illegalen,"* pp. 97-98.

Notes to Rudolf Bultmann,
A Sermon about the Parable of the Great Banquet

1. Unless otherwise noted, biographical material and the overview of Bultmann's work are from Charles Moritz, "Bultmann, Rudolf (Karl)," in *Current Biography Yearbook: 1972* (New York: Wilson, 1972), pp. 52-54. A condensed overview of Bultmann's work is: http://en.wikipedia.org/wiki/Rudolf_Bultmann; accessed July 17, 2012.

2. Moritz, "Bultmann, Rudolf (Karl)," p. 53.

3. http://en.wikipedia.org/wiki/Rudolf_Bultmann; accessed August 9, 2012.

4. Moritz, "Bultmann, Rudolf (Karl)," p. 52.

5. Rudolf Bultmann, "The Task of Theology in the Present Situation," in *Rudolf Bultmann: Interpreting Faith for the Modern Era,* ed. Rodger A. Johnson, trans. Schubert Ogden (Minneapolis: Fortress, 1991), pp. 269-77.

6. Eberhard Busch, *Unter dem Bogen des einen Bundes: Karl Barth und die Juden 1933-1945* (Neukirchen-Vluyn: Neukirchener Verlag, 1996), pp. 106-7.

Notes to Clemens August von Galen, A Sermon about *Aktion T4*

1. http://en.wikipedia.org/wiki/Clemens_August_Graf_von_Galen; accessed on May 22, 2012.

2. http://www.britannica.com/EBchecked/topic/223894/Blessed-Clemens-August-Graf-von-Galen.

3. http://www.britannica.com/EBchecked/topic/223894/Blessed-Clemens-August-Graf-von-Galen.

4. Michael Burleigh, *The Third Reich: A New History* (New York: Hill and Wang, 2000), p. 400.

5. Trence Prittie, *Germans against Hitler* (Boston: Little, Brown, 1964), p. 83.

6. Prittie, *Germans against Hitler*, p. 83.

7. Prittie, *Germans against Hitler*, pp. 83-84.

8. http://en.wikipedia.org/wiki/Clemens_August_Graf_von_Galen; accessed on May 22, 2012.

9. Prittie, *Germans against Hitler*, p. 84.

Notes to Wilhelm Busch, The Way of True Faith

1. Unless otherwise noted, biographical information is from the Wikipedia article on Busch, http://de.wikipedia.org/wiki/Wilhelm_Busch_(Pfarrer), accessed August 9, 2012.

2. Ulrich Parzany, *Im Einsatz für Jesus: Programm und Praxis des Pfarrers Wilhelm Busch* (Neukirchen-Vluyn: Aussaat Verlag, 1995), p. 151.

3. Parzany, *Einsatz*, p. 151. Unfortunately, Parazany does not indicate the date of the incident.

4. Wilhelm Niemöller, *Aus dem Leben eines Bekenntnispfarrers* (Bielefeld: Ludwig Bechauf Verlag, 1961), p. 129.

5. Parzany, *Einsatz*, pp. 163-64.

6. Parzany, *Einsatz*, p. 147.

Notes to the Appendix,
A Sermon about the Loyalty Oath to Adolf Hitler

1. Michael Burleigh, *The Third Reich: A New History* (New York: Hill and Wang, 2000), p. 274.

2. Schuschnigg's son has written a book on his family's strong Catholic faith and their hardships in the Third Reich (see Kurt von Schuschnigg, *When Hitler Took Austria* [San Francisco: Ignatius, 2012]).

3. Cornelia Schmitz-Berning, *Vokabular des Nationalsozialismus* (Berlin: Walter de Gruyter, 2007), pp. 456-59.

4. Jørgen Glenthøj, "Die Eideskrise in der Bekennenden Kirche 1938 und Dietrich Bonhoeffer," *Zeitschrift für Kirchengeschichte* 96 (1985): 378.

5. J. S. Conway, *The Nazi Persecution of the Churches: 1933-1945* (Vancouver: Regent College Publishing, 1968), p. 211.

6. Glenthøj, "Eideskrise," p. 378.

7. Eric Metaxas, *Bonhoeffer: Pastor, Martyr, Prophet, Spy* (Nashville: Nelson, 2010), p. 308.

8. Glenthøj, "Eideskrise," p. 378.

9. Glenthøj, "Eideskrise," p. 378.

10. Ferdinand Schlingensiepen, *Dietrich Bonhoeffer, 1906-1945: Eine Biographie* (Munich: C. H. Beck, 2006), p. 308.

11. Glenthøj, "Eideskrise," p. 378.

12. The story appeared in the Australian paper the *Courier Mail,* May 18, 1938; http://nla.gov.au/nla.news=article/40991095; accessed on July 27, 2012, using "Hitler Oath or Dismissal" as key words.

13. Victoria J. Barnett, *For the Soul of the People: Protestant Protest against Hitler* (New York: Oxford University Press, 1992), p. 157.

14. Barnett, *Soul,* p. 157.

15. Eberhard Bethge, *Dietrich Bonhoeffer: Eine Biographie,* 8th ed. (Gütersloh: Chr. Kaiser/Gütersloher Verlagshaus, 1994), pp. 679-80.

16. Eberhard Busch, *Karl Barth: His Life from Letters and Autobiographical Texts,* trans. John Bowden (Philadelphia: Fortress, 1976), pp. 255-56.

17. Bethge, *Dietrich Bonhoeffer,* p. 679.

18. Bethge, *Dietrich Bonhoeffer,* p. 678.

Bibliography

Aichelin, Albrecht. *Paul Schneider: Ein radikales Glaubenszeugnis gegen die Gewalt-herrschaft des Nationalsozialismus.* Gütersloh: Chr. Kaiser/Gütersloher Ver-lagshaus, 1994.

Barnett, Victoria J. *For the Soul of the People: Protestant Protest against Hitler.* New York: Oxford University Press, 1992.

———. "The Role of the Churches: Compliance and Confrontation." In *The Holo-caust and the Christian World: Reflections on the Past Challenges for the Fu-ture,* edited by Carol Rittner, Stephen D. Smith, and Irena Steinfeldt. New York: Continuum, 2000.

Barth, Karl. *The Epistle to the Romans.* Translated by Edwyn C. Hoskyns. Oxford: Oxford University Press, 1968.

———. *Homiletik: Wesen und Vorbereitung der Predigt.* Zurich: Theologischer Verlag, 1970.

———. *Predigten 1921-1935.* Vol. 1. Edited by Holger Finze. In *Karl Barth: Gesamt-ausgabe.* 6 vols. Zurich: Theologischer Verlag, 1998.

———. "Theologische Existenz heute!" In *Theologische Existenz heute,* edited by Karl Barth. Vol. 1. Munich: Chr. Kaiser Verlag, 1933.

Beste, Niklot. *Der Kirchenkampf in Mecklenburg von 1933 bis 1945: Geschichte, Dokumente, Erinnerungen.* Göttingen: Vandenhoeck & Ruprecht, 1975.

Bethge, Eberhard. *Dietrich Bonhoeffer: Eine Biographie.* 8th ed. Gütersloh: Chr. Kaiser/Gütersloher Verlagshaus, 1994.

Bethge, Eberhard, Renate Bethge, and Christian Gremmels. *Dietrich Bonhoeffer: A Life in Pictures.* Translated by John Kabitz. Philadelphia: Fortress, 1986.

Bonhoeffer, Dietrich. *Berlin, 1932-1933.* Vol. 12. In *Dietrich Bonhoeffer Works.* Gen-eral editors Victoria Barnett and Barbara Wojhoski. Edited by Larry Ras-mussen. Translated by Isabel Best, David Higgins, and Douglas W. Scott. Minneapolis: Augsburg Fortress, 2009.

Bibliography

————. *Predigten, Auslegungen, Meditationen.* Vol. 1, *1925-1935.* Edited by Otto Dudzus. Munich: Kaiser, 1998.

Bultmann, Rudolf. *Marburger Predigten.* 2nd ed. Tübingen: J. C. B. Mohr (Paul Siebeck), 1968.

————. "The Task of Theology in the Present Situation." In *Rudolf Bultmann: Interpreting Faith for the Modern Era,* edited by Rodger A. Johnson, translated by Schubert Ogden. Minneapolis: Fortress, 1991.

Burleigh, Michael. *The Third Reich: A New History.* New York: Hill and Wang, 2000.

Busch, Eberhard. *Karl Barth: His Life from Letters and Autobiographical Texts.* Translated by John Bowden. Philadelphia: Fortress, 1976.

————. *Unter dem Bogen des einen Bundes: Karl Barth und die Juden 1933-1945.* Neukirchen-Vluyn: Neukirchener Verlag, 1996.

Busch, Wilhelm. *Es geht am Kreuz um unsere Not: Predigten aus dem Jahr 1944.* 3rd ed. Neukirchen-Vluyn: Aussaat Verlag, 1999.

Childs, Harwood L., ed. and trans. *The Nazi Primer: Official Handbook for Schooling the Hitler Youth.* New York: Harper, 1938.

Conway, J. S. *The Nazi Persecution of the Churches: 1933-1945.* Vancouver: Regent College Publishing, 1968.

Ebeling, Gerhard. *Predigten eines "Illegalen": 1939-1945.* Tübingen: J. C. B. Mohr (Paul Siebeck), 1995.

Fant, Clyde E. *Bonhoeffer: Worldly Preaching.* Nashville: Thomas Nelson, 1975.

Fischer, Klaus P. *The History of an Obsession: German Judeophobia and the Holocaust.* New York: Continuum, 2001.

Galen, Clemens August Graf von. *Akten, Briefe und Predigten, 1933-1946.* Veröffentlichungen der Kommission für Zeitgeschichte. Reihe A: Quellen: Band 42. Edited by Konrad Repgen. Mainz: Matthias-Grünewald-Verlag, 1988.

Genest, Hartmut. *Karl Barth und die Predigt: Darstellung und Deutung von Predigtwerk und Predigtlehre Karl Barths.* Neukirchen-Vluyn: Neukirchener, 1995.

Glenthøj, Jørgen. "Die Eideskrise in der Bekennenden Kirche 1938 und Dietrich Bonhoeffer." *Zeitschrift für Kirchengeschichte* 96 (1985).

Gollwitzer. Helmut. *Dennoch bleibe ich stets an dir: Predigten aus dem Kirchenkampf 1937-1940.* Edited by Joachim Hoppe. Gütersloh: Chr. Kaiser Verlag, 1988.

————. *. . . und lobten Gott: Predigten — gehalten in der Gemeinde Berlin-Dahlem 1938 bis 1940.* Neukirchen-Vluyn: Neukirchener Verlag des Erziehungsvereins, 1964.

————. *The Way to Life: Sermons in a Time of World Crisis.* Translated by David Cairns. Edinburgh: T. & T. Clark, 1981.

Harder, Günther, and Wilhelm Niemöller, eds. *Die Stunde der Versuchung:*

Gemeinden im Kirchenkampf 1933-1945: Selbstzeugnisse. Munich: Chr. Kaiser Verlag, 1963.

Heschel, Susannah. "When Jesus Was an Aryan: The Protestant Church and Antisemitic Propaganda." In *Betrayal: German Churches and the Holocaust,* edited by Robert P. Ericksen and Susannah Heschel. Minneapolis: Fortress, 1999.

Johnson, Rodger A., ed. *Rudolf Bultmann: Interpreting Faith for the Modern Era.* Minneapolis: Fortress, 1991.

Kelly, Geffrey B., and F. Burton Nelson, eds. *A Testament to Freedom: The Essential Writings of Dietrich Bonhoeffer.* San Francisco: HarperCollins, 1995.

Kershaw, Ian. *Hitler, 1889-1936: Hubris.* New York: Norton, 1998.

———. *Hitler, the Germans, and the Final Solution.* New Haven: Yale University Press, 2008.

Klagges, Dietrich. *Das Urevangelium Jesus: Der deutscher Glaube.* Leipzig: Armen-Verlag, 1933.

Klemperer, Victor. *The Language of the Third Reich: LTI — Lingua Tertii Imperii; A Philologist's Notebook.* Translated by Martin Bradley. New York: Continuum Impacts, 2006.

———. *LTI: Notizbuch eines Philologen.* 17th ed. Leipzig: Reclam Verlag, 1998.

Lackmann, Max. "Herr, wohin sollen wir gehen? Ein Wort eines theologie-studenten an seine Kommilitionen." In *Theologische Existenz heute.* Munich: Ch. Kaiser Verlag, 1934.

Moritz, Charles. "Bultmann, Rudolf (Karl)." In *Current Biography Yearbook: 1972,* pp. 52-54. New York: H. Wilson Co., 1973.

Niemöller, Martin. *Dahlemer Predigten 1936/1937.* Munich: Chr. Kaiser, 1981.

Niemöller, Wilhelm, *Aus dem Leben eines Bekenntnispfarrers.* Bielefeld: Ludwig Bechauf Verlag, 1961.

Parzany, Ulrich. *Im Einsatz für Jesus: Programm und Praxis des Pfarrers Wilhelm Busch.* Neukirchen-Vluyn: Aussaat Verlag, 1995.

Richardson, Alan, ed. *A Dictionary of Christian Theology,* pp. 191-94. Philadelphia: Westminster, 1969.

Röhm, Eberhard, and Jörg Thierfelder. *Evangelische Kirche zwischen Kreuz und Hakenkreuz: Bilder und Texte einer Ausstellung.* 4th ed. Stuttgart: Calwer Verlag, 1990.

Rott, Wilhelm. "Was ist positives Christentum?" *Evangelisches Kirchenarchive.* Berlin, Bestand 50/4888, pp. 1-73.

Shirer, William L. *The Rise and Fall of the Third Reich.* New York: Simon and Schuster, 1960.

Schlingensiepen, Ferdinand. *Dietrich Bonhoeffer, 1906-1945: Eine Biographie.* Munich: C. H. Beck, 2006.

Schmidt, Kurt Dietrich, ed. *Die Bekenntnisse und grundsätzlichen Äußerungen zur Kirchenfrage des Jahres 1933.* Göttingen: Vandenhoeck & Ruprecht, 1934.

Bibliography

Schmitz-Berning, Cornelia. *Vokabular des Nationalsozialismus*. Berlin: Walter de Gruyter, 2007.

Schneider, Paul. *Der Prediger von Buchenwald*. Edited by Margarete Schneider. Neuhausen/Stuttgart: Hänssler, 1995.

———. *. . . und sollst mein Prediger bleiben: Zeugnisse von Paul Schneider*. Edited by Rudolf Wentorf. Giessen: Brunnen Verlag, 1966.

Scholder, Klaus. *The Churches and the Third Reich*. Vol. 1, *Preliminary History and the Time of Illusions, 1918-1932*. Translated by John Bowden. Philadelphia: Fortress, 1987-88.

———. *Die Kirchen und das Dritte Reich, Band 1: Vorgeschichte mit und Zeit der Illusionen 1918-1934*. Frankfurt: Propyläen, 1977.

Scholze-Stubenrecht and J. B. Sykes, eds. *Oxford-Duden German English Dictionary*. New York: Oxford University Press, 2005.

Steigmann-Gail, Richard. *The Holy Reich: Nazi Conceptions of Christianity, 1919-1945*. New York: Cambridge University Press, 2003.

Stein, Edith. *Aus der Tiefe leben: Ein Textbrevier*. Edited by Waltraud Herbstrith. Regensburg: Topos plus Verlagsgemeinschaft, 2006.

Torrance, James B. "Karl Barth." In *The Encyclopedia of Religion*, vol. 2, James Lindsey, editor in chief, pp. 789-92. New York: Thomas/Gale, 2005.

Wahrig, Gerhard. *Deutsches Wörterbuch*. Berlin: Bertelmanns, 1974.

Wentorf, Rudolf. *Der Fall des Pfarrers Paul Schneider: Eine biographische Dokumentation*. Neukirchen-Vluyn: Neukirchener Verlag, 1989.

Zahrnt, Heinz. *Die Sache mit Gott: Die protestantische Theologie im 20. Jahrhundert*. 3rd ed. Munich: Piper, 1996.

Worldwide Web

Biographische-Bibliographisches KIRCHENLEXIKON, Verlag Traugott Bautz (www.bautz.de/bbkl.)

On Bultmann: http://en.wikipedia.org/wiki/rudolf Bultmann.

On Gollwitzer: http://en.wikipedia.org/wiki/Gollwitzer; http://www.independent.co.uk/news/people/obituary-helmut-gollwitzer-15123667.html.

Hitler's speeches at http://www.hitler.org/speeches.

Holocaust Encyclopedia. http://www.ushmm.org/wlc/en/.

On von Galen: http://en.wikipedia.org/wiki/Clemens August Graf von Galen; http://www.britannica.com/EBcheckd/topic/223894/Blessed-Clemens-August-Graf-von-Galen.

Permissions

Without the permission to translate the German texts and to use the Augsburg/Fortress translation of the Bonhoeffer text, the book would have been utterly impossible. Therefore I offer sincere thanks to the following for their kind permission and support of the project.

Augsburg/Fortress for permission to use their translation of Bonhoeffer's sermon "Gideon" in *Dietrich Bonhoeffer: 1932-1933. Dietrich Bonhoeffer Works*, vol. 12, 2009, pp. 461-67. Scholars interested in Bonhoeffer should access this ongoing effort to offer in English a critical edition of all of Bonhoeffer's writings.

Theologischer Verlag, Zurich, for permission to translate Karl Barth's Advent sermon from Karl Barth, *Predigten 1921-1935*, vol. 1, 1998, pp. 297-305.

Neukirchener Verlag for permission to translate Paul Schneider's sermon "Crossing the Stormy Lake" from *Der Fall des Pfarrers Paul Schneider: Eine biographische Dokumentation*, by Rudolf Wentorf, 1989, pp. 95-98.

Dr. Heinz-Hermann Niemöller for permission to translate the Niemöller sermon and to the Evangelische Kirche in Hessen und Nassau for facilitating communication with Dr. Niemöller.

Brunnen Verlag for permission to translate Paul Schneider's Thanksgiving sermon from . . . *und sollst mein Prediger bleiben*, by Paul Schneider, editor Wentorf, 1966, pp. 148-58.

Landeskirchliches Archiv Stuttgart, Germany, for permission to translate the sermon by Julius von Jan.

Neukirchener Verlagsgesellschaft des Erziehungsvereins for permission to translate Helmut Gollwitzer's sermon of September 3, 1939, from . . . *und lobten Gott: Predigten — gehalten in der Gemeinde Berlin-Dahlem 1938 bis 1940,* by Helmut Gollwitzer, 1964, pp. 88-92.

Neukirchener Verlagsgesellschaft for permission to translate "Die Art des rechten Glaubens" from Wilhelm Busch, *Es geht am Kreuz um unsere Not: Predigten aus dem Jahr 1944,* 3rd ed., 1999, pp. 44-48.

Gütersloher Verlagshaus for permission to translate Helmut Gollwitzer's sermon on November 16, 1938, following the *Kristallnacht* pogrom from *Dennoch bleibe ich stets an dir . . . : Predigten aus den Kirchenkampf 1937-1940,* ed. Joachim Hoppe, 1988, pp. 52-60.

J. C. B. Mohr (Paul Siebeck) for permission to translate Gerhard Ebeling's sermon ". . . das ihr nicht jemand von diesen Kleinen verachtet!" from *Predigten eines "Illegalen": 1939-1945,* 1995, pp. 98-102, and for permission to translate Rudolf Bultmann's sermon on Luke 14:16-24 in Rudolf Bultmann, *Marburger Predigten,* 2nd ed., 1968, pp. 126-47.

Kommission für Zeitgeschichte for permission to translate Bishop von Galen's sermon of August 3, 1941 (Number 341), in Clemens August Graf von Galen, *Akten, Briefe und Predigten, 1933-1946,* in the series Veröffentlichungen der Kommission für Zeitgeschichte, ed. Konrad Repgen, vol. 42, Matthias-Grünewald Verlag, 1988, pp. 875-83.

The Evangelisches Kirchenarchiv in Berlin for their help during a research trip and for permission to publish the Hitler oath sermon. It was during that research that I found the essay on positive Christianity that I reference in the editor's introduction.